Setting Up and Managing a Small Practice

A Guide for Solicitors

by

Martin Smith LL.B., Solicitor

Martin Smith & Co.

THE LAW SOCIETY

113 Chancery Lane
London   WC2A 1PL

© Martin Smith 1995

First printed 1995
Reprinted 2000

ISBN 1 85328 348 7

Published by

THE LAW SOCIETY

113 Chancery Lane
London WC2A 1PL

Printed by Antony Rowe Ltd,
Chippenham, Wiltshire

Contents

CONTENTS

Preface

As a sixteen-year-old Classics student at King Edward VI Grammar School, Stourbridge, in the West Midlands, I began to wonder what I might do with three 'A' Levels in Latin, Greek and Ancient History. Apart from possibly being an archaeologist grubbing around ancient relics in Greece or Rome, or being a Classics teacher, nothing immediately sprang to mind. My Classics master came up with various suggestions, one of which was law.

Classics', he said, 'produces a logical mind which is ideally suited to law.'

I decided to bounce the idea off a Scout leader whom I knew and whose opinions I respected.

'What do you think of the idea of me becoming a solicitor?' I asked.

'Now there's a job', he said. 'Money for old rope! They get paid a fortune, they don't start work most days until 10 am and their secretaries do most of the work. You see them in the mornings in the magistrates' court. They haven't got a clue what the case is about and their secretaries sit next to them passing them all the right documents and telling them what to say next. If only I had my time over again, it would certainly be something I'd like to get in on.'

This, I thought, is the job for me. If ever I meet up with the latter individual I will strangle him!

Some years later, when I was aged twenty-two, I went for my formal interview in front of the Law Society. The general view in the queue of young hopefuls was that the interview was a pure formality and no one had heard of anyone who had 'failed' the interview and had been refused admission as a solicitor as a result. When it was my turn to go in, I went in front of three dark-suited, austere individuals who asked me a series of questions including why I wanted to be a solicitor. Ever one to tell the truth and shame the devil, I recounted the advice of the Scout leader. It may perhaps have come as a refreshing breath of stark truthfulness in what had probably been an afternoon of platitudes and well-rehearsed statements of entering an honourable profession and helping to underpin the fundamental principles of justice, law and order in a civilised society, but if it did, the three austere gentlemen betrayed no sign of it. Rather a look of horror and disbelief crept over their faces and one gentleman looked over his bifocals and said, 'I think that far from finding it is money for old rope you will feel you have earned every penny that you make.'

The moral of this story is threefold.

Firstly, even a crusty old Classics master has words of wisdom to pass on.

Secondly, never trust anyone's advice at face value, no matter how apparently learned, or wise, not even your old Scout leader.

And, thirdly, not everything uttered by the Law Society and its officers is complete rubbish.

This book is dedicated to these people, but first and foremost it is dedicated to my dear wife, Rachel, without whose unstinting hard work, help and encouragement when it was needed most, the practice of Martin Smith & Co. would have died shortly after birth.

Martin Smith
November 1995

Acknowledgements

It is often said that there are always plenty of candidates willing to take the credit when things go right, but very few volunteers to accept blame when things go wrong.

This book is unique for two things. Firstly, there is no other book on the market at the time of writing that assists solicitors with the formidable task of setting up a new practice.

Secondly, it is unique in that it disproves the earlier theory. The blame for any of the book's shortcomings belongs entirely to me. The persons listed below have given of their time and skills freely and unselfishly and as a result have turned the book into a much better work than would otherwise have been the case. In no particular order, they are:

Nick Hughesman of Lyall Youngman, Chartered Accountants, who prepared the business plan and assisted with accounts matters.

Vic Lyall formerly of Lyall Youngman, now retired, without whose assistance there may not have been a solicitors' practice on which to base my experiences.

Angela Deacon, Jennifer Israel, and the sundry **sole practitioners** and **outside consultants** who made time in their busy lives at the Law Society's request to read early drafts and contribute their comments.

Andrew Park who helped with the chapter on computers and computer systems.

Pat Skipwith, surveyor, who helped with matters relating to planning.

Carl Upsall of the Law Society whose good humour, tact and diplomacy was of vital importance when stamina and energy levels in the production of the book were running low.

No. 1 son James Smith, who at the tender age of 13/14 managed to turn my raw material into polished cartoons and still found time to do his homework.

My wife, Rachel, who despite her myriad other tasks both at home and in the practice devoted endless hours to typing and amending the text.

My very grateful thanks go out to each of the above.

To Victor Lyall

A first class accountant called Vic
Met a lawyer both stylish and slick
Who said, 'I need a place'
Vic said, 'I've got some space
You'd better move in a bit quick'.
Some seven years later up there
Although at first sight it's unfair
The world had moved on
And Victor had gone
But the sly stylish lawyer's still there.

PART ONE

Ears Back and Go For It!

CHAPTER 1

Setting Up – the First Steps

DO NOT LET SEEMINGLY INSUPERABLE DIFFICULTIES DISSUADE YOU FROM SETTING UP.

People start new practices for all sorts of different reasons. They may have been made redundant either from industry or from private practice. They may have been victims of partnership splits, or they may simply have decided that they like the idea of their name in lights and running their own show. Very often the reasons for starting a new practice in the first place will in themselves govern whether the practice will be that of a sole practitioner or whether it will be a partnership.

Sole Practice or Small Partnership?

The majority of people will probably try, at least in the first instance, to set up in practice with someone else. Unless the proposed partner or partners are themselves already in partnership together and are splitting off from an existing partnership or are close friends, the parties, in the main, rapidly reach the conclusion that the risk of things not working out is too great. The old legal adage that partnership is like marriage is only too true in this situation. In order to go into partnership under these circumstances, you will want to know your proposed partner extremely well. There must be a high degree of trust, mutual respect and confidence, and these qualities must be present in such quantities that they will enable the parties to stay together during the very difficult and worrying early periods as well as sustaining them in the later periods when hopefully the hard work put in will result in success. These times can be just as dangerous as the early periods since one party may credit themselves with being the architect of the success and may wish to enjoy rather more of the spoils than the others.

No one can help with these decisions any more than there is any point in calling in a marriage guidance counsellor when you are thinking of getting engaged. The only advice that I can give is to make sure that you know your future partners as well as it is possible to know them. If there are any parties who may be well known to one partner but not to you, ensure that you meet them and their spouses and see them in a domestic setting as well as in a working environment, on as many different occasions as you can manage. You should all meet as often as you can since people react differently when in the company of others to how they react in a one-to-one situation. You must talk about all the different aspects of setting up a partnership together so that the possible differences of opinion will come out at this stage rather than 12 months down the line.

The above process has seen off many a proposed partnership before it has got started, which is probably no bad thing since it may have been doomed to failure at the outset. The choice then is really fourfold, namely, stay where you are if that is possible and make the best of it, join another firm as an employee if you get the chance, leave the profession altogether, or set up as a sole practitioner. It is probably true to say that the majority of sole practices result from the first two options not being available and the third being an even more daunting prospect than the fourth.

Sole Practice – Advantages

The single most overriding benefit of being a sole practitioner is the freedom you have from day one to run your practice exactly how you please. You have no partners to worry about, you do not have to think about the possibility of people plotting your downfall or arranging your sudden departure whilst you are away on holiday, no one chases you for your time sheets or billing figures and there are no 'office politics'. When I was a partner in a City firm, I once remember attending a partners' meeting at which we spent two hours debating whether or not the firm should use window envelopes or plain envelopes. The manoeuvres which took place prior to a desire to change one's car would have impressed a Cabinet Minister angling for an increase in his spending budget. Plot and counterplot would be hatched with alliances being made so that one partner supported another partner's similar application three months further down the line and all being timed to coincide with the firm's greatest month of positive cash flow, and preferably the senior partner's absence on holiday. As a sole practitioner, such decisions, be they trivial or momentous, can be taken in seconds and implemented within hours. Even with a partnership of two, the constraints are immediately in place with your partner's feelings to consider, but as a sole practitioner you have a completely free hand.

Sole Practice – Disadvantages

The downside is the feeling of isolation, the fact that you have no one – at least in the early years – with whom you can discuss either business or legal problems. You have a strong sense of vulnerability since there is no one to look after the practice if you are ill and the feelings of being overstretched are even more apparent as a sole practitioner than they might have been as a partner. You have to be in at least six places at the same time.

All sole practitioners who are members of the Law Society are automatically members of the Sole Practitioners Group. The group exists to represent the interests of sole practitioners in the Law Society and to provide support both locally and nationally. Further information can be obtained from the permanent secretary to the group at the Law Society, 50 Chancery Lane, London WC2A 1SX. Tel: 0171 242 1222.

The Law Society itself operates a Solicitors Assistance Scheme (contact the Professional Ethics Department) whereby experienced practitioners give help and advice to colleagues in professional difficulties.

Nevertheless, when the rewards come you have the satisfaction of knowing that the credit belongs solely to you. Of course, your staff will have helped and no doubt there will be clients who have perhaps gone out on a limb for you and put their trust in you and there will be other people who will have assisted in providing the breaks when you needed them, but no matter, the applause is all yours! Your clients have come to you with their business because of their respect for your ability and skill and your integrity and reputation, and that more than anything else is immensely gratifying. It may only be a little baby and it may be fat and ugly, but it's all yours!

Setting Up – Law Society Requirements

In order to set up as a sole practitioner, a solicitor is required to wait until he or she has been admitted for three years. (See Principle 2.04 of *The Guide to the Professional Conduct of Solicitors 1993*, published by the Law Society.) Similarly, in new firms consisting of a number of partners at least one of the partners in the firm must normally have been admitted for at least three years. The Law Society has the power to grant waivers in suitable cases and may be perhaps rather more inclined to do so at present, when a great many solicitors have been made redundant early on in their careers and are simply unable to find employment elsewhere. Whether or not this is a good idea is a matter of opinion. In the case of solicitors who have only been in general practice for, say, two years with law being their first career they are likely to be aged between 26 and 30 and even if they have the management experience to run a practice and to be able to arrange the finance, their experience is likely to be fairly narrow and when any one of the various crises that can arise in a small practice does so, and there is no one else to turn to for help and advice, panic may set in. Having said that, the younger you are, the more energy and drive you tend to have and possibly fewer responsibilities, like spouses and small children, with more time than most to devote to making a go of it.

CHAPTER 2

Where to Locate

Where you decide to make your home is an interesting aspect of setting up. The importance of getting it right varies from nil to absolutely crucial. If you have a large client following, then your clients will probably want you to be fairly close to them. If you have a commercial following, then this in practice may mean that you are inevitably going to have to locate in central London, or if you are setting up in the provinces, in the nearest large commercial centre. Clients still have a certain 'snob attitude' towards their solicitor's location. If the image which you wish to project is that of a highly organised, switched-on commercial firm, you may have difficulty in obtaining instructions from commercial clients if you are located in an unfashionable and run-down suburb or a country lane. Clients will expect you to be in the thick of it, commercially speaking. It follows that certain key decisions must be taken at this stage. What type of practice are you going to market yourself as? What type of market are you going to aim at?

Locating According to Your Market

In my own case, I decided to offer a general high street type practice whilst at the same time marketing the practice towards commercial clients both in the area and outside of it so as to offer them the skills acquired by 12 years' practice in the City with the same kind of service they were used to with a City firm but at substantially less than City rates. Many provincial firms have followed this approach with very considerable success. As the recession has taken its toll, commercial clients have had to take a fresh look at the fees they are charged and the service they receive and have concluded that in many instances they can make substantial savings whilst experiencing little or no drop in the quality of service and in the quality of the advice and work provided in return.

The danger of my own strategy is that of falling between two stools, being unable to compete with City service because of size and resources whilst outpricing oneself from local markets because of the additional resources which need to be available to try to provide the City type service.

Again, these decisions must be made by the individual and it is difficult to advise someone on what type of market to go for. It will depend on exactly what your own experience is, the type of clients you feel able to attract, whether you have an existing client following and so on.

Locating Close to Home

If you are setting up in partnership, then you may wish to have premises that are more or less roughly equal in travelling time for each of you. However, if you are going it alone, then the choice is yours. Availability of suitable premises may make the decision for you since if the only premises you can afford and which are available are 50 miles away, then you may have no choice. At present, there is an abundance of vacant office premises and you have a rare opportunity to cut your travelling time down to say 15 minutes.

Practising from Home – Advantages

A further option is to set up in practice from home. At first sight this has enormous advantages – no travelling for a start. The disadvantage of never being able to get away from work is probably less than one might think. The important clients often ask for your home telephone number and will be offended if you are not prepared to disclose it. In the early days you will probably find yourself leaning strongly in the other direction and volunteering your home telephone number to all and sundry, inviting them to call you any time, day and night. Once things have taken off a bit, you may not be quite so forthcoming! You will probably find yourself working in the office or at home, certainly in the early days once things have got going, until 8 or 9 o'clock, and again, it does not really matter whether the phone is ringing at home or in the office. If you are working from home, the two become the same thing.

If you decide to work from home it is advisable to have an answerphone and an ex-directory telephone number for your family and friends, so that you are not on call all the time. The majority of clients to whom you will be giving your home telephone number will be business clients and by and large they respect the fact that you are entitled to time with your family in the evenings and at weekends and will only call you if it is something they are particularly worried about, or it is an emergency.

Practising from Home – Disadvantages

A much more important factor is probably going to be your own attitude. It is difficult to work from home for many people at the best of times, particularly with children running about and the television blaring. If the home is a place where you normally relax but sometimes work and the office is a place where you normally work and sometimes relax, the whole thing tends to work much better. You are better able to switch off when you get home and feel much more in the mood for getting on with things whilst you are in the office. To be successful in running your practice from home, you have to be very self-disciplined and have fairly spacious accommodation.

In my view, business clients tend to feel more comfortable coming to see you in the office than they do seeing you at home where they feel they are intruding. It also presents a much more business-like image if you are working from normal office surroundings rather than one room tucked away somewhere in the house. Make no mistake about it – our business is as much image as anybody else's. You can still have a professional image, even though you practise from home, but you may need to work harder at it. The Bohemian 'carpet slippers and Val Doonican sweater' look is all very well but it may not be what a commercial client is looking for.

If you run your office from home, unless you live in the high street, you will not be readily accessible to passing trade, banks, building societies, etc. Some building societies are not prepared to instruct you if you practise from home. You do, of course, enjoy the benefits of not having to pay rent and you may not pay full business rates. Nevertheless, whilst this is not an insignificant area of expenditure, it is not one of the most substantial. In our case, for example, accommodation charges including items like repairs, heat and light, account for only 10 per cent of total outgoings. Staff costs, by contrast, account for more than 46 per cent. Clearly, these figures will vary depending on how much you pay for your premises and staff and what other outgoings you have and the decision must be between cutting yourself off from the high street or other commercial centre, loss of image, etc., for a saving of probably no more than about 8 per cent once you have taken into account the additional heating and lighting costs involved in working from home. You may also find that you are required to pay business rates which would reduce the saving still further.

There is also the danger that when you move house the taxman will claim that you are not entitled to full principal private residence relief for capital gains tax purposes. If, for example, your house has six rooms and you use one as an

9

office, a sixth of the gain made when you sell your home may be liable to CGT if that one room has been used wholly for business purposes.

The answer is to ensure that no single room is dedicated exclusively to the business. The Revenue may point to the fact that you may be claiming running costs of one room as a business expense in your accounts as evidence of a room dedicated to business use, so it is better to claim a proportion of the costs of heat and light, etc., for part of two rooms rather than the whole of the cost of one.

ENSURE NO ONE ROOM IS DEDICATED EXCLUSIVELY TO BUSINESS.

The Revenue also like to point to the use of a fax machine to support the contention that the room is for business purposes rather than domestic, but if you can ensure that the room has a dual purpose, both business and domestic, by putting a cooker in the same room, or a library of non-legal books, you are likely to be able to resist an attempt by the Revenue to deny full relief.

You may be able to claim part of your council tax against the profits of the business. So long as you can demonstrate that the amount claimed is reasonable, there is no reason why such a claim should not be allowed. The best approach may be to put forward a global figure for 'use of home as office' with a suitable breakdown available if required.

There is also no reason why a proportion of VAT on fuel required for heat and light, etc., cannot be reclaimed in the same way if you are willing to take the time to work the figures out.

Sharing Premises – an Ideal Compromise?

One further option which is not often considered is the possibility of hiring out office space from business and commercial centres. Certain agencies will rent out fully furnished, staffed and equipped offices on a monthly basis and included in the arrangement is the ability to hire additional facilities such as a board room or a conference room and to have available catering services for a separate hourly rate. This enables you to have a prestigious address and impressive offices and other facilities at a fraction of the true cost, as the cost is being split between all the other occupiers of the building. It also relieves you of the dangers of signing a lease. If you sign a lease before 1 January 1996, even a short-term lease will mean that you will be liable for its duration, which may well be five, eight or 10 years, and whilst you would no doubt be able to assign it if you have read it properly and negotiated it correctly, there is still the possibility of no one wanting the premises or of them running up rent arrears and you being liable if you have given covenants or if you are the first leaseholder.

After 1 January 1996 the Landlord and Tenant (Covenants) Act 1995 alters the position so that the tenant's liability will cease on assignment for leases signed after that date except where the landlord's consent to assign is needed. Then, the landlord can require the old tenant to guarantee the assignee's performance of the covenants.

Informal Arrangements

The solution which we ourselves adopted was similar. We discovered, through a client, that other professional people had surplus office accommodation available within their own building. They were prepared to allow us to occupy part of the premises on an informal basis and to share with us the costs of partitioning them off. We also negotiated within an accommodation charge the use of their receptionist, waiting area, photocopier and similar facilities. The arrangement worked extremely well. They were paying for all of those underused facilities in any event and were glad to have part of that burden relieved by us sharing the facilities. We were not and never have been asked to sign any formal agreement and the whole thing was done on a handshake. If you have such an informal arrangement you run the risk of your 'landlord' suddenly asking for the space back which could cause you something of a problem!

It also meant that, professionally speaking, we had other level-headed business people with whom we could on occasions share our problems and they could do likewise. From their point of view they had instant access to free initial legal advice and were only too pleased to be able to recommend their own clients to us as a firm which they could observe operating at first hand and run by someone they felt they could trust.

Of all the various options available, this is the one I would recommend above others. It is cheap, low risk, good in terms of image and provides the opportunity for a steady flow of clients via your 'landlord' if the arrangement works well on a personal level. I can think of nothing more demoralising than starting off a practice with no clients from one room of a building where you may know no one else in the entire place and where the opportunities to get to know them are infrequent. Your whole working attitude is likely to be very poor, not the kind of bustling, confident atmosphere likely to arise where you are sharing space with others whose businesses have been running successfully for some years. Whether you have a formal sublease or take up occupation on the rather risky 'handshake' basis is up to you.

Getting Your Premises' Image Right

It is also important to make sure that the premises are 'approachable' from the point of view of the kind of client you are trying to attract. If the premises have thick, pile carpets, brass handles on the doors and mahogany panels along the staircase, then legal aid clients or first-time house buyers may well take one look at the premises and go elsewhere either because they think they are going to feel out of place or because they are afraid that the fees are going to be astronomic. At the other extreme, if the paint is flaking off the walls and the linoleum has holes in it and there is no shade around the light bulb, your commercial clients are not going to come back for a second appointment.

Choosing the Location – Check the Competition

Location will also depend to a large extent on what competition there is in the area. It is not a bad idea to get out a street map and then to look in the Solicitors' Directory and identify the locations of each practice address and to mark them with a suitable fluorescent, sticky label. At one time I thought of locating my practice in Enfield. It appeared to be a bustling area, only 15 minutes away from my home with good public transport arrangements. After 20 minutes with the map and Solicitors' Directory I had discovered about 16 separate practices all located virtually on top of one another, as a result of which I decided not to move to Enfield!

Considerations of this type may not feature largely if you already have a strong client following and have decided that you can probably do without passing trade. Depending on the type of practice you intend setting up, you may actively not want passing trade, but to rely on providing a good service for your existing client base whilst actively seeking to consolidate it with other clients of similar standing. If you have no, or a very uncertain, client base, then I would suggest that all work is likely to be work that you cannot turn away unless it is totally outside your field of expertise and you feel you would be a danger to the client if you tried to tackle it.

Even if it does not look particularly profitable work, it is still probably worth doing in the early days, unless it is clearly grossly unremunerative. Even poorly paid work in the first few months will bring in some cash and will help to spread the word that your practice has arrived and is open for business. At a later stage, when the practice has got off the ground, you may want to think more carefully as to whether you can accept such work.

What to Call your Practice

The way in which you style your firm is to some extent decided for you by the Solicitors' Practice Rules. Rule 11 (see *The Guide to the Professional Conduct of Solicitors*) restricts the firm's name to that of one or more of the principals or former principals, 'together with, if desired, other conventional references to the firm', which means 'and Co.' or 'Partnership', 'and Partners', etc. So, if your name is Bloggs and you set up in partnership with Mr or Mrs Smith, you can be 'Bloggs & Co.', 'Smith Bloggs and Partners', 'Alfred Smith and Tony Bloggs', or any similar combination.

If you are starting up in Aylesbury and want to call yourself 'The Aylesbury Law Practice' you would need to apply to the Council of the Law Society for express approval under Rule 11, or else find Mr or Mrs Aylesbury to come into partnership with you!

Alternatively, you would need to find an existing practice called Aylesbury and Co. and buy it. Since it would have had a former principal called 'Aylesbury', you would be able to use the name, or a variant of it, as the name of the new practice.

The Dilemma of Taking on New Fields of Work

You will, unless you come from a very general practice to start with, or are setting up with others so that the firm is able to handle a whole range of legal services, be faced with the dilemma of seeing work go elsewhere, possibly to a competitor, or tackling work which you may not have done before. There is a fine line to be drawn between being timid and overcautious and attempting things you have not done before and recklessly diving into something for which you have no aptitude or competence. As a litigator of 12 years' experience with virtually none of it in conveyancing, will-making or probate when I started, I had some hard choices to make. It may even be that some of the choices made were wrong, either in taking on work that I should not have taken on or in turning away work which, if I had had a little more courage and self-confidence, I could have dealt with quite easily, and certainly as well as the person to whom the work went. Everyone has to start somewhere and you should not shy away from work when you are setting up in practice simply because you have not done it before.

Using Available Reference Material

You can now buy a book relatively cheaply on a subject which might have been considered, at one time, a specialist area. With the assistance of such a learning aid and a decent precedent book if there is not a suitable set of precedents in the book itself, you can quite easily carry out a perfectly competent job for the client. The hardest part is in saying 'Yes, of course,' to the client when the client asks 'Could you handle this for me?' No one, not even experts, have all the facts at their fingertips all of the time. They all go off and look things up. The client is not only paying you for the knowledge of your subject but also for your objectivity, level-headedness and plain common sense – and for your professional training in how to consult specialist texts and other sources. Your general knowledge of the law and your years in business and experience of life will often tell you when something is wrong and when to call a halt to further progress until you have found, by leafing through the book, the answer to whatever is giving you an uneasy feeling.

There are also plenty of other people – barrister friends, accountants, friends who are solicitors and even other solicitors in the area – who you can ring up and pick their brains when something is troubling you. If they do not know the answer they may be able to point you in the right direction. It does not take very long at all before all of this becomes second nature and you are drawing up wills, administering estates and conveying away quite happily when only six months earlier the whole thing was a closed book.

As well as being spoiled for choice as regards text books on new areas, there is now a multitude of courses offered on all types of subjects, pitched at all levels of experience. If you wish to develop an expertise in an otherwise unknown area you can supplement your reading of textbooks with a short course at a training centre. As well as helping to absorb and consolidate the knowledge so far acquired, it will confirm what you have already learned, giving you added confidence, as well as raising questions you had not considered, making you less likely to stumble into something unexpected at a later stage.

If you have a friend who is a solicitor or barrister who specialises in a particular field you are interested in entering, why not ask if you can attend a trial or a conference with them to gain additional experience? Provided the agreement of the client and other partners in the firm is obtained, there should be no difficulty. Doctors think nothing of standing over an experienced colleague so as to acquire part of their skill and knowledge.

Advocacy for the Inexperienced Sole Practitioner

If you have never done any advocacy before, now is not the time to feel shy! You may feel that that this is something you are simply not cut out to do. The answer is that you are now facing the stark reality of having to earn your living very much at the sharp end. Put aside your bashfulness and just get on with it! The courts are full of barristers and solicitors not necessarily any more skilled than you, and all earning a decent living out of advocacy. If I did not feel tongue-tied, embarrassed and have my pulses racing when I got up to speak in a magistrates' court, I would feel that there was something seriously wrong. I clearly recall sitting behind one of the most experienced QCs in the land some years ago (the gentleman concerned is now a senior Old Bailey judge) when he was opening an appeal in the Court of Criminal Appeal. I marvelled at the way the words simply flowed without a trace of nervousness and how he seemed totally at ease. One of the Lords Justices then asked him if he had an additional copy of the document to which he was referring and he turned to me to see if there was a spare one on the file. As he did so, I noticed that his hands were trembling to such an extent that his own copy of the document was making a quiet rattling noise. As I looked up at him, I could see that he was perspiring heavily across his forehead and neck despite the fact that the appeal was heard just before Christmas and the courtroom was chilly. If people of that seniority and experience are entitled to work themselves up into a state when getting up in front of a Tribunal, so are you! Don't let confusion about claiming standard fees and not knowing the paperwork involved put you off. Get out there and earn the fee first and sort out getting paid later. Five minutes on the telephone with another solicitor or the Legal Aid Board will show you how to submit the first claim form. The rest are all the same.

If you are going to court for the first time or after a long absence, try to go on an earlier occasion, sit at the back and get acquainted with the court. Always give yourself plenty of time to get to the hearing and *never* arrive late. As well as creating the wrong impression with the client your own anxiety level will be much increased.

CHAPTER 3
Finance

One of the early key decisions you will have to make is how you are going to go about financing the practice, be it as a sole trader or as a partnership. The views of people in business, including professional advisers, can vary immensely as to whether you should try to borrow all the money you will need, whether you should try to borrow as little as possible or none at all if you can, or whether the firm's capital should be roughly half borrowed and half proprietor's funds. Once again, necessity may provide the answer – if no one will lend you the money, you will have to put up your own! On the other hand, if you have no money to put in, you can only commence by borrowing. The merits of these debates will be examined later, but if you intend borrowing money one thing is certain – you will have to put forward a business plan to demonstrate to your proposed lender (who is almost certainly going to be a bank) the fact that you have done your arithmetic and can make the figures add up. Not only that, but they will go into the figures themselves and make sure that they do add up and that the business is likely to trade sufficiently profitably to enable you to repay the money. Even if you are supplying the capital entirely yourself, you must prepare a business plan no matter how rudimentary.

Preparing the Business Plan with Professional Help

The majority of people setting up a new business will go to an accountant to prepare the business plan. There is no reason at all why solicitors should be sufficiently arrogant that they feel they need to do it differently. It is the kind of thing that any competent, qualified accountant (as opposed to a book-keeper type accountant) can do for you and the cost will not be exorbitant. You must do the necessary research into markets, profit levels, setting-up costs, etc. Although accountants will often have helpful ideas and suggestions they are really there to present in financial terms the business plan that you have put together. They will do it in such a way as to make your ideas make financial sense to a bank. They are not there to do all your thinking for you. Equally, a bank does not need to know down to the last penny what money will be going through the business. It simply needs to have sufficient information to ensure that the project is going to be viable. Some banks will even help you to put the business plan together, but first impressions are just as important in this situation as in any other. The bank may be one with which you have had no previous connection. In due course you may well be looking to the bank as a source of business. If you go in with a half-baked business plan scribbled out on the back of an envelope, the manager is unlikely to be impressed by the way you go about things and that impression may stick. If you go in with a properly prepared business plan which you fully understand and which has been well thought out and you can go through it and explain it the bank manager, it is the perfect opportunity to strike up a good rapport which may well lead to a long-lasting and mutually profitable business arrangement. Keep the accountant's bill – that will form part of your set-up costs which are tax deductible – and so with luck, the Revenue will be paying a good 25 per cent of the bill in any event.

If you are not intending to borrow but to put forward the bulk or all of the capital yourself, then your preparations need not be so elaborate. You may be able to get away with the 'back of an envelope' approach so long as you are taking a realistic view of the figures and you are reasonably sure that you have not left anything out.

Example of a Business Plan

Appendix 4 sets out a very rough business plan which you would present to a bank manager when asking for his or her help to finance the new venture. Appendix 5 sets out a costings plan which simply shows how much money you will need to get started and you will see that the capital requirement is likely to be in the region of £12,000. This is for a very basic sole practitioner's office and involves no staff other than a secretary. If your spouse is able to help you out with secretarial work or book-keeping your staffing costs can be kept very low. Whoever does the book-keeping must know all the accounting rules – this is essential for any practice but perhaps even more important for a sole practitioner as there are fewer people available to sort things out if they get in a mess.

Clearly, the amounts involved are a very rough guide just to give you an idea of what items you should be thinking about and what they are likely to cost, but you may decide to go for more elaborate premises or to work from home. You may decide to invest in more advanced systems and equipment right from the start and employ back-up staff right away. All these items will cause the business plan to change dramatically and the items in Appendix 5 should be used more as an aide memoire than anything else. It does, however, show you how, with only a fairly modest investment by business standards, you can get the show on the road.

Opening Bank Accounts

You will need to open a bank account even before you have opened an office. Although at this stage you may not have any client funds to put into it, you will still need to talk to the bank manager about opening a client account and setting the account up. Paying-in books and cheque books will need to be printed.

Even if you have not gone to a bank to provide the finance, it is a good idea to negotiate an overdraft facility of, say, £10,000 in case cash flow does not go quite the way you intended it to. The time to arrange the overdraft is at this stage rather than when you are in trouble. Even a fairly friendly bank manager is unlikely to give you a higher overdraft facility than that initially since you have no trading record. Any trading record that you might have had as a partner elsewhere is not terribly relevant.

Choosing a Bank

The choice of bank and its location is very important. If you have a good relationship with a bank already and you are going to be setting up not too far away, then you may do well to stay with the same bank and keep the relationship with someone you know. It may pay you to retain your connection with that bank even though you are moving away and since you can in that instance make your day-to-day transactions with the local branch whilst maintaining the account elsewhere. The main problem with this arrangement is that credits take two days longer to get from the branch to the account than if you were paying directly into the account.

If you decide to set up with a bank near your office, you have an excellent opportunity to make an impression. Banks are generally keen to get solicitors onto their books and you should find a very positive response from any bank that you approach.

Bank Charges

Most banks will offer you a year's free banking which is extremely good news when you are just setting up. Nevertheless, you must enquire what the charges are likely to be once that year has run out, and cost it into your business plan. Banks are generally now familiar with the practice of some small traders of moving their bank account once a year to obtain perpetual free banking. It is galling for any practice to have to pay 75p for the privilege of paying a cheque into their account for their bank to have use of their money and then to have to pay another 75p to write a cheque to draw it out again. The rate of interest that banks are willing to pay on client account balances also varies quite significantly. Some banks will charge a fee for transfers from client account into office account whilst others do not. Charges for individual items, like telegraphic transfers, can also vary appreciably. There is, regrettably, no substitute for doing the homework and getting from banks their individual charges, negotiating the best deal you can with them and then applying a notional number of debits, credits and transfers and telegraphic transfers, a notional average client account credit and therefore interest sum, and seeing which bank is charging you the least at the end of the day. It is a tiresome exercise but a necessary one. Having done your homework, you are then in a position to sit down with the bank manager and talk in fairly stark terms to him or her. If the bank manager wants your account, and we are talking long term – up to 20 years, then you need a bit of flexibility. This is again no time to be shy. Equally, it is not the time to be aggressive. Local managers are now, in general, controlled by regional offices and a lot of their discretion has been taken away. There is, therefore, no point in pushing them too hard, but what flexibility there is you should exploit as best you can.

Your Bank as a Source of New Business

This is also a good time to talk to them about any minor legal work the bank may have. Banks now have what they euphemistically refer to as 'Realisations' Departments, or a central debt collecting unit, so that individual managers are not free to select a local solicitor to carry out debt collection work, but there are nevertheless considerable opportunities for bank managers to point their customers in your direction if they are so minded for such matters as wills or conveyances.

Deposit Accounts

You will probably not at this stage have sufficient time or inclination to start looking at deposit accounts. You are required by the Deposit Interest Rules to ensure that any money that you are going to be holding for a client for anything more than a few days is properly invested, but it is generally a lot simpler just to ask the bank to place the funds in a deposit account. You are unlikely, in the early few months, to have any substantial sums to hold on behalf of a client, but if you do, then the best answer is likely to be to go into a local building society and indulge in the same exercise with the building society as you did with the bank manager. Building societies are also a good source of client referrals and you should not miss the opportunity to make yourself known and to make it clear that you are the introducer of the funds. If at that stage you are not licensed under the Financial Services Act to give investment advice, then you must be careful not to advise your client to place the funds with a specific building society since you may infringe the Act. This does not prevent a client from directing you to open the account with that building society and you carrying out those instructions. Don't forget that these accounts will have to be reconciled at no more than five-weekly intervals in the same way as the client account with the bank.

Borrowing Requirement or Putting Up Your Own Capital

As stated earlier, this may come down to what is available and if you have ready cash from, for example, a redundancy payment or capital repaid from your partnership capital account if you have split from a partnership, it is financially unsound to leave that in a building society account whilst you then go out and borrow your working capital to set up your firm. The exponents of the contrary view argue that they would never put their own funds at risk. This is a view I have never properly understood since the bank tends to attack your money and your assets if it wants its own funds back because the business is failing and you won't repay it. To my way of thinking, borrowed money is in much the same category as your own money except that it costs a lot more to get hold of and to hang on to and people have a nasty habit of asking for it back when you can least afford to repay it!

It became very fashionable in the 1980s to borrow heavily in order to finance solicitors' practices since there was a plentiful supply of cheap money and the economy was booming. The idea was that you took the bank's money, made it work to earn greater profits and expand your firm to a degree that would never have been possible without the outside finance. Many of those firms were caught out quite disastrously when the recession hit and interest rates went through the roof. Being a cautious individual, I set up my own practice entirely from my own funds. I borrowed nothing from the bank and have never used a penny of the £10,000 overdraft facility which the bank kindly afforded to me. The result was an enormous sigh of relief as I watched interest rates climb progressively way beyond any level that people thought they would go.

Many large firms were brought up very sharply by banks who rather abruptly told them that not only would the overdraft not be permitted to rise any further but would actually be called in unless there was an immediate injection of partners' own funds in some very uncomfortable amounts. These are the risks that you run if you use other people's money to finance your practice. A better way would be to adopt a policy of borrowing as little as possible and only for specific areas of expansion. The scope of the borrowing should be limited so that you have a definite and workable plan to repay the borrowing within, say, a three to five-year period. In other words, you would be treating it in the same way as buying a washing machine on hire purchase. The monthly outgoings would not be too great, you are not paying substantially more for the washing machine and yet you have the use of it during that time. As practitioners, we are all aware of those households that not only get the washing machine on credit but also the TV, the video, the freezer, the car and the microwave. The income of the household is so strangled that it cannot cope. Any firm in that situation becomes very vulnerable. If the bank decides to pull the rug from under your feet, it can bring the entire practice down and you must never let yourself get into that position.

Putting up Your House as Collateral

Any bank making a loan for setting up a practice is almost certain to want you to put your house up as collateral. Again, if you are playing with your own money, this is something you need not worry about.

Bear in mind that it may not be just your money you are putting at risk. If you are married, for example, it will be the family's savings. Your partner will need to be consulted on these decisions and indeed consent even if he or she is not going to be working in the new firm. It is important that they are a willing party to the arrangement and not pressurised into it.

If the house is being put up as security for bank finance, your partner will probably be required to have separate legal advice as to the wisdom of putting the family fortune at risk and will be required to sign documents putting his or her share of the house up as security, especially in the light of the House of Lords' observations in *O'Brien* v. *Barclays Bank plc*. These issues should be tackled at an early stage, not left until the filing cabinets are on order and the estate agents are asking for the first month's rent on the office.

The reality is that the house is at risk anyway, simply by virtue of the fact that you are in business. If the business fails, your creditors will attack your assets and the main one is the house. All you are doing by putting the house up as security is to give them a head start on the rest!

CHAPTER 4
Professional Indemnity Cover and Insurance

The profession has its own professional indemnity cover up to the minimum compulsory level of £1 million for each and every claim through the Solicitors Indemnity Fund Limited. The Indemnity Fund is a statutory fund which provides indemnity cover and contributions are received by the profession based on the gross fee information of the practice. In the case of a 'new practice', i.e. one with no established client base being introduced, the contribution payable is a flat rate of £500 per principal plus VAT. The cover needed for a new practice depends on the type of practice and what work, if any, the sole practitioner or partners concerned bring into the new practice. The partners or sole practitioner will be asked by the SIF what client base they are bringing with them to the new practice and what level of fees that base is likely to generate during the first year. From this, the SIF will be able to assess whether the practice can properly be termed a new practice or a successor practice.

Unless you are quite clearly carving out a section of an existing practice with a readily identifiable fee income, you are likely to be classified as a new practice and the flat fee of £500 plus VAT will apply. The logic is fairly obvious. In the first trading year, the business is likely to be fairly quiet unless it is in fact part of an existing business that has been lopped off. The risk to the SIF is therefore less than in later years since the principal or partners concerned will have more time than they would wish on their hands to ensure that work is done in a controlled and careful manner. If the practice subsequently takes off, it is then that the dangers set in with the work being done at a frantic pace and the consequential dangers of insufficient attention being paid to matters and lack of supervision of staff. The risk, therefore, in the first year is likely to be comparatively less than in future years, and after the first year the firm has a track record and the fee income generated in that time is a known quantity.

Although under the standard arrangements there is cover of £1 million, the first £3,000 of the claim must be borne by you, and this could happen three times in a year, i.e. £9,000, unless you pay an extra premium to reduce or remove the deductible (i.e. the part you pay) or the number of claims you pay in a year.

Also, there is probably a vested interest in the SIF making sure that the new practice is not overburdened in the first year with a massive insurance premium that puts its survival in danger. The more firms in the scheme, the more the risk is spread and the better it is for everyone.

You may find that after five or six years of running your own practice you get a rather unpleasant shock. You should bear in mind that for PI claims loading purposes, you remain liable as a principal even after leaving a firm in which you were a principal. You are jointly and severally liable not only whilst you are a partner with a firm but even after you have left for acts which occurred up to the date you left. From SIF's viewpoint, they are concerned with who the principals were when an act of negligence was committed. If, therefore, a claim is paid out in 1996, but the act of negligence to which it relates was committed in 1985 and it has taken 11 years to settle, you will be treated as a party to that act of negligence if you were a partner in the firm in 1985. You may have no knowledge that a claim was notified, you may never have dealt with the client concerned and, almost certainly, you will not be involved in the settling of the claim, unless your former partners have chosen to involve you. You will nevertheless have the PI contribution payable on your new firm loaded against you for the following five years and your former partners are entitled to look to you for payment of your part of the deductible. This is perhaps something you might like to cover if you are in a position to negotiate the terms on which you leave the former practice.

Premises and Contents

You may think that there is not much to insure and perceive this as an overhead that can be avoided. Whilst this may be true in the first few months, it will be a devastating blow if what little equipment has been purchased is either stolen or destroyed by fire. With even basic computers costing £1,000 a time and fax machines robust enough to withstand the wear and tear of everyday use costing £2,000 each, not to mention the precedent library, the desks, chairs, etc., it is surprising how much it can cost to furnish an office for a second time. Much will depend on the type of premises you have chosen. If you are practising from home, it is as well to check with your insurers that such usage is covered and you may have to pay a small additional premium. At the very least, the level of cover will need to be increased to take account of the purchase of the additional equipment since otherwise you run the risk of having a claim only partially met on the basis of underinsurance. If you fall to the temptation of not bothering to insure in, say, shared premises, do not give way to the temptation for the second year. The expense is a deduction from profits and, once again, the Inland Revenue is making at least a 25 per cent contribution to the premium.

You may be in possession under a lease which requires you to insure the fabric of the building or provides that the landlord does and recovers the premium from you, in which case there is no temptation available to which you can fall.

Business Interruption

There is no requirement to take out this kind of cover, which is a policy which will provide you with a guaranteed minimum income in the event that you are unable to continue to practise due to, for example, a fire. The ordinary building and contents policy will cover you for the cost of putting the premises back into one piece and replacing the equipment, but if during the time it takes to restore the premises to their former glory you are unable to trade for a period of, say, six months, then you are going to be many thousands of pounds out of pocket. Business interruption insurance will cover this eventuality and may also cover such things as the cost of replacing your files from photocopying other people's documents, the cost of temporary accommodation elsewhere, etc. Whether you take out this insurance or not is up to you. It may be available as an add-on to a policy which is essential and may represent good value for money. The risk to the insurers is comparatively small and therefore the premiums are likely to be relatively user-friendly and the benefit to you if you need to rely on it can be enormous.

Employer's Liability

All employers are required by law to provide cover for staff who may injure themselves whilst at work. The Employers Liability (Compulsory Insurance) Act 1969 requires employers to arrange £2 million of cover in respect of employees sustaining injury arising out of, or in the course of, their employment. Whilst £2 million of cover for each and every claim sounds a lot, this type of cover is generally available for an unlimited amount as part of an employer's general insurance policy covering loss and damage to equipment of around £10,000, accidental injury to visitors to the premises and all the usual kinds of cover an employer would want or must have by law for a basic price of around £150. You are also required by law to display a copy of the employee's insurance certificate in a prominent place within your place of business. These provisions do not apply where the only employees in the business are husband or wife, father, mother, son, daughter, brother, sister, etc.

You will have to take extra care on the question of disclosure. Insurance companies are very mindful of people operating businesses from home without taking out a business policy. If you have a burglary at home and a fax machine and computer are stolen, insurers may try to argue that they are not covered on a domestic policy. So long as you check the terms of the policy you are buying to ensure the cover is wide enough for your needs and make full disclosure, you should not have problems. When choosing a business policy, pay special attention to the section relating to equipment and whether it covers equipment used at home as part of another office base. Tell insurers that you sometimes work from home and so does your spouse and confirm that the equipment there is covered on the office policy, and if necessary, pay an additional premium.

No matter how safe your offices accidents can happen and you are required by virtue of the Health and Safety at Work Act to report the matter to the Health and Safety Executive, which is likely to be located at the local Town Hall. They will institute an investigation depending on the level of severity of the incident and any injuries sustained in it. If they discover you have no insurance cover, then you are very likely to be prosecuted. This is unlikely to impress other staff or clients. As stated earlier, this cover is comparatively cheap and is available as part of a package deal providing for several different types of cover normally associated with running a business.

Ill Health

There are three ghosts which perpetually haunt sole practitioners. The first is the prospect that business will dry up and they will have no clients. The second is that they may die leaving a practice with no one at the helm and partner and children unprovided for. The third is that they may be struck down with long-term illness. The first ghost is taken care of in this book. The second can be catered for by life policies, and by making a suitable will (dealt with in Chapter 15), and the third can be insured against. Once again, whether you take out such a policy is up to you. The insurance is readily available but it may be fairly expensive and the majority of policies exclude liability for the first two months or so. If you were suffering from a long-term illness and were unlikely ever to recover sufficiently to be able to make a go of the practice you should possibly be looking to dispose of it rather than trying to stagger on with some form of long-term insurance. Nevertheless, many practitioners may feel happier with such insurance in place knowing that at least the mortgage and general household expenses will be paid up to a certain level if disaster does strike.

Public Liability Policy

As well as having cover for accidents happening to your employees you will need to consider your responsibilities to visitors, e.g. clients, who come to your premises. This cover is obtainable as part of the general office 'package' of insurance referred to earlier at minimal cost and you would be foolish not to have it. If operating from home, you may find such visitors are not covered under your household public liability section if you are operating as a business and have not taken out specific business cover. As described earlier, insurers may refuse to pay out if you have a burglary and it is business equipment that has been stolen, such as fax machines, if you have not told them you are running a business from home.

CHAPTER 5

Tools of the Trade

Computers or Manual Systems

When starting a new business many people and particularly solicitors rush out and buy a computer. Those with lots of money rush out and buy several computers. There seems to be a belief that no business today can succeed or be in the least bit efficient without a computer. If you have never used a computer before, consider buying a basic computer with perhaps a simple word-processing package on it in order to familiarise yourself with computers and their basic operation. If you intend operating from offices but want to have a facility for doing some work from home, to include a word-processing facility, then it is worth purchasing more advanced equipment. If you do so, however, it is likely that when you eventually decide upon the type of system to buy for serious office use it will be incompatible with the one you have at home which is too basic. The worst thing that you can do unless you are fully computer literate and know what hardware and software is on the market, and how they can improve the effectiveness of your business, is to buy a computer system without fully considering all the consequences. Alternatively, bring in a computer consultant to advise you on what equipment to buy.

Your approach will be different if you are two or more partners with an existing client base that you know will come with you when you set up rather than if you go solo with only one or two clients coming with you for certain. In the former situation it may be worth taking professional advice from a computer consultant. The advice will not be cheap, but if it looks like you are going to need a full-blown system within a matter of days, not weeks, of setting up and you are fairly confident that you will get full use out of the system and will not need to change it for at least three or four years, then the advice would be worthwhile. The cost of the advice will need to be built into your set-up costs and business plan.

For those people whose initial venture may be rather more modest, the likely solution will be to invest in something fairly cheap with the intention that it will be obsolete within about six months to a year. Within a couple of weeks you will need a word-processing facility that will produce a reasonably good quality result and there are many systems on the market that will do exactly that. There is no point in investing in anything more substantial at this stage. The Law Society publishes lists of suppliers of both computer hardware and software. Whilst they are not 'approved' as such, you have the reassurance of knowing that they have had to reach certain criteria laid down by the Society before being admitted to the list.

So far as accounting systems go, the advice is very much along the same lines. If you are a two or three-partner firm, then there is going to be a great deal of financial information processed almost immediately and you are going to need comparatively sophisticated software to run on a computer. Notwithstanding this, it is undoubtedly a good idea to have a manual system in operation for the first six months and to run the two together. If something goes wrong with the computerised system or you put the wrong information in, then you have the manual system to fall back on. It is more or less twice the work, but it is well worth it. There are reasonably priced accounting software packages specifically geared for sole practitioners. The Law Society's *Gazette* produced a survey of such accounts packages on 25 May and 6 July 1994, copies of which are reproduced at Appendix 9.

With a sole practitioner, it is essential to have a manual system in the first instance, either with or instead of a computerised system. There will be a great deal to be going on with in the first few months and if you have to cope with a computer malfunction or software fault which loses you all your financial information, the resultant chaotic scene may be sufficient to make you want to call it a day. If you have a manual system in place, you may add up figures wrongly, but it is nothing that cannot be sorted out. Suitable manual systems are obtainable from Moore Paragon U.K. Ltd. (tel. 0171-928 9022) and Oyez Stationery Group plc (tel. 0171-232 1000) for less than £500.

Unless you are fully conversant with computers, you will find that when you first put in a computerised accounts system alongside a manual one you will not dare to trust the computerised system. Once you have got used to it and can see how much time it is saving you and how more accurate it is – computers do not make arithmetical mistakes, unlike book-keepers – you will quickly find the situation being reversed so that you are putting more trust in the computer system than you are in the manual system. Once that situation is arrived at, you can abandon the manual system at a convenient juncture. The importance of getting the accounts system right cannot be emphasised too strongly, be it a manual or a computerised system. It is well worth getting an accountant to oversee the design of your systems and their implementation and carrying out a mini 'audit' after, say, three months, to pick up any mistakes before they become habit or things get out of hand.

Furniture

Many people, as with computers, will rush out and buy brand new furniture. They will furnish a waiting room with leather upholstered armchairs and sofas, with mahogany desks for partners and try to make their premises look as sumptuous as possible to impress clients. Bearing in mind that many clients are far from impressed by such offices and can actually be put off (see Chapter 2), this uses up valuable capital resources which may be put to good use elsewhere or held in reserve for later. If, for whatever reason, six months or a year into the practice you decide to move, you may find that the furniture will not fit in the new premises, is out of place or you need more of it and that particular type of furniture is no longer made and you have to have other furniture alongside it which looks incongruous.

A much better solution is to buy secondhand. Even before the recession, there was a thriving market in secondhand furniture. Such entrepreneurs advertise in The Thomson Directory and Yellow Pages and are not at all difficult to find. You must take the time to go and look at the furniture before you buy and select the pieces yourself, making sure that any faults are simple to remedy, but it is a small price to pay for the considerable savings you will make at a time when your capital resources are limited and your business is vulnerable.

Library

Whilst the cost of acquiring individual textbooks is not cripplingly high, comprehensive libraries for solicitors are nevertheless surprisingly expensive items. As employees or partners in larger firms, a library is something which we have come to take for granted. No longer will it be simply a question of walking into the relevant room and there it is – textbooks and law reports as far as the eye can see. Having set up your new business there will, sooner or later, come a time when you need to look something up and you will find that your usual textbook is not there anymore. When setting up, a library is a substantial expenditure of capital which cannot really be justified. You must, therefore, be highly selective in what you acquire, which will depend exclusively on what type of practice you have. If you do no divorce work you do not need a book on divorce.

The best compromise is to purchase a few new books dealing with those areas of law which you will definitely be practising on a day-to-day basis and to make do with secondhand for everything else. You will find that in the Law Society's *Gazette* there are regular advertisements for individuals or firms wishing to dispose of major works and also professional booksellers who make their living by acquiring entire libraries from practices that are merging. In this way you can generally acquire the current edition of a major work for roughly half the cost of buying it new.

With these items, you will need to be particularly selective. You will be spending £2,000 or £3,000 on one work such as a *Halsbury's Laws* or *Atkins Court Forms* and there may be the odd volume or two missing which will have to be replaced and then inevitably, there is the cost of the updating service, which will be a continual drain on time and money. It can be quite demoralising to find each month a brand new release of the *Encyclopaedia of Forms and Precedents* arriving together with an invoice for £100 or so and even more demoralising when you have several such volumes arriving for different major works and it dawns on you that the profit costs produced from the last dozen wills you have just done have been wiped out. Books must pay for themselves. If you purchase a set of books which sit on shelves and do not help you make money, you have made an unwise investment.

The other extreme is also true. There is no point holding up work for the sake of a book. One case on its own may justify you going out and buying the latest work on that subject.

Designing Your Library

You must also have somewhere to put books. They take up a surprising amount of space and they are somewhat less than impressive if they are just lying in a pile on the floor. They will have to be properly shelved or put in proper bookcases, all of which will add substantially to the cost of providing the library. Before you lay out the money on acquiring 20 or 30 volumes of a work, think first of all where you are going to locate it, what you are going to keep it in and how easy it will be for yourself and other people, possibly not yet recruited, to have access to them without disturbing other people. Be sure to build the cost of suitably displaying them into your calculations.

Staff

Employing Your Spouse (or Close Relative)

As a sole practitioner without a client base you know you can count on, the requirements of staff are going to be very limited. You may be extremely fortunate, as I was, in having the ideal member of staff available in the form of your spouse.

Many people have commented that it can be a dangerous course of action to have your spouse working for you in the business. Whilst there are clearly dangers of tensions from work being brought home and family squabbles being ventilated in the office, spouses working in solicitors' practices either as a principal or in some other capacity and vice versa not only can work well but generally do. Firstly, there is the added motivation that the venture must succeed if the family finances are not to end in ruin. There are very few members of staff who will be quite so highly motivated as that! Secondly, people get married because they share common aims and dreams. A spouse will share your aspirations, fears and excitements in setting up a new practice and you are likely to be able to count on him or her for 100 per cent support in achieving those same dreams. Your success will be very much jointly shared, provided you don't try to take all the credit. Thirdly, your spouse may often be prepared to work well above and beyond the call of normal duty. Very few members of staff are prepared to start work again in the evening and type from 8 p.m. to 1 a.m. to get some essential piece of work out of the way – and cook the dinner into the bargain!

Your spouse or close relative may also be an ideal book-keeper. If they are not trained they may be prepared, unless they are working in a career of their own, to acquire the necessary skill by going on courses. Should you have a wife who has more time on her hands than she would like after children have just started school and is hesitant about resuming a career elsewhere, the idea of being a key player in a brand new venture may not only seem appealing but positively exhilarating. Precious funds are kept within the family unit. Your spouse will also have their own tax allowance which can be used up against income received by the practice.

The other side of the coin is that if your spouse keeps their own job you avoid putting all your eggs in one basket and are thus assured of at least one income coming in each month. Whether you both work in the practice or not, school holidays tend to become something of a nightmare. They can be counteracted to a large extent by duplicating the office facilities at home so that typing can continue whilst the children are creating mayhem in the rest of the house, but it is someone less to answer the telephone in the office and do a lot of the running around, and there is always something of a sigh of relief once the holidays are over. It does also mean that to a large extent you are more exposed. If your spouse becomes ill, or if the relationship breaks down, you will have lost your secretary, book-keeper and partner at one fell swoop.

Part-time Help

You may well find that within about six months of trading there is a sufficient profit pattern emerging that you can recruit a part-time secretary. Choose someone who does not have the same schooltime problems as you so that a good deal of the pressure is taken off during school holidays. There are many able people who, for one reason or another, do not wish to take on a full-time responsibility but are quite happy to work four or five mornings a week. It is always a good idea to give preference to those people who live locally. If an emergency crops up and you need them in a hurry, you can always see if they can spare you a few extra hours and they are unaffected by bad weather and train strikes. They are also likely to work for less money than those applicants who spend an appreciable part of their wages on travelling.

Sharing Staff

If you have been able to find a corner in someone else's offices under the office-space-sharing scheme described in Chapter 2, you may have been able to negotiate, as part of the package deal, a sharing arrangement of certain members of staff. In the early days, the value of this facility cannot be overstated. If the staff concerned are co-operative and do not feel that they are being put upon, it means that you have the full-time service of a receptionist and/or telephonist and/or typist with none of the responsibility or full cost. If the arrangement is put to them in the right way, things can work very well. For many people, there is a certain fascination in watching a business grow from absolutely nothing and they take a certain amount of satisfaction from having given it a gentle shove in the right direction. Believe it or not, there are still many people who will do things without expecting any more reward than your grateful thanks and reasonably frequent expressions of gratitude. Show them that you appreciate what they do and what a help they are being to you and they will do all they can to assist you without asking for anything more than a few words of thanks and perhaps a rather thoughtful present at Christmas.

Expanding

As business increases, the helping hands of such treasures may soon prove insufficient. The time may quickly come when you need to arrange your own separate receptionist and telephonist facilities. Do not leave it too late so that a problem arises between your office-sharing 'landlords' and their staff and yourself. If you do, the facility is likely to be withdrawn and possibly your licence to occupy the premises along with it. If you do not let a problem arise, then if business later subsides and you decide to reduce your staffing levels to correspond with the downturn in business, you will probably find that the same people who helped you before will help you again.

Recruiting – Factors to Consider

Taking on staff is one of the biggest decisions that you can make. Wages are the single biggest overhead of any solicitor's practice. It is vital that you obtain value for money. You cannot afford to have passengers. It is even more critical in a small business to ensure that you have no more staff than you absolutely need (always allowing a little flexibility to cope with sudden influxes of work and expansion) and to recruit the right people who will be a credit to your business and who will work hard. Always obtain references and take them up, but in the final analysis, trust your own judgement as to whether the individual will fit in. They may not have a particularly good reference from their last employer, but this need not be the critical factor in deciding whether to take them or not.

Their academic record is likely to be important, but people with straight As and good degrees are not necessarily going to be the best people for your practice. You must imagine that you are a client and they are dealing with you as a fee-earner. What sort of impression do they make on you? Would you have confidence in them in dealing with your case? The fact that they can remember huge amounts of information and regurgitate it later when called upon to do so is not nearly as impressive as the ability to win a client's trust and confidence and make them feel reassured that they are going to put everything they can into a case and that they care about the result. Contracts of employment, etc., are dealt with in Chapter 16, but do not forget when you have taken someone on to write to them immediately confirming their appointment, when they are to start and with a summary of their job description and conditions of employment. If you fail to do so, the employee may think you have changed your mind and not turn up on the agreed date and even if they do, you may, by that stage, have forgotten quite what the terms were that you offered them.

Telephone Systems

No business today can even begin to trade without having a telephone system in place. You will find it very difficult to operate successfully from home with just one or two lines. True, if you have many more you will have lines ringing and no one to answer them. Nevertheless, if you decide to trade from home, then to a large extent you are cutting yourself off from expansion. There will be something of a vicious circle. People will become frustrated if the telephone is not answered or if they get the engaged tone. This means fewer clients. If you have fewer clients, you are not expanding and so you confirm yourself in your decision to restrict yourself from operating from home. If you are going to have three or four lines, you will need three or four people to answer the calls. Unless you have an exceptionally large house, you are rapidly going to need office space.

If you accept the above principles, then the telephone system you will require will probably have at least three lines. You may also choose to have an additional private line purely for you to be able to make outgoing calls. This applies equally to two and three-partner firms. If you go for a system which can accept at least five incoming lines and possibly as many as 10, you can start, in the case of a sole practitioner, with say three lines on which you can make both incoming and outgoing calls with a skipping system so that if one of the lines is engaged an incoming call will automatically skip to a line that is free. As the business expands, you can then add additional lines and extensions to the system. Both BT and major suppliers such as Merlyn or Mercury have excellent systems so that you are now rather spoilt for choice. The simplest thing to do is to contact their sales representatives who will willingly attend at home and demonstrate the equipment and you can decide what system is likely to suit your needs. Make sure that any agreement you sign does not tie you to the equipment for an inordinate length of time. The shorter the period, the better. It is also probably better to rent the equipment than to buy since you can then take advantage of improved products as well as spreading the cost. Most agreements impose no penalty provided you stay with the same company if you are upgrading the equipment. Read the contracts carefully to see what happens if you terminate before the agreement expires or wish to reduce the size of the equipment. Look carefully to see what the terms are of any maintenance contract, which is normally obligatory.

Installing Lines

You have rather less of a choice when it comes to telephone lines and although BT's monopoly in many areas has been ended there is still very little choice when it comes to the allocation of lines. It is important to ensure that an early approach is made to the area sales department who will discuss your requirements in detail. You should have a clear idea before you make contact of how many lines you will need, the number of extensions and the system's eventual capacity in terms of maximum number of extensions. Don't forget to allow for expansion, and don't forget the separate lines for your private line and the fax machine. It is important to ensure that the lines are allocated as far in advance as possible. It is better to have the lines available a month before the business opens than to find that for whatever reason you have been let down and you are somehow expected to run a business with no telephones.

Fax Machines

Fax machines were recently described by my local District Judge as being the instrument of the devil. Faxes are a much abused instrument with people faxing things that could more conveniently and cheaply be sent by post or document exchange, but they can, on occasions, be life-savers. No modern day practice can do without them. It is not worth buying a cheap or secondhand fax machine or trying to use a fax line which is shared with a telephone line. You must have a dedicated fax line. However, there are many fax machines on the market with all kinds of gadgets, which will store messages and only transmit them at off-peak times, will remember millions of regularly dialled numbers, will store messages even when paper has run out, and so on. There is no need to bother with gadgets of that sort in a small practice unless you are a niche practice specialising in international work. Inevitably, you will find yourself signing a maintenance contract for which the maintainers are likely to do very little at vast expense, but if you do not have the safety net of a maintenance contract, you may well have great problems in getting anyone to repair your fax. It is not really practical to delay installing a fax since, if you follow my advice and have a dedicated line, you will need to put the fax number on your notepaper. It is best to have all the telephone and fax work carried out at the same time and all the equipment in place before you start trading rather than trying to instal the fax after you have been going a few months.

Document Exchange

Similarly, at this point you may decide to put yourself on the document exchange system. There are still some solicitors who are not on it and many people setting up feel that it is an expense that they can do without for the first year or so. In my view it is simply not worth trying to make the saving. Most other solicitors are now on it, as are many banks, building societies, etc., and it is extremely reliable.

Notepaper

Two and three-partner firms may well want to have their notepaper designed by graphic designers. The charge involved is not inconsequential. If it is spread between two or three partners, it is bearable, but a sole practitioner is likely to shy away from what is perceived to be an unnecessary set-up cost. That is fine, so long as you are going to have a reasonable product at the end of it. Notepaper is the solicitor's shop window. If the notepaper looks of poor quality and amateurish, it will reflect very badly on the solicitor's practice. I recently saw a newly-founded sole practitioner's notepaper which he had designed himself and had produced off a laser printer from his computer. The quality of the paper itself and the appearance of the notepaper were pretty poor. He offered the opinion that anyone who had a computer with a laser printer and was still paying out money to have letterheads printed was a mug. I made no comment, but I did feel what a pity it was that with only a very small investment he could have substantially improved on the image that his practice projected to his clients and the public at large.

There is no doubt that quite a good quality product can be produced from laser printers and you may wish to experiment if you have decided to invest in one or have friends who have one. They are certainly not bad for producing mock-ups of notepaper and trying out different ideas. However, once you have decided on what the notepaper is going to look like and you are ready to produce the finished article, it is far better to ask a printer to do it. Ultimately, you may decide that with a few adjustments you can do just as good a job as the printer and, once your stock of professionally printed notepaper has run out, you can always not re-order and produce your own, but I doubt if it will look nearly as good.

Do shop around and haggle, but make sure you show a specimen of what you have already and ensure that it is clearly recorded in correspondence that any quotation must be for letterheads that are of at least as good quality as the sample provided. Other printers may be able to produce cheaper notepaper but if the overall appearance is not as good, then you want to be in a position to walk away from the order on the grounds that they have not fulfilled their part of the contract.

The set-up costs are quite high initially for professionally printed stationery and the printer will then encourage you to order in large quantities since it dramatically brings down the price. By and large you should resist such offers, particularly if you are a sole practitioner. Larger practices will obviously use more paper, but a sole practitioner may take two years to get through what would be a normal print-run for a two or three-partner firm and in that time you may have moved premises, taken on additional staff and would like to put them on the notepaper, merged, changed telephone numbers, etc. Also, by keeping large stocks of notepaper, you take up valuable storage space and tie up cash.

Setting Up a Precedent Library

When you left your last place of work and decided to set up on your own, you probably took with you, in so far as you were able, every kind of precedent you could possibly lay your hands on. These might include drafts of pleadings settled by counsel, specimens which appeared in the Law Society's *Gazette*, precedents photocopied from standard but expensive precedent books, or a pleading served on you by someone else which you thought looked particularly good. You must always bear in mind the question of copyright. It is not a bad idea to check with counsel that they do not mind you adopting their pleading as a basis for others in the future. With a bit of flattery in the right place as to what an excellent pleading it was, they probably will not mind. Precedents taken out of precedent books which you have not bought yourself may need a little more care. You do not want to start your practice on the wrong end of a copyright action.

Every practice needs to have a precedent library of some sort. This will take two forms, precedents stored on word-processor and precedents contained in text books. You may feel that what you should be doing before you actually start work is to rush out and buy masses of material which other people have already put on disk so that you can be all set to go on the first day. This is both unnecessary and a waste of time and money. You will also probably fill up an entire hard disk of a computer with things that you may or may not use. There is no harm in including a few things, such as a standard precedent for a will, a fairly common form of consent order in a divorce matter, and so on, which you are fairly certain you will be using on a regular basis, but other than that it is much better to wait and see. Then, when you have occasion to use a particular document and put it on word-processor, you may decide to keep it as a future precedent. By buying a book containing precedents which covers a specialist area in which you practise, you will obtain the benefit of a ready-made precedent and also help and advice from the author on how and when to use it. Having put that onto disk for the particular job, you will hopefully be paid for the job itself and have the precedent ready and waiting for a similar one in the future. If time goes by and the work is not repeated, you can always delete it. You have still been paid for putting it on there in the first place. By creating a precedent on your computer's hard disk and then periodically trawling through it to delete those items which you have not actually used again, you will acquire your own computerised database of precedents in an economic and cost-effective way. Other information is much more neatly stored away on a bookshelf and is just as easily accessed as if it were on computer. You may wish to consider indexing your precedents alphabetically. All too quickly you may acquire so many precedents that it takes an age to find the one you want unless you have a paper index.

Forms

Similarly, whilst you may want to put on your word-processor certain forms which you use virtually daily, it is far better to order a stock of those printed forms which you think you are likely to use rather than to spend hours putting every conceivable divorce and probate form on your computer only to find, with the benefit of hindsight, that 90 per cent of them you almost never use. Whether you decide to put the information on computer or use the printed law forms approach, you will, without question, need quite a large stock. Most law stationers have minimum quantities but if they can see that you are going to order enough stock to set up a new practice, they can often be persuaded to bend their own rules and let you have five of something rather than their usual minimum quantity of, say, 20. You will need to go through their catalogue picking and choosing the forms you think you might need, but if in doubt, do not order it. All too often the forms are changed and you find yourself throwing away large quantities of forms that are no longer current. You will find that they will normally despatch forms overnight through the document exchange so that if you need one at short notice you can get one.

Another advantage of using printed forms is that a new form is likely to be right up to date whereas you may have missed changes in the law and failed to update the one on your computer. If you have a regular order with a law stationer they will always keep you up to date with new forms and many now issue information sheets to warn of impending changes and invite you to order new forms. If you decide to use printed forms rather than your own maintained on a word-processor you will need a conventional typewriter to complete them.

Don't be afraid to approach another firm if you need a form in a hurry. If you constantly run out of forms and are always begging them off other people, you may outstay your welcome, but if you enlist other people's help once in a while they will not feel bashful about asking you. Co-operation between fellow professionals is always a good thing and such small beginnings can lead to other things.

CHAPTER 6

Advertising

Advertising may be defined as telling people who you are, where you are and what you do. Marketing is persuading them to buy what you are selling once you have told them who you are, where you are and what you sell. You may feel that when you are first setting up there is no point in devising any marketing or advertising strategy, that there is not enough time and you do not have the financial resources. You are wrong on both counts. The business of a solicitor is the selling of legal services. To get customers you have to let them know who you are, where you are, what it is you can do for them and why they should choose you rather than anyone else. If you are able to get the first three across, then there is a reasonable chance that they will choose you anyway. At least you are in the running. This really is the advertising side of things. Even if you are taking with you an existing client base, you will be foolish to rely on that alone. What you need is a steady stream of customers past the door. Even your established clients are not going to want to be using your services the entire time. There will be gaps and those must be filled. For most of our professional lives, we as solicitors have been unable to advertise our services to the general public. This has now changed.

Where to Advertise

Where you advertise will depend on who it is you want to reach. For the average, ordinary high street general practice, you should consider advertising in Yellow Pages and The Thomson Directory. The Law Society runs an excellent 'banner advertising' scheme in Yellow Pages whereby local solicitors can have their name put in a general advertisement so that you have a display advertisement for little more than the price of a lineage advertisement. They have expanded this recently so that there are now several different types of banner advertisements and you may have to choose between a general type of advertisement and a more specialist one. Thomson Directories do not run a similar type of advertisement, but it is already a lot cheaper, since the areas covered by the individual directories are smaller and so the same size advertisement tends to be cheaper.

Local newspapers are another option, but you have to bear in mind that nobody reads last week's news and a local paper will last, at best, for one week. To have any real effect, an advertising campaign in a local paper must be spread over several weeks and you have to compare the cost of doing that and the number of people you are likely to reach with what it will cost to advertise in Yellow Pages or Thomson, an advertisement which will run for a year. You must also place yourself in the position of someone looking for a solicitor and consider where you are likely to look. In the main, people are likely to look in a dedicated directory rather than a local newspaper and if they see your details in a local newspaper it is likely to be more by accident than a deliberate attempt to find a solicitor there.

Once you have set up and your advertising is having some sort of an effect, you are likely to be contacted by all sorts of other people suggesting that you place an advertisement with them. Consider each one carefully. My experience is that in the main most other forms of advertising do not work. Local authorities will suggest that you have your name in a box on their calendar. Counselling services will sometimes send bereaved relatives brochures and will sell the space in the brochures to those persons who are there to help bereaved relatives and friends. They may offer to sell you space in that brochure so that you can assist with the administration of an estate. Again, my experience is that people do not respond to such advertisements.

Advertisements do not work for all sorts of reasons. It may be that you have put the advertisement in the wrong medium, that the advertisement itself is not eye-catching, or gives the wrong information or creates the wrong impression. It may be that the timing of the advertisement is wrong.

Designing Your Advertisement

Any advertisement must leap off the page to someone who is looking for a solicitor. Put yourself in the shoes of a prospective client. Look at the other advertisements in the particular medium being considered and see which advertisements you find attractive and then ask yourself why. Is it their size, the nature of the services offered, the price, or the general impression and friendliness created by the advertisement? What is likely to be attractive to you will probably attract other people. You can go to an advertising agency, but if you are a small practice the fees are likely to be prohibitive. For the time being, you are probably going to have to be your own advertising executive. Do a mock-up of the advertisement that you propose to put forward and show it to your friends. Ask them what they think of it and what impression is created of your practice by the advertisement. Ask them where they would look if they were trying to find a solicitor cold rather than one who was recommended.

If your practice is a two or three-partner firm, your approach may be slightly different. You may have specialist skills within the practice and want to advertise to a particular section of the public either as well as or instead of a general advertisement. The basic rules are still the same. Who are these people and where are they likely to look if they want to find a solicitor? Will it be a specialist trade publication and if so, which one? How many other people are advertising in that trade publication? How many clients will you need to persuade not only to respond to the advertisement but also to instruct you as their solicitor before the whole thing becomes cost-effective? Do not leap forth with an entire advertising campaign before putting your toe in the water. Place a few advertisements in a fairly modest way to see what sort of response it brings. If you are deluged with enquiries then you know you have found the right place to advertise, but if there is a deafening silence then it is unlikely that you will substantially improve on the response simply by increasing the size of the advertisement and the frequency with which it appears. On the whole, it is better to be cautious with your advertising rather than flamboyant. This is not to say that you can place a few bits of lineage in a local newspaper and expect the clients to roll in. The size of the advertisement must be sufficient to be eye-catching. There is no point in a tiny advertisement tucked away in a directory surrounded by massive advertisements of other people. It would be better not to advertise there at all.

The timing of an advertisement is likely to be crucial. Directories such as Yellow Pages and Thomson have fixed copy deadlines and if you miss the deadline for submission of your advertising copy in an annual publication then you may not be able to promote your firm through this medium for another 15 months. You will either have to do without any advertising or find a less favourable publication whose copy date you can make, or content yourself with periodic forays into local newspapers.

The advertisement itself is crucial. Having made your advertisement sufficiently eye-catching so that the prospective client has actually taken the trouble to look at it, you will have something in the region of one to two seconds to sustain that interest before the potential client becomes bored and starts to read someone else's. The message should therefore be interesting, short and to the point. There is an old saying in advertising that you should never sell the product – you should sell the idea behind the product. If you accept this maxim, then you do not simply put in your advertisement 'We do conveyancing'. The customer does not want to buy a conveyance; what they want is to buy the services of someone who will take the burden and worry of the whole house-moving process off their shoulders. Accordingly, your advertisement will be more along the lines of 'We take the pain out of conveyancing'. This is what the customer is looking for. You have hit the right note and they are now prepared to read on. Your references to experience, personnel, fast, reliable service and written quotations available the same day will all serve to reassure the customer that you are the firm they are looking for.

If, in your opinion, you feel that the client is not terribly interested in claims to reliability and speed but is only interested in price and will simply go for the lowest quote, you may prefer to centre your entire message around price. In that case, your advertisement is likely to put the price per conveyance, if that is the way you operate your firm, as the most prominent feature. If you opt for this idea, you must be sure that your potential customers are concerned solely with price and not quality of service and you can be sure that your competitors will be explaining away your very low price on the basis of the low-grade service you will be providing for the low fee charged. Whether the work goes to you or to them is all part of the fun.

Personally, I have never sought to advertise myself as the cheapest firm in town and would rather be thought of as someone who provides a good standard of work for a sensible fee. In the days of cut-price conveyancing and price wars between firms, that may be something of a luxury. Time alone will tell.

Once the phone has started ringing with people asking how they enlist your services, there is one crucial question you must ask them – 'How did you get my details?' Introduced at a suitable juncture in the conversation (not too early as it may sound rather unfriendly, and clients want to talk first about their problems before they talk about anything else), it provides key information as to which advertisements are working and which are not.

The answer may be that they have found you in one publication or another or that they have been recommended by someone else. In the case of a recommendation, it is important to telephone or write to the person making the recommendation and thank them for it. Not only is it good manners but it also makes that person feel that their contribution towards your business is appreciated and not taken for granted, which hopefully will lead to further recommendations. There is no need to send them a gratuity (words of thanks are usually enough) and gratuities can lead to slippery slopes (such as a breach of the Introduction and referral Code 1990 – see *The Guide to the Professional Conduct of Solicitors*, published by the Law Society) but there may be occasions where people have gone to inordinate lengths to secure the work for you and in those exceptional circumstances, a modest donation to their drinks collection may not be out of place.

Where the client has found you as a result of an advertisement, you must make a note of it. It is also important that your staff make a note of it if they take the call, as and when you have risen to the stage where you can afford to employ staff. It is important to know where every single client has come from.

Write down the sources of your business and count them up at the end of the week/month/year. Once you have moved on to, or possibly started with, two or more partners, then you undoubtedly will have to write down and collate the information at the end of the month somewhere centrally so that you can get a precise picture of the cost-effectiveness of your advertising. You can start to analyse precisely where your recommendations are coming from and possibly why and see if further efforts in that area will bring yet greater rewards.

You have placed your advertisement, the prospective client has telephoned you and has started asking questions about the practice, your prices, your experience and may have started telling you some of the problems that they face. So far, so good. You still have not converted the telephone enquiry into a real, live client. All you have is an opportunity to do so and you should not let that slip away. You have paid a lot of money to get this far and that money will be wasted if the client puts down the phone and chooses another firm. Inevitably, you will only convert a comparatively small number of your responses so do not get too despondent if you have a few days or even weeks where none of the people you have spoken to on the telephone actually make an appointment and give you the business. It is, however, an opportunity to review the position generally and to ask yourself if there is something you are doing wrong.

A certain impression will have been created by your advertisement itself. This is something over which you have a good deal of control. As discussed previously, you should consider what sort of an image you wish to project for the firm and this image should be contained within your advertisement. What are clients looking for? How can you project this, both in your advertisement and from the moment the telephone rings? Having obtained a certain mental picture of what the firm is going to be like, the client's next contact with the firm is with the person who answers the telephone. You may have a dedicated telephonist and you will either have chosen him or her for their pleasant, friendly and helpful manner of answering the telephone or you will have trained them to do so. If you have a group pickup system so that the telephone can be answered by anyone in the office, it is important to listen to how people are answering the telephone and dealing with clients. There should also be a standard response so that the opening words are the same, which is likely to sound more professional than a whole variety of different openings. Imagine that you yourself were on the other end of the telephone when you hear a member of staff answering the call and ask yourself how you would react if spoken to in that way.

Telephones must be answered quickly. If a telephone is allowed to ring for any more than three or four rings, then it tells the client that the firm is not run particularly efficiently – you have already begun to lose the image battle. Never allow clients, or anyone else for that matter, to be put on hold for more than about 15 or 20 seconds. It is far better to explain that the person they wish to talk to is likely to be some time and take their number so that they can be called back. If a caller must be put on hold, they must be reassured that they have not been forgotten and that Mr. Bloggs has almost finished and should be off his present call in just a moment.

Winning the Client

A caller has now been put through to you. You have about 30 seconds in which the client will decide whether they like you or not and whether you sound the kind of solicitor with whom they would like do business. What you say in that time is vital. Again, you must analyse what this particular client is looking for and then match your response to fulfil the need. If the client is looking for a sympathetic ear, then no amount of your telling the client how efficient and reliable the firm is will be of the slightest use. They want someone to sit there with their mouth shut so that they can pour their heart out. That is not to say that you must sit there endlessly allowing the client to tell you their entire life story only to find that at the end of a free half an hour call the client tells you that you are far too expensive when you get down to the sordid business of hourly rates.

Similarly, the client may simply be trying to get free advice, or they may have a serious problem which needs attention. By commenting on specific areas of the problem that they have outlined, you may be able to demonstrate that you have the right legal knowledge and the confidence to deal with their matter without actually getting too involved. The one thing you should be aiming for is to arrange for the client to come into your offices at the earliest possible opportunity. It may be prudent to find out at a fairly early stage in the conversation whether the client is likely to be eligible for legal aid or whether they will have to pay for the advice. If you have not had to deal with such calls yourself previously and have simply been fed a steady stream of clients, this process may be rather difficult for you, but you will fairly quickly be able to recognise what parts of your conversation put clients off and what elements of it they find attractive. There is no point having a client who is clearly ineligible for legal aid and who feels that your hourly rate is far too high. Such clients are likely to be nothing but trouble anyway. Nevertheless, there are abrasive ways in which one can put the question of fees (such as, 'Well, I am sorry, but that's my hourly rate. If I don't charge that I go out of business') and more diplomatic ways, ('I can appreciate that it may sound a lot, but there is a certain minimum level at which we have to charge in order to make the figures add up. Perhaps we could get together for half an hour and see how far we get with that. Would that help?'.)

The Free Interview

You may feel that it would be worthwhile offering clients a free 10-15 minute interview either as a general policy, possibly advertised, or just in suitable cases where it looks as though the client may not be eligible for legal aid and is not happy with the idea of paying for the advice. If you get them into the office, then in that 10 or 15 minute period it may become clear that they are in fact likely to be eligible for legal aid or that from what you have said in the interview the cost of the legal services may not be quite so prohibitive as they at first thought. At worst, you have lost 10 or 15 minutes of your time but you have ceased to be a name in an advertisement. The client may have future problems and may turn to you for help and by that time they may be eligible for legal aid or have the funds available to pay you privately.

CHECKLIST

- Work out marketing and advertising plan.
- Set budget.
- Decide on type of media to be used.
- Contact media for copy deadlines and prices.
- Design adverts.
- Place in chosen media.
- Check advert has correctly appeared.
- Monitor response.

CHAPTER 7

Putting in Systems

COMPUTERS

Depending on what type of practice you were in previously and what you did in it, you may or may not be 'computer literate'. You may have been aware that computers were around in your previous practice but had no real knowledge of how they worked and probably had no particular interest. This section is intended for those people who have not the slightest idea of how a computer works, still less what points to look for when buying one. If this does not apply to you, please skip ahead to the next chapter.

As discussed in Chapter 5, computers are not the answer to everything. They are a tool of the trade, nothing more. You do not buy an office shredder just because everyone else has one. You buy one because you have decided that the volume of material you have to dispose of warrants such a purchase, you can fit it into your budget and it is cheaper than getting someone else to take it away and shred it. You have good, sound, logical reasons. You should buy a computer for exactly the same reasons. There are a great many instances where a manual system is far superior to a computer. A manual system never breaks down and does not cease to operate during power cuts. Whilst you can lose the data in a manual system by losing the book in which you have written your notes, or it catches fire or drops in the fish tank, it cannot be lost by pushing the wrong button or because somebody inexperienced did all the wrong things. Having said that, it is much more difficult than you might think with today's computers to lose data by pressing the wrong button. Computers are now far more user friendly than they ever used to be and most computer systems will give you a very clear message that by doing what you are about to do you will lose certain data and ask you if you really want to do it. It is virtually impossible to lose data by accident, such as by pressing the wrong button. You normally have to press two buttons at the same time.

A manual system needs no warm-up period. You simply get the notebook out of your desk and look up the relevant page. Computers need to go through a warm-up procedure when you first switch them on. This can be rather annoying if you need the information quickly. An ordinary address book with A–Z sections can normally locate a client's address and telephone number at least as fast and sometimes faster than a computer. They can be operated by you without any training rather than by an employee brought in specially and trained at vast expense.

Where computers score over manual systems is in their ability to handle very large amounts of information and to retrieve that information at amazing speed and with incredible accuracy. They are therefore absolutely vital within a large organisation but far less important in a small practice. At exactly which point you need to computerise is a matter for your professional judgement. Unless you already have a large amount of information, such as a substantial client following, lots of active cases and probably two or three employees, you may well have little use for a computer system of any sort, apart from perhaps a word-processor. It is unlikely that you will have any difficulty in deciding at which point you need to computerise. You will simply find it very difficult to manage to do everything manually.

At this stage, you will realise that you have certain problems. You will need to analyse exactly what those problems are and then apply your mind, or possibly that of computer consultants, to the question of how a computer may be able to help you. By approaching it this way, you are much more likely to invest in a computer that will suit your practice rather than ending up with a white elephant. The trick is to have the problems first and then adapt the computer and software that runs on it to solve the problems rather than to get the computer and the software and then think what problems you can put it to work to solve. You will also need to think one stage ahead. You will look at your business plan and see where you are likely to be in about three years' time and then take a conscious decision that you will either get rid of your computer at that stage and buy a completely different one, or a different system, or buy the kind of computer now that can be expanded to meet your future needs as and when they arise.

Types of Computer System

Computers fall largely into two different systems for the purposes of a small practice. They are either stand-alone systems or networked systems. Stand-alone means precisely that. The computer sits on its own and doesn't talk to anybody except hopefully you who are operating it. If you have two or three computers in the office that are stand-alones, they cannot talk to each other directly. You may be able to pass information from one to another but that will be rather like a carrier pigeon system as opposed to a telephone system. That is not to say that the carrier pigeon will not do its job remarkably well. Stand-alone systems are, generally speaking, less complicated and more suitable for the sole practitioner and even two or three-partner firms. They are simpler to use and cause fewer problems. If one machine goes wrong, you can always use another one if you have two stand-alones. If you are using a network and the system goes down, then effectively you have no computers at all at one fell swoop. Stand-alones are also cheaper to buy and the support services are less expensive.

Networked systems are a series of computers which are all part of the same system. They are all able to have access to the same information from a central point. They are a little bit like the extensions on a telephone system. Accordingly, if you have several people who will need to use the computer, either at the same time or at different times and they will all need a computer screen on their desk, then the networked system is the right one for you. On the other hand, if you are the only person who will use the information most of the time, or perhaps your secretary is the only person using a word-processing system, or your accounts person is on an accounting system, then there is not much point in having a networked system unless you are going to have one master software package which can be accessed by each of the above persons at the same time. That is likely to be rather expensive both in terms of the hardware (the computers themselves) and software (the computer program which runs on the computer, without which it is useless).

Storage or Memory

Information on a computer is stored either on a hard disk or a floppy disk. In the beginning most disks used were floppy disks which were 5.25 inches square and looked like small pop records. The software, usually purchased on one or more of these disks, was put into the computer. This could take a number of disks, depending on the size and complexity of the program. The information on these disks was then absorbed by the computer into its Random Access Memory ('RAM'). In human terms, this is the conscious mind of the computer as opposed to its subconscious mind where all sorts of other information might be stored. You would then add the information which you wanted the computer to sort out for you and work on. You had to be careful that the information going into the computer's RAM (or conscious memory) was not too great so that the memory was filled up. New information was recorded on another disk (your working disk) which was then removed. When you switched the computer off, all the information was lost except insofar as you still had a record of it on your original software program disks and your own working disk.

The 'hard disk' was then developed. This is a kind of drum inside the computer which rotates as the computer finds the right bit of it to store information. The hard disk is capable of storing the same amount of information as is recorded on a great many floppy disks. You could, if you wanted to, feed the information from the floppy disks into the computer and then get the computer to copy it onto the hard disk. The next time you wanted to access the information you only had to ask the computer to put the information it had stored on its hard disk back into its conscious memory – the RAM – thus saving a great deal of time and trouble. Not only that, but if you wanted to you could alter the information stored on the hard disk and call it up again in the same way. With the vast increase in computer sales in recent years, virtually every computer sold for office use today has a hard disk.

With stand-alone computers, the hard disk is contained normally within the computer itself. With networked systems, by and large the hard disk sits as a large box plugged into all the other computers working off it since, generally speaking, they need to be able to store a lot more information.

Nowadays, most floppy disks used are 3.5 inches square and despite their name are contained in a hard casing. Do not confuse the floppy disk in a hard case with the term 'hard disk'.

The memory on computers is measured in megabytes (Mb). For a sole practitioner or possibly two and three-partner firms using stand-alone systems you will need a computer with at least a 30 or 40 megabyte hard disk which also has a 'drive' for a floppy disk. The memory capacity on machines is constantly increasing with most manufacturers offering computers with over 250 megabyte hard disk capacity.

Windows

Windows is a comparatively recent feature on computers and is becoming more and more popular. Unfortunately, it uses up a great deal of computer memory. Basically, the idea of Windows is that instead of having two or three different software programs on your computer all performing separate functions and only one of which can be used at any one time, you can pause with a Windows program half way through one function leaving the information still on the screen and call up something else as a little 'window' on the screen, perform the function with that and then go back to where you were in the first function. It is like being able to put a bookmark in a book and then skipping further on to find some other information before returning to your original place, without having to start right back at the beginning.

Because of the popularity of Windows and its 'user friendliness', many computer suppliers will sell a machine with Windows software already loaded on it by the manufacturer. Two points to watch for are firstly whether you will have sufficient space available left on the machine if you are going to run Windows, and secondly whether your computer chip is fast enough. The latest version of Word for Windows only runs on a 486 chip or faster. First, of course, you must decide what it is you want to put on your machine in addition to anything that the manufacturer may have included. To run an accounts or word-processing package within Windows you will need at least four megabytes of main memory. If you install the whole of Word for Windows, Version 6, including games, screensavers, etc., it will use up 25 megabyte of memory on your hard disk. The most basic installation of the programs uses 5 megabyte of memory. Bear in mind you have not yet started putting information of your own on the disk which will use up more space.

Speed

Computers work at different speeds. The speed at which they work is determined by the type of processor in them. Processors have got faster and faster due to the improvement in the quality of the computer chips inside them: the 286 processor has been replaced by the 386 and now the 486 processor. The name of the computer generally has this identifying feature somewhere in the title. As well as being able to process the information faster, the speed of the computer to some extent governs the type of program that can be run. Windows, for example, takes up a great deal of space because there is a lot of information which the computer needs to handle. If you have a computer with a 286 processor, it might just be able to get Windows to run on it, but it will be so slow that the program will be totally useless. To run Windows, you will need at least a 386 and preferably a 486 type of computer. The current version of Windows has been doctored to prevent it being run on a 286 processor.

Printers

The printer for an accounts package is really not important since all you need from that is to be able to see what the figures look like. They are not normally presented to anyone else and so their appearance does not generally matter. If you need to send a client a print-out of a ledger, he or she is more concerned with the transactions shown on it than how pretty the figures look. When it comes to the presentation and appearance of legal documents or letters, then it is quite the contrary. For those you need a much better quality printer which means that despite the letter quality mode which most dot matrix printers can produce, you are really going to need a bubble/ink jet printer (really the same thing) at least, and preferably a laser printer. You will find huge differences in price between the three different types. Remember, your legal documentation and letters are your 'shop window' and both clients and other professionals will judge you by both the quality of your work and the quality of its appearance. Your choice of printer is, therefore, important.

Types of Printer

There are several different kinds of printer but for the solicitor the choice can be narrowed down to three: dot matrix, ink jet or laser.

Dot Matrix

Dot matrix printers work by firing a series of pins onto a ribbon leaving an imprint on the page. They usually are designed with either nine or 24 pins, the more pins used, the greater the clarity. In draft mode they are quite fast but must slow down to produce letter-quality print. They are the only one of the three types of printer mentioned here which can be used to produce multi-carbon copies for items such as invoices. They are the noisiest and cheapest, and starting at around £100 are good value for money.

Ink jet

The technology used is similar to that of the dot matrix but the print head fires ink at the paper instead of pins. The quality of print is excellent, such that it may be difficult to distinguish it from a laser-produced document. Their running costs are lower than those of a laser printer. They are quieter and faster than a dot matrix but not as quiet or as fast as a laser. A reasonably good quality ink jet for a small office will cost £200-£300 and will print at about three pages a minute. The print itself has a life of about seven years, which is fine for most purposes with the possible exception of wills. You also have to be careful not to smudge ink jet-produced documents whilst the ink is drying.

Laser

Lasers work on a quite different principle to dot matrix and ink jet printers and are more akin to photocopiers. Their print quality is superb, they are almost silent in operation and can print at a speed of about 12 pages a minute. Do, however, bear in mind that the time it takes to print out a document may have more to do with the computer you are using and the software you run on it.

The printer only prints something when the computer tells it to. If, due to the slowness of the computer and the software used, the command takes two minutes to come through, as is often the case, it might take two and a half minutes to print out a couple of pages, even with a laser printer.

Choosing a Printer

The disadvantages of lasers are their relatively high capital and running costs. They have come down in price dramatically over the last five years but even so, be prepared to pay £2,000 for a good 'workhorse' laser printer for a busy established office.

Considerations to bear in mind when choosing your printer are:

- Will its main use be to produce a high-quality finished product (letters, affidavits, etc.) or simply to record information (accounts, time-sheets)?
- Where will it go and will it fit?
- How much will it cost to run?

- Does it matter if it is noisy?

- How long do I think it will be before I change it for another printer?

If you have an established client base which you are taking with you and are confident your output will be large from the beginning you will probably need a laser printer and possibly more than one, depending on how many secretarial staff you have, from the inception of the practice, and probably a dot matrix for the accounts.

If you are starting a practice from nothing with little or no established client base, buy an ink jet if you are confident with using computers and a dot matrix if you are not. It makes sense to operate with a low-cost dot matrix printer until you have sorted out a workable system and can see how much of a workload will be passing through it.

If you suddenly find you are extremely busy you may decide to invest in a laser at an early stage, but more probably you will wish to graduate to an ink jet, keeping the dot matrix for the accounts.

Setting up Your Computer

Having selected your hardware, loaded your software or had it done for you, and chosen your printer, you then have them all delivered. Then comes the shock. The delivery man dumps the whole lot in the middle of your office floor with the instruction manual sellotaped to the top, waves a cheery goodbye and disappears. You open the instruction manual, which is the size of *War and Peace*, and start trying to plough your way through it. You then find that this is the instruction manual for the computer and there are separate ones for the printer and the software, each of which are themselves the size of volumes II and III of *War and Peace*. At this time a degree in Japanese comes in handy.

If anything, sorting out the printer is likely to be the biggest problem. Annoyingly printers operate to different page lengths (i.e. the amount of text you get on one page) because the size of the print varies from one machine to another. The printer itself may need to be told to what page length it is operating since it may be capable of printing in more than one print size. In turn, the software on the computer needs to give certain instructions to the printer on such matters as page length, so the two need to be able to communicate effectively.

You OPEN THE INSTRUCTION MANUAL
AND START TRYING TO PLOUGH
THROUGH IT.

Accounts Packages

There are many accounts packages available specifically geared to small practices. They vary in complexity and prices range from about £600 up to £4,000. The more expensive, then generally speaking, the more the package will do for you and the more matters it can handle. Because of its additional complexity, it will take up more space on the computer. Our own solution to these various difficulties was to have a basic word-processing package on a fairly basic and cheap machine. This did not affect the quality of the finished product since its appearance is governed not so much by the computer or the word-processing software that is run on it but more by the type of printer that is used. We ran the word-processing work on that and had a separate and more sophisticated computer solely for the accounts work. This meant that when the point came when we needed the two functions to be dealt with at the same time the book-keeper did not have to stop work to allow the word-processor operator to type an important document.

It is, in my opinion, undoubtedly better to start off with a manual accounts system until you get used to running your own accounts and then find a suitable software package and run the two together until gradually you move off onto a fully computerised system. Again, neither the software nor the hardware needs to be sophisticated. Go for something rudimentary to start off with and then when you appreciate all the problems and the shortcomings of the system you are running, you can afford, both in terms of time and cost, to upgrade.

In the same way, you can do without databases, spreadsheets, computerised debt collection systems, conveyancing systems, etc., in the early days. Once you get used to using computers and seeing what they can and can't do, then is the time to decide whether those additional tools of the trade can be applied usefully to your particular tasks.

FILING

When I was in partnership, each file had a number. In fact, it had several numbers. As someone who is very bad at remembering numbers, I found this particularly irksome. Each file had a number so that I could find it in my filing cabinet. It had a different number on the accounts system. It had a third number for time-recording purposes. It had add-on numbers to show who supervised it, what type of matter it was and who the fee-earner was, and when it was put into store, it had yet another number to enable it to be retrieved from the dead files system.

The reason why files need several different numbers is because each system comes in at a different time. When setting up a new practice, you have a unique opportunity to have one number for a file throughout its entire life since you are starting all your systems in one go. This gives you an amazing advantage over all those people spending collectively millions of hours looking up all the different numbers each time when they want to do something with a file.

To start off, you need a card index box with A–Z dividers and two A5 size books, one of which has A–Z pages on it. You then start numbering your files. If you have taken some files with you from another practice, there is nothing wrong with adopting one of the several numbering sequences and using that as your starting point, so long as any new files that are opened are numbered sequentially from the highest number of the existing files. Put all your files in correct numerical sequence in your filing cabinets and then make out an index card for each one. The top line on the left-hand side will be the client's surname followed by any first names with the file number in the top right-hand corner. The nature of the matter will then appear underneath it. The file is then cross-referenced in the other two books. You will go through your files systematically in this way and if, like myself, you took hardly any clients with you from your previous practice, this takes a depressingly short amount of time so that when you have indexed all 10 of your files, you can sit down and make a cup of tea!

The index card should then look something like this:

```
┌─────────────────────────────────────────┐
│ BLOGGS, MRS FREDA              7483       │
│ Re: Road Traffic Accident                 │
└─────────────────────────────────────────┘
```

Mrs Bloggs' name is then put under 'B' in the A5 book with 'Re: Road Traffic Accident' opposite it and at the end of the line the file number 7483. It is a matter for you as to whether you start your numbering sequence at file no. 1 or file no. 1000, thus in the latter case giving the impression to the rest of the world that you have thousands of files and not just 10! You then turn to the other A5 book and you write '7483' on the left-hand side and 'BLOGGS, MRS FREDA Re: Road Traffic Accident'.

Having listed all your files in this way, you then give instructions to your secretary that any new file that is opened must be allotted the next number and at the same time as a label is done for the file cover an index card is created and the two entries made in the two A5 books with the index card put in the appropriate place in the filing card box.

As your practice expands and you have individual fee-earners with their own set of files and filing cabinets, it is important to insist that people stick to the system. A great many people try to create their own system, which spells disaster. They will tell you that they find it much easier to put things in their filing cabinet in alphabetical order. Insist they do it your way. The day will come when they are not in the office and you need to find one of their files in a hurry. If the client's name is McDonald, you will not know if it is filed at the front of all of the Ms, or in a separate section for Mc or Mac. If the file number is 7483, the only possible place that the file will be is between 7482 and 7484 in the filing cabinet. It may be necessary to check more than one filing cabinet, but the possible places for the file to be become substantially limited.

As a sole practitioner, the buck stops very much with you. If the file cannot be located, it is very much your fault. If someone else is operating the kind of filing system more appropriate to a neanderthal cave dweller, it is your fault. Setting up a new practice, you have the opportunity to lay the foundations of a highly efficient filing system and keep it that way. It is your fault if it goes off the rails because your staff subsequently demolish the system over a period of time.

Having set up the card index system, this number then becomes the number either for a manual accounts system or a computerised accounts system – it makes no difference. Again, when you swap from one system to the other, it normally does not matter. Occasionally, some computerised systems have to have a certain number of digits, but you can often get round this by putting noughts at the beginning or end. Certainly, with the simpler systems more appropriate to small practices, they have no problem at all in accommodating four-figure reference numbers. The same number can be used for a time-recording system and for the dead filing and storage system. We have always had a system whereby a file is moved out of a live filing cabinet into a dead file cabinet. Critics of this may well say, with a certain amount of justification, that you are taking up valuable office space and cluttering up the place with a load of dead files. Inevitably, you will find that if you take a file out of a live cabinet when you think it is finished and you put it into some kind of long-term storage, within 24 hours someone will write you a letter on it. We keep files in a dead file system for at least a year after we think the matter is ended where we can have ready access to it. It does mean that every now and then you have to go through the cabinets and 'flush' them through by taking out files and putting them into dead filing cabinets, but it is an exercise well worth the effort. Then, after a further period of inactivity or your dead file drawers become full, suitable candidates can be removed to longer term storage and should at that stage be marked with destruction dates. So far as the filing system is concerned, you can maintain the same number right the way through live, dead and storage systems.

STORING

Quite how long you should store files is a matter of opinion. *The Guide to the Professional Conduct of Solicitors* gives certain advice and guidance on this topic. The safest and, generally speaking, most unattractive option from a practical point of view is to offer the file back to the client. If he or she declines to accept it, then there is at least an argument for saying that the client cannot complain if you dispose of it and suddenly it is required. However, it does mean that you have the problem of transporting the file back to the client at some expense, almost certainly to yourself, or asking the client to come and get it.

If you are not going to arrange for it to go back to the client by some means or another, then you will have to store it – but for how long? The real cost of storing documentation is always fairly high, unless you are going to take it home and keep it in the attic, where it is going to be difficult to get at, will be in the way of all the other things you want to store there, and will probably end up getting filthy and damp. Clearly, the shorter period of time you store it, then the better for you. However, if you destroy a file too soon, you are taking a chance. It is always difficult to explain to a client why you have shredded the file and the word 'negligent' will constantly be seen to be passing through the client's mind, even if it is not uttered.

Personally, I take the view that comparatively minor criminal matters can be destroyed after as short a time as two or three years (but see the Guide on the relevance of VAT problems). If the client re-offends, there is every chance you will not be instructed anyway – criminal litigation clients can be notoriously fickle. The chances are that the client will not remember which firm represented him or her and in any event, there will be no need for the file to be retrieved. If there is such a need, key information such as previous convictions will be on record elsewhere. You will presumably have a copy of your bill in the office which should assist you with the VAT problem referred to above.

Similarly, with conveyancing sale files, the client has disposed of the property and so why is there any need to retain the file for any great length of time? The answer is likely to be the danger of a possible action for misrepresentation despite any exclusions you may have put in the contract. If those are going to happen at all, they are probably likely to happen within a period of, say, three years. A client is unlikely to complain about being misled as to what exactly he or she was buying after that time. The exception to that is defects in title, but in that event the client is probably likely to turn first of all on his or her own solicitors and you do have the maxim of caveat emptor on your side in that situation. You may be prepared to take the view that you can dispose of such a file after three years if you are prepared to accept the VAT risk referred to earlier. Six years may be safer. It is a matter for your judgement and a question of how much storage space you have available.

Is it ever safe to dispose of a purchase file? The client may stay in the property for 20 years and a defect in the conveyancing work may only come to light when that client comes to sell the property and the defect is pointed out by the would-be purchasing solicitors. It may, therefore, only ever be safe to dispose of such a file two or three years after you know for sure that the property has been sold on again, even if that may not be for 20 years. In all other types of cases, you are really going to have to wait for at least six years.

The best time to judge how long to keep a file is when you first put it into long-term storage and the best person to do the judging is the fee-earner who worked on the file, unless they are quite junior. At that stage all the relevant factors should still be reasonably fresh in the fee-earner's mind. No file should be put into store without a destruction date marked in red on the front. This makes the job of destruction far easier. The selection of files for destruction should only ever be undertaken by a principal, or at least a working party of senior fee-earners under the supervision of a principal. If a file has been recalled from storage for any reason, careful consideration should be given to the question of reassessment of the destruction date. It is foolish to leave a destruction date intact if it is clear from further developments on the file that it is not going to the shredder quietly.

ACCOUNTS

At first sight, setting up your own accounting system seems horrendously complicated, particularly if you have never concerned yourself with the workings of a firm's accounting system before. In fact, it is not at all difficult. Because it seems such a formidable task, it is tempting to go out and buy a computerised system so that it has got everything on it. As discussed in earlier chapters, this would be a big mistake. Once again, it would be a case of getting a computer and then trying to see what problems you could load onto it rather than identifying the problems and then finding out how a computer could solve them.

Who should be your Book-Keeper?

If you are fortunate enough to have a spouse who enjoys book-keeping, then you have an ideal choice. If not, it is best to employ someone, albeit on a part-time basis. It is normally a bad idea to try to do it yourself. It usually ends in disaster and, in a great many cases, an appearance before the Disciplinary Tribunal.

If you use a part-time outside book-keeper, don't just select one from the telephone book. Get a recommendation, preferably from another solicitor with a small practice, or at the very least from an accountant whose judgement you can trust. It is an easy matter for someone to get your accounts into a mess and an enormous task getting them straight again. It is no defence to an allegation of breach of the Accounts Rules that it was the book-keeper's fault.

Another alternative is to use an outside book-keeping agency. There are a number of companies who will provide a computerised book-keeping service for you. You send off your financial information to them in the post and they will do the rest. Whilst at first sight this may seem attractive, it is not particularly cheap and you do not have a lot of control over it. If, for any reason, the book-keeper needs to have access to the files, then the file is likely to be out of the office for three or four days. There is also a tendency to feel that you have covered that particular problem and not to look too closely at what is going on because it is now someone else's problem. If this system is to be used, it should have a close eye kept on it, and in the early stage of practice this can be a difficult thing to do.

Assuming that you are going to do the job 'in house', you will need to keep the following:

1. a system of slips or vouchers;
2. ledger cards (one for each client);
3. bills delivered book;
4. clients' bank book;
5. office bank book;
6. petty cash book;
7. wages book.

If you are starting with a computerised system, most of these books will be on the system.

System of Slips or Vouchers

You may well be familiar with a system of slips. You may have complained bitterly in the past that you cannot get anything out of your cashiers department without filling in a piece of paper first. Now that you are on the receiving end of people asking for things without slips of paper, you will come to realise their value and how they hold the system together. Slips are generally colour-coded and you can choose any colour system you like. The four that I have always used is a *pink* slip as a cheque request slip (or anything else where money is going out of the firm such as a telegraphic transfer that is being sent); a *blue* slip for any form of money received (including in-coming telegraphic transfers); a *green* slip for transfers, be it between office and client account or one office account to another office account or one client account to another client account; and a white slip for petty cash. All of these should be duplicated by means of carbon paper so that whenever you create an original for the accounts department you can put a copy on the file. At this stage of the proceedings, the accounts department may well be you or your spouse sitting in the next room! It is amazing how often the carbon file copy comes into its own. By checking the file you can see if you really did send off the deeds to the Land Registry because there will be a carbon copy of the pink cheque request slip with the Land Registry fees shown on it, etc.

Once the original slip has been actioned, e.g. by the drawing of the cheque to which it relates, or the conversion of a petty cash slip into money, it should be crossed through or a big red tick put on it, or whatever other device you want to show that the necessary action has been taken, so that you do not end up drawing two cheques for the same amount, or paying yourself your expenses twice out of petty cash. The slip is then placed on a tag and given a number. That number will find its way on to the ledger card in due course.

The following example involving a county court summons illustrates how the system works.

Fill out the pink cheque request slip for the court issue fee (check with the court what the correct fee is first!), put the carbon on the file and pass the original pink slip to the book-keeper/cashier. Again, as a sole practitioner this could be you! The cheque is then written out and the slip crossed through and placed on the tag and given the next number, e.g. P (pink)1. As this is a new matter, you will be opening a new client ledger card. Write the details out on the card, add the date and in the narrative column put 'court fee'. In the debit column of the office account section put the court fee, e.g. £60. In an appropriate column on your sheet write 'P1'. This tells you the number of the pink slip used to draw the cheque.

MR ALBERT BLOGGS		FILE NO. 0068		
Re: SHODDY ENGINEERING LIMITED				
Date		Office A/C		Client A/C
		Dr Cr		Dr Cr
1/4/95 Of you on a/c costs	B2			£100.00
4/4/95 Ct fee on summons	P1	£60.00		

In months to come, no doubt during your audit by your accountants, someone will ask you something about the cheque that was drawn. You will then look the matter up on the ledger card, see that the cheque request slip was P1 and will dig it out from your bundle. This will give you information such as who requested the cheque to be drawn, the payee and perhaps more information as to what the cheque was for than was recorded on the ledger card. The same system applies for each type of slip.

Ledger Cards

A number of companies including OYEZ and Moore Paragon UK Limited (telephone numbers are on page 30) have fairly simple ledger cards. Use a new ledger card for each new client matter with the name of the client and the details of the matter at the top and keep them in numerical order with a new number being allocated to each client as the files are opened. There is no need to open a ledger card for a client until there is a financial transaction happening on it, the first normally being a payment on account of costs or possibly a court fee or a local authority search fee. As outlined previously, your new system will have the same file number and accounts number. Such a system is perfectly adequate for small practices. Indeed, most practices have run perfectly satisfactorily for most of their history on a manual card ledger system, since computers are a comparatively recent invention. Even in terms of speed, whilst a practice is relatively small, there is little to be gained on the question of speed. It takes virtually the same amount of time to enter in a few transactions per day manually as it does on a computer. The big advantage of a computer is that it does not make arithmetical mistakes.

Once the practice starts to take off and there are lots more entries to be made, then the case for going computerised gets stronger and stronger. You will also need a number of 'nominal' ledger cards on office account where records are kept of office expenditure, e.g. housekeeping, wages, stationery, etc.

Bills Delivered Book

This is a record of all invoices you raise, showing to whom you have rendered an account, when and for how much. You will need an A4 size book with at least seven columns on each sheet. Head it up across a double page to include the following:

- Year/Date
- Client's Name
- Client's Account Number
- Invoice Number
- Fees Rendered (Gross)
- VAT
- Net Fee (i.e. Profit Costs)
- Disbursements net of VAT
- Date Paid
- Method Paid (i.e. cheque/cash/transfer, etc)

As you raise an invoice, fill in the columns with the relevant details, and when the client makes payment, make sure to complete the remaining columns.

Any spare columns can be used for extra information, e.g. if the client pays by instalments, these payments can be noted down with the relevant blue/green slip numbers recorded.

At the end of each month, total the money columns, leave a small gap and then commence with the next month's transactions.

The invoice pads I use are self-carbonating with a top copy for the client, one copy for the client's file and the third copy placed in a ring binder marked 'Accounts Rendered'. The pads are printed with my firm's headed paper details and are pre-numbered. Although these are a little pricey, I feel they are well worth the extra outlay.

The ring binder with the copy invoices constitute the bills delivered book for Accounts Rules purposes but the A4 book will prove exceptionally useful from a management point of view. In addition, you may, as a fee-earner and principal, wish to keep a separate list of all bills which go out, in your desk drawer. This will not be quite so scientific as the other records, but will give you quite an accurate idea of how well or badly you are doing without having to go and switch on a computer or interrupt the book-keeper. Also, the fact that the information is immediately to hand will encourage you to use it.

A sample entry would look like this:

1995	CLIENT	A/C No	Invoice No	Fees £	VAT £	Net Amt £	Date Paid	Fees Paid £	Method
1st Oct	Mrs L Jones	6600	2356	117.50	17.50	100.00	10th Oct	117.50	Transfer

Clients' Bank Book

This is a record of all financial transactions regarding clients' money.

Again, you will need a book roughly A4 in size, but wider if possible, with at least seven columns per page. As for the bills delivered book, head it up across a double page as follows.

On the left-hand page you will need the following columns:

• Year/Date

• Client's Name

• Client's Account Number

• Detail (i.e. how much money received from client)*

• Slip Number (i.e. number of blue slip)

- Bank (i.e. amount deposited in clients' account)*

* These two figures should be the same!

The left-hand side of the clients' bank book is, therefore, for lodgements at the bank.

It will be of little surprise, then, that the right-hand page of the clients' bank book is for payments out of the bank. Head the right-hand page up as follows:

- Year/Date

- Client's Name

- Client's Account Number

- Cheque Number

- Slip Number (i.e. number of pink or green slip)

- Amount paid out

The Solicitors' Accounts Rules now require a running total to be shown. At the end of each month, total the money columns, and reconcile them with the amount shown on the latest bank statement. The Accounts Rules provide for five-weekly maximum periods in which the figures must be reconciled, but this is really only to allow a little flexibility. It is sensible and generally more convenient to do it monthly.

Office Bank

This is a record of all financial transactions involving the firm's money as opposed to clients' money. You will need a book of similar size to the clients' bank book but with at least 15 columns and preferably 20, on the right-hand page.

As for the clients' bank book, the left-hand page will be for money received and the right-hand page for payments made. Head the left-hand page up as follows:

- Year/Date

- Details (i.e. who has made payment)

- Client's Account Number

- Slip Number (i.e. blue slip number)
- Banked Gross
- VAT
- Net Amount

Head up the rest of the double page (including any of the remainder of the left-hand page still available) as follows:

- Year/Date
- Details (i.e. who cheque made payable to)
- Cheque Number
- Slip Number (i.e. pink slip number)
- Gross Amount
- VAT
- Nominal Ledgers*

* The remainder of the page should be divided into columns for the following items: stationery, salaries, fax/phone, rent/rates, motoring, books, furniture, repairs, insurance, advertising, clients' disbursements, PAYE, VAT payment, practising certificate, professional indemnity contribution, etc. The amount of space available will determine how many headings you can have.

At the end of each month, total the financial columns and reconcile the amounts with the latest bank statement.

Petty Cash Book

This is a record of all cash payments made from the firm's petty cash.

You will need a book identical to that used for office bank. Again, the left-hand page is for money received, the right for payments made. Head up the left-hand page as follows:

- Year/Date
- Details (i.e. where money has come from. This will almost always be 'bank', i.e. cash withdrawn from office account)

- Amount Received

The remainder of the double page can be used for the following headings:

- Year/Date

- Details (i.e. what has been purchased, e.g. milk, stamps, etc.)

- Slip Number (e.g. white slip number)

- VAT

- Nominal Ledgers*

* As above, the remainder of the double page should be headed up with the various nominal ledgers you feel are appropriate, e.g. refreshments, postage, papers, cleaning, sundries, fares, etc. As before, at the end of each month total the various financial columns and reconcile the total with the amount left in the petty cash box.

Wages Book

This book will be a record of salaries paid to all employees. An A4 size book will suffice with approximately seven columns per page. One A4 page should be adequate for the necessary information. Head it up as follows:

- Year/Date

- Employee's Name/National Insurance Number

- Gross Salary

- Employer's and Employee's National Insurance Contribution

- Income Tax

- Employee's National Insurance Contribution

- Net Payment

At the end of each month, total the columns for employer's and employee's national insurance contribution and income tax and add the two together; this amount will be the PAYE payable by the 18th day of the following month.

Whilst on the subject of wages, you will, of course, have to work out using the various tax tables supplied by the Inland Revenue how much tax and national insurance to deduct from each employee's gross salary. The booklets provided by the Revenue are fairly self-explanatory, but if you are in any doubt, contact your local Tax Office. They are usually able to sort out any queries quickly. Do not put off contacting them – if you are interpreting the procedures incorrectly, it is much better to find out as soon as possible.

Reporting Procedures – Legal Aid Franchise and Law Society Practice Management Standards

As a sole practitioner starting a sole practice, you will probably not wish to be too concerned at this stage with a legal aid franchise and Law Society Practice Management Standards unless at a fairly early stage you are going to have several staff and the client base to go with them. In that instance, it would be well worth putting in the systems strictly in accordance with the Practice Management Standards both from the point of view of opening the way to a legal aid franchise application at a later stage and because they will assist the practice to be run efficiently and, hopefully, profitably. The day may not be very far off when copies of the Practice Management Standards will be brandished in industrial tribunals and partners grilled as to whether the firm complies with this aspect or that in the context of an unfair dismissal claim and, likewise, before disciplinary hearings. Rather like the Highway Code in the magistrates' court for driving offences, the plea that the Standards are advisory only will ring very hollow when you are trying to justify something that you have done or failed to do if your actions run contrary to the Practice Management Standards.

From a sole practitioner's point of view, if you have perhaps only one or two members of staff, you may feel that much of what is in the Practice Management Standards is irrelevant. This is true up to a point, but it does not stop you having some sort of business plan and a marketing strategy, and even your one or two employees will feel all the better for you having a chat with them about their performance over the last year, discussing their strengths and weaknesses and generally making them feel as though what they say and do in the course of their work is noticed and that it matters.

The chances are that if you are starting a brand new practice, the last thing on your mind will be legal aid franchises and Practice Management Standards. If the practice is going to start from very humble beginnings, then the solution is likely to be to make yourself aware of what those standards are and to implement them selectively as time goes on with those that are most relevant to your particular type of practice taking priority.

Perhaps one of the first items you will need to attend to will involve writing out a job description for any staff that you take on at the outset or are likely to take on within the first 12 months. You will also need to draw up contracts of employment. A simple way around these and many other problems associated with maintaining the Practice Management Standards is to acquire a copy of the Law Society's *Solicitors' Office Manual*. The *Office Manual* is designed specifically to assist with compliance with the Practice Management Standards and the precedents are easily adapted to suit your own firm. Since compliance with the Practice Management Standards is a pre-requisite in applying for a legal aid franchise, you are already half way there by complying with the Practice Management Standards.

In a small practice, reporting procedures can be kept fairly informal. It should be you who opens the post and so you should see every letter that comes in as well as signing, or at the very least, approving every letter that goes out. Handing a fee-earner their post provides an ideal opportunity to go through what is in the post and discuss anything that looks as though it might become a problem. This does not mean that you have to go through every letter in the morning with your staff. Grilling an employee about every piece of post is not only offensive to the intelligence of the employee and will undermine their confidence but is also unnecessarily wasteful of time. If your employee is a trainee solicitor, then you will need to have regular meetings anyway in order to comply with the training regulations. Either have a set time each month to talk through any particular problems and ensure that you both feel the level of supervision/degree of responsibility is suiting each of you, or just address that particular topic when a suitable opportunity arises. The only danger with the second approach is time tends to go rather faster than both of you expect. Encourage an open door policy so that trainees, and other staff, are encouraged to come to you with their problems rather than you spotting danger signs only to discover it is the tip of an iceberg, the bottom two-thirds of which should never have arisen and would not have done if you had been more approachable. It is very easy as a busy sole practitioner to delegate a matter to a fee-earner and then to feel that it is his or her responsibility. It always remains your responsibility and you should know exactly what is happening on any file that you have delegated virtually on a daily basis. Do not be afraid to ask to see the file. They are your files first and foremost. If done in the right way and with a high degree of frequency on a variety of files, the fee-earner will not feel his or her authority is being undermined. A file examination and discussion will be usual and not exceptional and the fee-earner will welcome the security of knowing that work has been looked at and approved and that he or she is on the right course. It is a good idea to pass one of your files to an assistant and ask him or her to look at it and come back with their views. This interchange of ideas with you looking at their work and they looking at yours builds confidence, and a request from you to look at someone's files is then not perceived as an intrusion.

With larger firms, the system becomes very much more complicated, as indeed it does once you have three or four fee-earners. In order to keep matters under control, it will at that stage be necessary to have regular diaried staff meetings, preferably with individual fee-earners separately. File lists will need to be maintained and, if not computer-generated, will need to be kept by hand.

At the staff meeting, which should be at least monthly if not fortnightly, the file list should be reviewed and after consulting with the member of staff in the meeting a view taken as to whether the fee-earner is under or over-employed and work re-allocated where necessary. Time records should be carefully scrutinised. A fee-earner keen to make a name for himself or herself may try to persuade you that there is no problem in dealing with the work that you have given him or her. The time sheet may show that he or she is working ridiculously long hours and that should be seen as a problem which needs to be addressed every bit as much as the fee-earner who appears to be unproductive.

An annual performance appraisal system needs to be implemented and again, the Law Society's *Solicitors' Office Manual* comes into its own for these purposes. The appraisal system set out in it will be entirely suitable for the vast majority of practices with only minor modifications. The strengths and weaknesses sections may be amended to suit individual tastes and the qualities sought in a particular employee, but the system adopted in the *Office Manual* has the benefit that it can be applied to different types of staff so that senior fee-earners and secretaries can all be assessed with one type of form which has the benefits of both simplicity and fairness. Whilst the system outlined has a number of options, I would suggest that appraisals are carried out on the anniversary of the staff's entry into the firm and that it should be explained to the member of staff that whilst the outcome of the appraisal will not be irrelevant for the purposes of pay review, the two are separate issues and the outcome of the appraisal is only one factor in the review of an employee's salary.

CHECKLIST

COMPUTERS

- Decide whether or not you need a computer.

- Analyse the tasks you wish the computer to perform.

- Decide how long you need your computer to last, e.g.

  (a) one year, as an experiment and then replace;
  (b) three years, then replace;
  (c) five years, then replace.

  If in doubt, buy something cheap and throw it away after a year.

- Research market to determine what software is most suitable for your needs, bearing in mind likely number of clients, employees, accounts, etc., in the period identified above.

- Having selected software, research market to ascertain which is the most suitable hardware in terms of capacity, reliability, price and back-up services.

- In addition, decide on networked or stand-alone system.

- Obtain references from other firms operating the system and talk to several of them as to suitability, reliability, etc.

- If appropriate, obtain advice of a computer consultant.

- Make your purchase, or lease, depending on overall cost.

FILING SYSTEM

- Buy card index box and A–Z dividers.

- Buy A5 book with A–Z indexing and one A5 book without.

- Go through your current files allocating file reference numbers and entering details on card index and cross-referencing them alphabetically in the A–Z indexed A5 book and numerically in the other A5 book.

- Put files in numerical order in filing cabinet, highest numbers towards the front.

- Label filing cabinet drawers with the range of numbers contained in each drawer.

- Put up large notice detailing consequences, preferably fatal, for anyone who transgresses the rules of your filing system!

STORAGE

At this stage, you should have no files to put into store, unless certain old clients from a previous practice have asked for their papers to be transferred to you even though they are considered completed matters. If so, label a filing cabinet 'Dead Files' and treat in the same way as a live file, except put the index card into a second card index box marked 'Dead Files' and put the file into the dead file cabinet.

Your card index box will need to be much larger than the one for live matters. As time goes on, more and more files will go out of live and into the dead system. It is usually a bad idea to destroy the index card even if the file itself is destroyed. If someone says you acted for them and wants their file many years later, you may be able to check through the card system and tell them with confidence you never acted for them since there is no card for them and it must be the firm down the road. You can't truthfully do this if you destroy cards as you go along.

ACCOUNTS

- Buy:

  (a) pink, blue, green and white transaction slips;

  (b) client bank book;

  (c) office bank book;

  (d) bills delivered book;

  (f) wages book;

  (g) petty cash book.

  You may wish to discuss size of books, number of columns, etc., with your book-keeper before purchase.

- Make out ledger cards for any existing/transferred files you have, using the file number as the account ledger number.

- Write out headings in your wages book and make entries for each employee (this may not take very long!). There is no need to make out a section for principals as they are not employees, but you will need to keep a record of what draw you take and when. You will also have to pay a self-employed persons National Insurance Stamp (details obtained from your local DSS Office – do not put off contacting them). The wages book may be a convenient place to keep such records.

REPORTING SYSTEMS

If you are starting a sole practice with few or no staff, there will not be much reporting to be done. You might usefully make a diary entry for six or nine months' time to consider what systems you need to implement and plan an action timetable. If you are starting with three or four staff then you will need to:

- Draw up and issue contracts of employment.

- Put in place a staff appraisal system.

- Put in hand a scheme for fortnightly/monthly management meetings.

- Implement a time-costing system.

- Allocate files to fee-earners.

- Set date for first partners' meeting if two or more partners!

CHAPTER 8

VAT and Tax Considerations

How to Register

Registering for VAT purposes is remarkably simple. If you decide to involve an accountant in your initial period of setting up to deal with such things as presenting a business plan to obtain finance from the bank, advising on your book-keeping system, tax considerations on when to set up, etc., then you may also ask him or her to deal with the registration of the firm with Customs and Excise for VAT purposes. There is, however, no real need to do that as will be explained below.

Firstly, do you have to register, and if so, on what basis? If your taxable supplies are or are likely to be above the specified limit for a period of one year, then you must register. The current limit set in November 1993 is £45,000. If you are below that level, you do not have to register, but if you decide you wish to register, then Customs must register you for VAT purposes. You may be wondering, looking at the three files that you have just taken with you from a previous firm, whether or not you are going to be anywhere near the £45,000 limit. But rest assured you will be. Accordingly, the decision is made for you – you will be registering for VAT purposes.

Cash Accounting?

There are two bases on which it is possible to register, the cash accounting system and the imaginatively titled 'ordinary scheme'. If you are a sole trader or a two or three-partner firm, then your turnover is unlikely to exceed £350,000 a year. If it is likely to exceed that amount, then you cannot join the cash accounting scheme or you must leave it if you are already in it. If you are allowed to, opt for cash accounting. There is only one disadvantage in part payment of VAT (set out below), but it is in other respects preferable.

The principal difference between the two systems is that with the cash accounting scheme you only have to pay over the VAT collected to the Revenue on bills that have been paid. If a client fails to pay your account you do not pay the VAT element of the account over to Customs and Excise whereas under the ordinary system the VAT must be paid over irrespective of whether your client has paid the bill. Most small practices will therefore want to take advantage of that benefit and will opt for cash accounting. One particular trap is the position where a client pays part only of an account. If that happens, you must apportion the payment between VAT and the rest of the bill. If the bill contains vatable disbursements, then it may not be a straightforward task in deciding whether to apportion the payment between non-vatable disbursements and vatable ones and profit costs. The regulations require that there be a 'fair and reasonable apportionment'. There is no problem in apportioning if the bill was simply for profit costs and VAT, or indeed if all the disbursements are vatable. The difficulty is remembering to include the VAT element of the part of the bill that has been paid in your VAT return. It is easy to forget, which results in an underpayment of VAT.

There is now no longer any requirement to stay in the scheme for a set period but you must leave it if you think your supplies are likely to exceed £437,500 at the start of the next cash accounting year. You can withdraw on a voluntary basis at the end of a prescribed accounting period where you derive no benefits from remaining in it or are unable to comply by reason of your accounting system with the requirements of the scheme. Anyone complying with the Solicitors' Accounts Rules will meet those requirements so this element should pose no problem.

Another advantage of the scheme is that the persons in it obtain automatic bad debt relief.

There are complicated rules on when and how Customs and Excise must register a person who applies for registration but these really need not concern solicitors. The gist of the regulations is that Customs want to be sure that you really are setting up in business of a kind that is going to involve VAT and not simply trying to set up a VAT fraud. A simple covering letter to the local VAT office (a phone call to an accountant will tell you which the local one is, or for that matter any local trader will probably do the same) enclosing the application form, imaginatively entitled Form VAT1, is all that is needed. Your letter will no doubt be on headed notepaper of some sort even if you have not had the final version back from the printers and will merely say that you are setting up a new solicitors' practice from a particular address, that you intend trading from a particular date and that as you will be making regular supplies of vatable services you wish to be registered for VAT and you have duly completed form VAT 1. Within a couple of weeks you should receive your VAT registration number. You will immediately need to telephone the printer so as to include the VAT number on your invoices.

You will need to notify the local VAT office (not the VAT central unit) of any changes in the business. These changes include a change in the name and/or the address of any partner, an alteration in the composition of the partnership or a change in the principal place from where the business is carried on.

Completing the first few VAT returns will no doubt fill you with dread as you are mostly relying on information produced for you by other people and yet it is you who has to sign the VAT return. You and you alone bear the responsibility and yet unless you are going to repeat totally the work that others have done, which may be several hours of work, you will have to rely on them for its accuracy. This is a fairly daunting prospect since the penalties for misdeclaration can be severe and Customs and Excise are not normally noted for their high degree of tolerance and flexibility. You may, however, draw comfort from three psychological 'crutches'.

Firstly, in a solicitors' practice it is probably more likely that the error you make will be in favour of the VAT man than yourself. The only kind of supply that any solicitor is likely to make is in the provision of professional services to a client. All of those services will be vatable with the possible exception of carrying out work for foreign clients, and even those services may well be vatable. The VAT calculation is comparatively simple and involves adding up the value of supplies made **and paid** for the VAT quarter, i.e. totalling up the bills, and extracting the VAT element from those bills and the disbursements that carry VAT. This constitutes the VAT output. You are, however, entitled to credit for the VAT that you have paid out to other people, including the VAT on counsel's fees. You will therefore go through all the monies that you have paid out to other people in the course of your business and see which ones not only have you paid VAT on but on which you can prove you have paid VAT, i.e. that you have a VAT invoice/receipt for. You will then extract the VAT from those invoices/ receipts and that constitutes your VAT input. You take the one from the other, which will normally leave you with a sum to pay over to Customs and Excise. In the first quarter you may not send out any bills at all and yet you will have paid out a lot of money in setting up, which includes a VAT element. In those circumstances it is just possible that you will have a credit, but this system of Customs paying you money instead of the other way round will very rapidly change. If it does not, you are probably best advised to cease trading as you are not doing any business! Book-keeping can easily be organised to show the VAT position without any special calculation if working on cash accounting, so you can see what your VAT liability is as it mounts up.

Pitfalls

Accordingly, the calculation should be relatively straightforward for a book-keeper, so that provided you include VAT where only part of the bill is paid and you do not include VAT credits where you should not have had one, you should be alright.

The trap is to forget to include the VAT in your next VAT return when someone pays a bill in stages. The tendency is to include the VAT element in the first payment but not the further payments. Or else, to treat the first payment as VAT exclusive instead of a VAT inclusive payment. You should extract VAT from each payment by multiplying by 40 and dividing by 47. If, for example, you send a client a bill for £230, i.e. £200 plus £30 VAT and your client pays you £115 in month one and £115 six months later, you should treat the first payment as one of £100 plus £15 VAT and the second payment the same way. If you credit the whole of the £115 to yourself and don't pay the £15 VAT, you have made an underpayment of £15.

VAT and vehicles

Another possible pitfall is in relation to motoring where you are using a car in the course of the business and you are claiming some or all of the running expenses out of the firm. If so, you are probably also setting off the VAT. Both the Inland Revenue and Customs and Excise will insist that not all of the expense is claimable. They will point to the fact that there will be an element of private use involved and therefore a proportion of the running expenses will not be, strictly speaking, incurred in the running of the business and you will have to extract that proportion together with any VAT on it. You should contact your local VAT office for further information.

One option is to pay your own car expenses but charge travel expenses in connection with your business. As you are only charging purely for those costs directly involved in running your business, there will be no private use element to be extracted for VAT and income tax purposes. The problem is that detailed records and receipts will need to be kept to show what the actual expenses are.

However, you may be entitled to claim some of the VAT back on your home telephone as it is highly probable you will be making at least some of your business calls from home. Again, speak to the VAT office about what percentage of the VAT they feel it would be appropriate for you to reclaim.

The second 'crutch' is that fairly early on in your trading period, i.e. within the first six months, you are very likely to receive a visit from a VAT inspector. Such a visit is not necessarily to be feared. The purpose of the visit is to pick up any errors you have been making before they lead to serious difficulties. If you have been claiming the full cost of the petrol for the mileage covered by your car (as indeed we did) it is far better to find out about it at an early stage where the amount of VAT underpaid is £60 or £70 than to wait until the firm's fleet has risen to several vehicles with the consequential increase of VAT underpaid. Any problems such as this can be ironed out at this stage. You are also very likely to receive a similar visit when you computerise your accounts system. The purpose of such a further visit is exactly the same. Mistakes may have been made in the transition, or there may be a problem with the software so that the wrong amount of VAT is computed. The sooner that is spotted and dealt with the better.

The third weapon in your armoury is that other dreaded annual event – the accounts audit. This is when you pay other professionals a fortune to crawl all over your books and papers to be told just before they present their bill that you have been doing all sorts of things wrong and it is going to cost you the earth to put them right. If this is indeed your perception of the annual audit, try looking at it this way. Any lecture that you may receive at the hands of your accountant will be nowhere as severe as the talking to you would get from the Inspector of Taxes or the VAT man and if you listen to what you are told, then you will avoid those mistakes in the future. The bill from the accountant is likely to be more palatable than the bill you would have got from the Inland Revenue or Customs and Excise had the accountants not taken the time to do the job properly.

Is everything lost and will you be carted off in chains if the accountants discover that you have got your VAT calculations wrong? This depends on the extent of the error. Customs and Excise accept that people can make mistakes. They are not going to pounce on every underpayment and impose every penalty when you have made a mistake. For that reason, they have a system whereby if you discover an error in your return and if the net amount of your error during that period is no more than £2,000, then you simply adjust the VAT and include the correction in your return for that period. You are not charged interest on any errors you disclose in this way. In calculating whether you have gone over the £2,000 limit, you must go back through all previous VAT periods and what matters is whether mistakes discovered in each of those periods and not yet remedied when added together total more than £2,000, not whether it is £2,000 in any one period.

For these purposes, you can take into account any overpayments so that if in one period you have underdeclared £1,200 and in another period you have over-declared £500, then the sum total is a net underdeclaration of £700 and you simply add that to your next VAT payment. There is no need specifically to tell Customs about it other than to record the error in your VAT account. You should also write a note about it for your accountants and keep the note with your other accounting records.

If you are over the £2,000 limit, you can make a voluntary disclosure by sending full details of the error in writing to your local VAT office who will send you a Notice of Voluntary Disclosure confirming the amount of your disclosure and any interest payable. Once you have made a voluntary disclosure of an error, you cannot incur a 'serious misdeclaration' penalty for the error. The basic message is, therefore, to tell them if you find you have made a mistake rather than waiting to see if they find it first. If you opt for the latter course and you get caught out, it is then that it starts to become painful.

Any good book-keeper or accountant will be fully aware of all of these matters, but as the person responsible for signing the VAT return, the buck stops with you. It is therefore very much in your best interests that you familiarise yourself at the outset with your responsibilities for VAT. Before you turn yourself in to Customs and Excise clothed suitably in sack cloth and ashes, there is one final thing that you might try to do to get yourself off the hook in the event that your errors exceed the £2,000 limit. Go through all the things that you have paid for, not only in that VAT period but all previous ones, and see if there is anything on which you have paid VAT which might not have been included in a VAT return. On the occasion when it was pointed out to us that we had breached what was then the £1,000 limit, I went through this exercise and managed to find a seminar which I had attended on which VAT had been charged. The majority of courses of that type do not carry VAT but this particular one did. It was a full-day course and because my book-keeper had been used to treating these courses as non-vatable, it had not been included in the figures. We were able to write off and get a receipted VAT invoice and the VAT element of the bill was sufficient to bring us back under the £1,000 limit.

Customs and Excise publish a very useful little pamphlet, number 700/45/900, entitled 'How to Correct Errors you Find on your VAT Returns'. It is well worth having a copy in the office and copies can be obtained from your local VAT office.

Income Tax – the New Self-Assessment System

The new rules for assessment and payment of income tax apply immediately to any business commencing on or after 6 April 1994. Existing businesses will move onto the new system from the tax year 1997/98. Under the old system, income tax was assessed on the partnership as a whole, but the new system makes each individual partner assessable.

Each partner will have to file a tax return for the previous accounting period ending in that tax year. The return will show that partner's share of profits. Partners will therefore have to agree between themselves how the profits will be allocated for tax purposes and how the money will be found to pay the tax.

For new businesses, the first tax year will be the year in which the business started and its 'basis period' will run from the day on which the business first traded to 5 April of the following year. Thus, in year one, if you start your business on 1 September 1994, your first tax year is 1994/95 and the basis period is 1 September 1994 to 5 April 1995. You will pay tax on the actual profits made in this period.

There is nothing to stop you having a trading year through to the following 31 August 1995 but for tax purposes your first tax year will be seven months long and you will be taxed on seven out of your 12 months in that tax year.

For your second tax year you will be taxed on the profits made over the 12-month period (assuming the accounting date is at least 12 months after the commencement date). In our example, the second trading period would be 1 September 1994 to 31 August 1995. Part of these profits will, of course, have already been assessed in the first tax year and are called 'overlap profits'. This 'overlap' is adjusted either on retirement or where there is a change of accounting period, but the effects are not indexed to take account of inflation. As you may have guessed, it is best to try to avoid overlapping of profits.

Individuals will need to take their own advice as to the best date for commencement and how long the first accounting period will be, but for the majority of people, the most favourable date is likely to be an accounting year running from 1 April to 31 March.

Existing Businesses

There are transitional arrangements for existing businesses in 1996/97. An average will be taken of the profits of the previous two years. It may be preferable to accelerate one-off payments of income or to delay major items of expenditure so as to boost the level of profits earned in this two-year period, as the profit level will be averaged over two years and thus diluted. It will pay most people to take advice on their circumstances as they are likely to recoup the cost of the advice from the tax saved as a result. You will also need to watch the legal and accountancy press as the Revenue have indicated they will press for legislation to counter tax-saving schemes if too many people try to save too much tax.

The Assessment

Tax returns will have to be filed by 31 January following the tax year. If the return is sent by 30 September, then the inspector will calculate the amount of tax payable for you. If filed after that date, then the taxpayer must do the calculations and the inspector will then agree them, or disagree. In reality, there will be little change from what happened under the old system. Although in theory the inspector set the level of tax, the majority of small businesses, including solicitors, submitted their accounts and tax returns via accountants, who calculated the amount of tax due. The inspector checked through the figures and if they were not acceptable, discussions would take place and an accommodation reached. If this was not possible, the inspector would raise an assessment and leave the taxpayer or their accountant to argue against it at a hearing before the Tax Commmissioners, but in most cases agreement would be reached before that stage. The option is still retained for the inspector to do the calculations, provided the taxpayer submits the necessary information sufficiently early.

Time for Payment

The relevant tax for the relevant period under the old system was payable in two instalments on 1 January and 1 July. (This will continue for existing businesses until the new system is in place.) More or less the same system is retained, except of course the tax being paid is for the current accounting period and is no longer on the preceding year basis for new businesses, and will no longer be in respect of existing businesses once the transitional arrangements have worked their way through in 1997/98.

A payment on account of the tax due will have to be paid on 31 January in the year of assessment and a further interim payment will be due the following 31 July (which is in the year following the year of assessment as it is after 5 April). These interim payments usually will be based on the tax payable in the previous year. It is a bit like an estimated electricity bill or a service charge arrangement on a flat. Then the following 31 January a further payment will be due. This will be partly a payment on account of the next tax bill and partly a settling-up of the actual tax due for the earlier period now that the figures have been agreed, always assuming that the inspector and your accountant have reached the accommodation referred to earlier. Any capital gains tax payable will also be due in the 31 January payment.

Timetable

New Business, i.e. commencement date on or after 6 April 1994 – new rules apply immediately.

Existing Business
Tax Year
1994/95 – penultimate assessment on preceding year basis.
1995/96 – final assessment on preceding year basis.
1996/97 – transitional rules apply.
1997/98 – first assessment on current year basis.

Tax Planning

If you have been a partner in a large firm, tax planning considerations will be something which will have passed you by. Even in a fairly small partnership, these aspects are usually dealt with by the accountants in conjunction with the senior partner. If you are now a sole practitioner, or perhaps a two-partner firm, then you are the senior partner and this aspect of the matter is something which you cannot afford to neglect.

As explained earlier, on 6 April 1994 all rules on how self-employed persons and partnerships, etc. are taxed, changed. This could well be good news, at least in the short term, since it may give rise to a 'tax holiday' of the kind experienced by partnerships that merge. Thereafter, the plan is that you will pay tax as you go along rather than building up a tax liability based on what you earned in previous years. The present system, to my way of thinking, has always been rather bizarre and almost invites a situation where the trader fails to make a proper tax reserve or does so and then spends it because he or she runs out of money. If you have a good year followed by a bad one, you will be in the position of having to make a substantial tax payment at a time when you can least afford it. When faced with a severe downturn in trade and bills piling up, it seems, at the time, folly not to dip into the reserve and pay off your creditors out of it.

To avoid getting into difficulties, you need to establish a tax reserve. This should all be part and parcel of your business plan. Keep an eye on what money you are making in a year and only take out by way of drawings at the very most what you would pay yourself if you were an employee. In this way, you leave the tax element still in the business. There is no need to be particularly scientific about this. See how much profit you have made for the month and take out 75 per cent of it. If there is no real need to take quite that much out, then simply leave it in the business. In this way, you will start to build up a credit balance on office account. When the balance gets more than your everyday needs, transfer it into a building society account. This will be the office deposit account, but to a large extent it will also be your tax reserve.

In your first year your start-up capital should assume you will not take a draw at all, so in effect you will live off your savings, or borrowed money, until you have a year's trading behind you and can assess what sort of profits you are making. Your budget for the first year will in any event be very haphazard. There will be unexpected expenses, and perhaps even the odd piece of particularly profitable work, each of which will distort your budget. You may, however, feel there are months, especially in the second six months of trading, when you can feel adventurous and have a draw.

87

You will need to be very conservative in your drawings policy for years one and two. Once this somewhat turbulent period is over and patterns are emerging, you can start to exercise a little less caution and still take a draw (although perhaps not a full one) even in a bad month, taking a yearly view of the position rather than focusing on just that one poor month.

If you have a particularly bad month, you will still need to pay your bills. You must bear in mind that you are taking out money which is not really there. Provided you are not drawing out the full level of profit in the better months, then things will even themselves out.

Periodically, review the whole situation as you go through the year and estimate what your tax liability for that year is going to be and make sure that what is going into the building society account is going to be adequate to deal with the tax situation which will arise, albeit not for a year or two.

Again, at the end of the year, look back and see over a couple of years what the tax liability is that has built up and make sure what is in the building society account is enough to deal with it. If it is not, then you have been overdrawing and must do something about it during the following year, both in terms of working harder and drawing out slightly less each month.

The need to build up a tax reserve of this kind will not arise if you started trading after 6 April 1994 since you will come under the new rules, but you will need to ensure that you save the instalments of tax due as you go along.

The Annual Accounts Examination

In order to comply with section 34 of the Solicitors Act 1974 and the Accountant's Report Rules 1991, you will need to have your accounts examined by a qualified accountant during the period specified. A qualified accountant for these purposes is a Member of the Institute of Chartered Accountants of England, Ireland, Scotland or Wales or of the Chartered Association of Certified Accountants. Section 34 of the Act, which is set out in Appendix 10 defines the period as covering not less than 12 months and beginning at the expiry of the last preceding period for which an accountant's report has been delivered.

You will need to obtain advice from your accountant as to how long your first accounting period should run. The accountant's report must be delivered to the

Law Society within six months of the end of the accounting period which you have chosen. Your further accounting periods will normally be of 12 months, following on consecutively from the end of the first period, with further accountant's reports delivered within six months from the end of each. This rule is now applied rigidly. It caught a lot of solicitors, and even more accountants, unawares when it first came in to force. The delivery of the accountant's report was once considered something of a formality and if it was a few days or even a few weeks overdue, then provided there was nothing known about the firm which would give rise to undue alarm, the overdue report and letter of apology would be all that was necessary. Gone are those days. If you are so much as one day overdue, the provisions of section 12(i)(ee) of the Solicitors Act 1974 will be vigorously applied against you. This will mean that you will not be able to apply for your practising certificate at the same time as everyone else and you will join the queue of those persons who have been out of practice for several years, those who have been in prison, struck off or made bankrupt. You will follow the same procedures laid down for them, which include obtaining references from at least two of your professional colleagues to say that they consider you are a fit and proper person to practise. In addition to this, you will have to pay an administration fee of £50 to the Law Society for the additional paperwork which it involves. That is a small price to pay for the considerable uncertainty which follows, as practising certificates arrive on everyone else's desk except yours and the time rapidly approaches when to comply with the law you will have to close down your practice until the certificate arrives. I speak as one who has gone through this ignominious and worrying procedure due to my previous accountant's computer flagging the report as having been delivered by him to the Law Society when in fact it was still on his file. The Law Society has no discretion to waive this provision as it is laid down by Act of Parliament. The previous latitude given to solicitors arose out of a rather relaxed attitude towards the provisions of the Solicitors Act and the Rules made under it, highlighted by subsequent litigation designed to bring this point to their notice and something which they are unlikely in the future to disregard.

The message is therefore very simple. Make sure that the examination of your accounts is put in hand in good time and that you diary the final date for delivery of the accountant's report, i.e. six months after the end of your financial period which you will have decided upon after receiving suitable advice from your accountants. Press the accountants for the report well before that date, i.e. a number of months rather than weeks, and get them to send the report to you. Do not rely on the statement from them that they have sent it to the Law Society.

Your accountant's fees are likely to be slightly higher for the first year whilst they are finding out about your business and your financial affairs generally. You will have to give them details of all building society and bank accounts that you hold, not only in your own name privately but also for clients. You may, for example, have opened up and operate a designated building society account on a client's behalf. Full details of all of these accounts will have to be passed to your accountants and it takes time whilst they record the information, for the most part on computer. There may be one or two problems with the first year's accounts whilst any errors that you might have made are sorted out. The accountants should allow for this in any estimate that they give you. Since these set-up costs will not need to be repeated, you will be in a stronger position to argue fees with the accountants for the subsquent years. Hopefully, the business will have expanded, but the additional work which they will have to carry out in conducting the accounts examination and preparing a set of accounts for submission to the Inland Revenue will not be nearly so great as the amount of work involved in setting up the job originally. The choice of accountants is important and it is as well to have a recommendation from another solicitor and to question the accountants as to the number of solicitors' practices on behalf of which they carry out the annual accounts examination and to press them to obtain their clients' permission to talk to you. Solicitors tend to think that most accountants will have had experience of conducting the examination, but this is far from being the case.

It is essential to obtain a definite quotation from the firm concerned, not only for the first year but also for subsequent years. You will need to build an important item like this into your annual budget and whilst there are plenty of examples of solicitors who will spring a nasty surprise in relation to their fees on their client, there are also plenty of examples of accountants who will do likewise. It may well be difficult for an accountant to quote for the first year since you are more likely in that year to get something wrong which may take a good deal of time on the accountant's part to rectify. This should not preclude a quotation from being given.

CHECKLIST

REGISTERING FOR VAT

- Obtain Form VAT1, complete it and send it to local VAT office (obtain address from your accountant or another local trader).

- Pass details to printer for inclusion on invoice pads once VAT number is allocated.

ACCOUNTS EXAMINATION

- Draw up shortlist of accountants.

- Invite them to attend your offices separately to talk about their services, inspect your accounting system and submit a written quotation, to include accounts examination under the Solicitors Act 1974 and completion of report, preparation and submission of a set of accounts to the Inland Revenue and their agreement with the Revenue and completion and submission of your tax return and that of your spouse.

- Ask each firm for a reference from a firm of solicitors whose accounts examination they currently conduct.

- Take up references.

- Select firm and agree a start date no more than six weeks after your accounts' end of year.

- Diary a date one month later for chasing draft accounts if not submitted.

- Diary a further date six weeks prior to final submission date of accountant's report to insist report produced immediately if not already submitted to you.

- Diary final submission date, i.e. six months from accounts' year end.

- Send off report to Law Society prior to submission date.

CHAPTER 9

Starting to Trade

Publicity

So this is it - you've got your premises and you're in them, the phones are on (hopefully!), you've chosen the start date and the great day has arrived. Other than sitting behind your secondhand desk in your swivel chair waiting for the telephone to ring, is there anything else that you should be doing?

The first thing you should do is to get out your diary and make a note of the exact date on which you started to trade. It is remarkably easy months later to be unsure of the exact date on which your new firm was born. As you will probably feel like celebrating its birth every year and possibly using it as an excuse for a party to invite clients along and make them feel a part of the firm, it is important to know exactly when the occasion took place. It is also necessary to know the date for tax reasons.

Should you be sitting behind the desk waiting for the phone to ring at all? The first few months for any new business is an extremely difficult and uncertain time. You will probably be afraid to leave the office for fear that the telephone will ring and you will miss a client. It is particularly important in the first few months to reassure existing clients that you are still very much around and available. Especially with small firms, clients have the perception that given a couple of heavy cases you will be unable to cope with theirs. Bereft of the substantial resources that you may have enjoyed at a larger firm, you will be submerged in other people's paperwork and their affairs will be neglected. You have to prove that this is not at all the case and you must therefore be totally available to your clients and fulfil their every need. Once this psychological barrier has been overcome, there will be no difficulty when a member of staff tells a client that you are unavailable for the moment and you will get back to them shortly, particularly when you have a good track record of a few months of the new firm's performance behind you. They will be quite happy to accept that situation and will not feel that this unavailability is the start of a deterioration in the service they have always enjoyed when you were with a larger firm and that it is time to look for a firm that can cope. In the meantime, however, you have got to give them not simply a good service but an excellent one so that, if anything, they feel that the start of the new firm on your part is a big step forward compared with the slightly less than adequate service they might have enjoyed previously with either your old firm (if they were clients of that practice) or any other firm they may have instructed.

Chapter 6 deals with advertising and the timing of the appearance of your advertisements in various types of media. If you are in time for annual directories such as Yellow Pages and Thomson, etc., then to some extent you will have taken care of the publicity side of things, but inevitably there is going to be a delay between the start of the firm and the appearance of advertisements in that type of directory unless you are setting up on the very day that the advertisement comes out. As discussed in Chapter 6, the gap can, to some extent, be filled by advertisements in local newspapers, but there are other ways of publicising the fact that you are in business.

Signage

Perhaps the most obvious form of advertising will be your firm's sign on the outside of the building telling potential clients and existing clients where you are. If you have decided to take a lease of premises which have a shop frontage, then you will no doubt be arranging for a sign writer to put the traditional gold lettering 'Solicitors' sign in the window. You may want to opt for a brass plate with your name on it. Brass is quite expensive and needs to be regularly polished. It also will take a few weeks to order. An alternative is the 'brass effect' plastic sign with a metal overlay which still costs £60 or £70 but can look surprisingly good. There is a also a silver effect version available which looks equally good. Many office stationery outlets can supply the plastic sign. The brass sign can give some clients the impression of being expensive and unapproachable. On the other hand plastic type with a metal overlay can give many people a more modern and friendly impression.

You will have to consider whether or not you need permission to put any sign up outside. If you have taken out a lease then the erection of such a plate may be controlled by the provisions of the lease. The terms of the lease may not cover the exterior of the building and the exterior may not form part of the demise. In either case, you may well need the permission of the landlord to put up any signage at all and this is something best negotiated at the outset when the landlord may be keen to have you sign a lease rather than as an afterthought when you are already installed in the premises.

The other consideration is planning law. The position is governed by the Town and Country Planning (Control of Advertisements) Regulations 1992. These Regulations permit the display of an 'advertisement' up to a certain size relating to any person, partnership or company separately carrying on a profession, business or trade at the premises where it is displayed. 'Advertisements' fitting this description are given deemed planning consent without the need for a separate application to the planning authority. Your nameplate is, after all, an advertisement since it advertises the fact that you are trading from the premises as a firm of solicitors.

The advertisement must not exceed 0.3 sq.m. in area (approximately 3.229 sq.ft), and no character or symbol on the advertisement may be more than 0.75 metres in height (2.46 ft) or 0.3 metres (0.984 ft) in an area of special control. No part of the advertisement may be more than 4.6 metres (15.08 ft) above ground level or 3.6 metres (11.81 ft) in an area of special control.

Only one such advertisement is permitted unless the premises have more than one entrance on different road frontages, in which case you may have one sign at each entrance subject to a maximum of two.

Illumination is not permitted at all for solicitors and if you wanted such a sign it would need to be the subject of a separate planning application.

If the building which you occupy is a listed building, or if you are in a conservation area, different provisions may apply. In those circumstances, you would do well to check with your local Planning Officer before putting up the sign. It is unlikely that no form of signage will be permitted, but it may be rather less in terms of size and prominence than would be the case in an area which was not subject to such controls. The relevant section of the Regulations appear at Appendix 11.

If you have managed to enter into an office-sharing arrangement, then you will need to have an arrangement with the people you are sharing the space with and this in turn may need the agreement of their landlords. Again, this is something best dealt with at the outset rather than later.

At this stage, you should also give some thought to internal signage. If you are on the third floor, then you are going to want a prominent sign downstairs directing clients up to your reception area.

Spreading the Word

The other form of publicity is word of mouth. Tell anyone and everyone you can possibly think of that you are setting up in practice. Tell your friends, the neighbours, existing clients, clients you have not spoken to for years and ask them to support you if they can. This is no time for being bashful! You are going to need every client you can lay your hands on. You must also make yourself known in the locality. Contact all the bank managers and building society managers and arrange to see them. If you go into the newsagents to buy a newspaper, start chatting to them about business generally and then introduce into the conversation at a suitable point the fact that you have just opened up down the road from them and that if there is anything that you can help them with at any time you would be only too pleased. You may have slight pangs of unprofessionalism and feel that you are being a little bit like a door-to-door encyclopaedia salesman, but this is precisely what everyone else in business does. It is open to you to do the same so long as you do not infringe the Publicity Code by 'cold calling'. (See further Chapter 18.) There is no need for the hard sell. Simply tell people who you are and where you are and that you would welcome their business if they chose to instruct you. Don't forget to leave them a business card.

Informing Clients

You may be leaving an existing practice either as an assistant solicitor or as a partner and quite clearly an obvious source of business for your new practice is the client base of your existing practice. Whether or not you can make use of this will depend on your exact status in the firm. If you are an assistant solicitor with a contract of employment there may well be a restraining clause preventing you from taking clients with you. If you operate in this area of the law, then you may be able to take a view yourself on the precise effect of the clause and how enforceable it is. Be careful – the last thing you want to have when you are trying to wrestle with the problems of your new firm is a lawsuit from the old one. It does, unfortunately, happen. It is fairly common for people to put in restraining clauses which they know from the outset are probably not going to be upheld if challenged in the courts but they take a deliberate decision to put in a fairly restrictive clause on the basis that the restrained employee is not going to want to take on their organisation in the courts.

A rather superficial statement of the law is that such a clause will only be enforced by the courts if it is reasonably necessary to protect the interests of the employer and is not in unreasonable restraint of trade. If the courts decide that it is in unreasonable restraint of trade, then the entire clause stands at risk of being struck out completely. There is a good deal of case law on the subject and if you think that your employers or partners are likely to be upset if you take certain clients from them, you would be well advised to take some serious advice on the clause to the extent of going to counsel.

Further guidance on what ethically you can and cannot do can be found in Principle 3.14 of *The Guide to the Professional Conduct of Solicitors 1993*.

Once you are satisfied that you know what the position is it would be a good idea to make a list of those clients who you think or know would follow you and to approach the partners and ask them if they would have any objection to you acting for those clients. You will probably find that most of the clients on your list are people that you have introduced to the firm anyway and you may be pleasantly surprised at the approach which the partners take. If the reaction on their part is a bad one, then you will clearly have to be rather careful in what you do. Keep strictly to the terms of the restraining clause unless you are certain that it will not be upheld by the courts. In the final analysis, the court is unlikely to prevent a client from giving you instructions where it is clear that the relationship with the former firm and the client has deteriorated through no fault of yours, other than the fact that you are offering a choice simply by setting up.

If you have been a partner in an existing firm then the situation may be very different. Again, you will have to look to the terms of the partnership deed, but in the absence of a lawful restraining clause there is nothing to stop you from circulating every single client of the firm with notification of your intention to set up in practice and to ask them whether they wish to have their files transferred to the new practice or to stay with the old one. (See Principle 3.14 of the Guide.) A most useful precedent for such a letter is contained in Annex 3G of the Guide. This letter is phrased as being written jointly by the continuing partners and the outgoing partner but can be suitably adapted if either side wishes to write unilaterally. However, if the firm is unwilling to follow the advice given in the Guide it does place you in a rather difficult position. It is sometimes helpful if the parties are able to talk to someone in the Law Society's Professional Ethics Department for clarification of the relevant principles in the Guide and the commentary to the principles and this may be enough to cause the parties to go along with the guidance or you could perhaps confine yourself to ringing round people and passing the information that way. Principle 3.13 says that where there has been an alteration to the composition of the firm, *all* clients *who may be affected* must be informed promptly. Also, if the client's work would suffer from a restraining clause being enforced then it would be proper to transfer the client's file despite the restraining clause.

In reality, there is no point in approaching clients who are wedded to the firm or to particular partners within it. It can, however, be surprising who follows you and who does not. People with whom you felt you had a close professional relationship will decide to stay with the present firm and others whom you had thought would never have followed you will go to considerable lengths to trace you if news of your departure has not reached their ears. You can often find that when you discuss this with them and say that you thought they were the client of another partner that they will come out with comments such as 'Yes, he's great company in the pub but he's useless if you want to get anything done.' To have such people endorse your professional qualities in such a way can be heartening in the extreme at a time when you feel at your most isolated.

In so far as clients have made their choice and they are coming with you, get your hands on the files. You do not want to have to wrangle with other people at a later stage over the actual transfer of the files to you. Get the files under your own control and get them billed up to date and explain to the client that the file can only be transferred once those costs have been cleared. When this has been dealt with, get the files ready to be uplifted and taken home in so far as this can be properly done without interfering with work on that file.

Principle 3.13 and the commentary make it clear that the client's work must come first and that any disagreement with the old firm should not be allowed to interfere with the proper conduct of the client's business. This is often easier said than done. Where a client has unequivocally decided to come with you, and has paid their bill, it would be difficult for someone to criticise you for trying to get hold of the file, since in doing so you are trying to comply with Principle 3.13.

Obtaining New Clients

You will find that in the first three or four months of opening there is a plethora of things to do. Whilst there will undoubtedly be times when you are sitting there doing nothing, for the most part you will be wishing that there were more hours in the day to get everything done. The initial shockwaves of opening the new practice will have begun to subside and the telephones will have started to ring with comforting reassurance.

By this stage you will have consolidated what business you have managed to take with you and you are able to set out to create new clients for the firm. You have introduced yourself to as many people as possible and generally put the word about that you have arrived in town and are ready to deal with whatever work comes your way. You now need to put in hand a series of marketing initiatives to make sure that you are taking the business to the clients as well as waiting for the clients to come to you.

If you have a lot of experience in business or have run a marketing campaign before, you may wish to start a major promotion of your practice right away. Running such a marketing programme is dealt with in greater detail in Chapter 18. Even if you feel it is not yet the right time for a full-scale marketing campaign, for which you may not, at this point, have sufficient time or money available, you still need to consolidate the ground you have gained. But the question is, how do you find new clients?

One answer is the inaugural party. This is simply an excuse to put on an enjoyable social engagement for as many people as possible with the intention of placing your name before as many potential clients as possible. The excuse can be a summer barbeque, bonfire night, the 'anniversary of one month and still in business' party, or anything else that seems appropriate. The cost of such a party is likely to be £200 or £300. If it results in a single conveyance or divorce or landlord or tenant dispute that you would not otherwise have had, then it has paid for itself and that client or those clients that have arrived as a result of your marketing initiative will be clients not only on a single occasion but for a number of occasions in the future.

The Business Lunch

Nearly all the tax advantages of business lunches that existed in the past have been removed by the Government. This does not necessarily mean to say that they are a bad idea. Clients are still flattered, by and large, by a free afternoon out. From their point of view, they are able to convince themselves that they are acting in the best interests of their own organisation, which indeed they may well be if they are able to replace a mediocre firm of solicitors with one like yours which is able to do the job better. It also means that they are able to get to know a solicitor on a personal level and develop a relationship and a rapport. All of these things are not only crucial from the solicitor's point of view but also from the client's. If you are in business, you are going to need a solicitor whom you can trust. There is a multitude to choose from and the business lunch provides the opportunity to make your mind up about someone. As a marketing tool, it still has its place.

Joining an Organisation

The more societies, organisations and clubs you join the more people you will meet who are potential clients. Again, they will be able to see you at first hand and decide what kind of individual you are. Join as many organisations as you can and be as active as time permits and get the exposure to as many people as you can that a young business needs.

Citizens' Advice Bureaux

The 684 main offices and about 700 'extensions' of the Citizens' Advice Bureaux around the country fulfil a very important need within our society, and with the reduction in legal aid eligibility their importance has perhaps never been greater. There are many people in society who are faced with problems that they simply cannot deal with and they turn to the CAB for help and advice. Introduce yourself to the local CAB at an early stage and offer to provide them with such assistance as you can. Most CAB have an evening at which their clients attend by appointment to see a lawyer free of charge to deal with problems with which the CAB personnel are not qualified to deal. It is unlikely that this form of referral will result in a vast increase in your business, but this is precisely the kind of additional inflow of work that a new practice needs. In addition, there is no harm in letting people know, in appropriate places, that you are prepared to do such work. If you are prepared to devote such time as you can willingly to help those less fortunate in society, then sooner or later the good works you have performed will reap their reward. People may respect you for the work that you do and be bonded to the firm that bit more as a result.

Talks and Seminars

Many organisations will jump at the chance of having a lawyer attend for free to give a talk, especially if it is a topical matter. The initiative must come from you. Find something on which you feel you can talk for half an hour without making too much of a fool of yourself, put the talk together and then approach a suitable organisation. The whole exercise will probably cost you two hours in terms of time in getting the talk together and in presenting it. If that results in two hours' worth of chargeable time later on, then it is an excellent investment. The probability is that it will result in rather more than that and over the next five years you may find that your time and effort has been repaid many fold. It is not at all difficult to do. The biggest difficulty is in the discipline required to take time out from the ordinary routine of daily practice to set aside the time to do the research and then to fit the presentation into the daily schedule. From a marketing point of view, you take the floor as an expert in the particular field on which you are about to hold forth. Make sure that in the course of that talk people know who you are and where you are and what you can do for them. You should not go so far as to turn the whole thing into one gigantic sales pitch, but there is no point in giving up your time and putting in vast amounts of effort if at the end of it people haven't the slightest idea who you are.

Newspaper Column

Another marketing exercise you may be minded to carry out is to contact your local newspaper and ask them if they would like you to write a legal column. You will be fortunate indeed if they will pay you anything at all for doing so, but it will give considerable publicity for you and your practice in the locality. As with seminars, you start off on the footing that you will be regarded by your readers as an authority on the law and as something of a minor celebrity. It is perhaps not the likely influx of clientele which is the value of writing a local newspaper column as the increase in esteem in which you are held by your existing clients who get to know of it.

The Existing Client Base

Within a few months of being in practice, you will have a clear idea as to who your existing clients are. If you analyse those clients and the type of business they conduct, you will see that with their co-operation you will be able to reach a great many other people and those customers of your client's business will have considerable trust in what those clients say to them. It is a rather difficult and sensitive area, but with tact and diplomacy you may be able to persuade your existing clientele to introduce you to their clients. Many of your clients will themselves have set up on their own at some stage and may be only too acutely aware of the giant leap into the dark that this represents. If so, they may be very sympathetic to an approach in which you ask them to introduce you to their customer base. It is a rather slow process but can reap considerable rewards. If they do allow you access to their own client base, then it is even more important that the job you do for their clients is a good one. If it is, your clients will rise in their own clientele's esteem. If you make a mess of it, then your clients will feel betrayed and you stand not only to lose their clients but also the client himself. Tread carefully, but if handled in the right way you could pick up some extremely valuable clients by this method of marketing.

Credit Control and Billing

Bills to clients were rightly described by a former senior partner of mine as the 'lifeblood of the firm'. The design and appearance of your invoice will be almost as important as that of your notepaper. Work should be billed, to quote the same former senior partner, 'whilst the tears of gratitude are fresh in the client's eyes'. Do not be bashful about putting in a bill. The bill should go in at the earliest opportunity. Those clients who make the comment that you are rather fast at putting in the bill are those clients with whom you are likely to have a problem. It is certainly wrong to put in a bill prematurely, but once the actual work involved is completed, the bill should go in immediately. As well as the main office's bills delivered book, it is not a bad idea to make your own (as described earlier). It can be as informal as having a counsel's notebook divided into five columns with the following headings:

Client	Matter	Date Bill Delivered	Date Bill Paid	Profit Costs
J. Bloggs	Matrim Procs	1/11/93	1/12/93	£250.00

In this way you have at your fingertips a complete summary of the entire billing of the firm. This may, depending on the stage of the evolution of the firm, consist of simply yourself or yourself and one or two others, but no matter. You have the same up-to-the-minute information as a senior partner of a 20-partner 80-fee-earner firm with a multi-million pound turnover. The only difference is that he needs a multi-million pound computer system serviced by a great many computer operators to give him that information whereas you have the same level of information at virtually no cost. One must ask oneself the question: who is managing whose business most efficiently? This is the advantage of being a principal in a small practice.

Giving Credit

Many businesses inform the client on the invoice that they have 30 days or so in which to pay the account. This is an invitation to the client to take at least a month in paying the bill. Our invoices have always stated quite clearly on their face that they are payable immediately with the words 'this amount is due now'. They then go on to state:

> 'Under the Solicitors' (Non-Contentious Business) Remuneration Order 1994 clients have the right within one month of the receipt of a solicitor's bill to require the solicitors to obtain a certificate from the Law Society that the amount charged is fair and reasonable and to require them to refund any part of the bill which is not. The client will be required to pay part of the bill unless the Law Society waives this requirement. The Solicitors Act 1974 also contains provisions enabling clients to have solicitors' bills taxed (i.e. checked by an officer of the court). If this bill is not paid within one month interest at the High Court judgment debt rate is chargeable from the date of the invoice'.

Apart from being a gentle warning at the outset that you expect to be paid promptly and that otherwise there will be certain repercussions the above notice on the bill also operates as the required notice under the Solicitors' (Non-Contentious Business) Remuneration Order 1994 which enables the interest provisions in non-contentious matters to run and also serves as the necessary notice that is required to be delivered in a non-contentious matter before you can sue on a bill. Displayed in a reasonably prominent position on an account in this way, clients are unlikely to take umbrage. Commercial clients are used to seeing other people's standard conditions of sale and, if anything, the display of such a notice on the face of a bill is likely to convey to them a favourable commercial approach by the solicitors rather than any kind of an aggressive stance. In any event, you cannot get away from the fact that in order to litigate against a client effectively, if they fail to pay the bill in a non-contentious matter, you must serve a notice in the required form and by failing to serve that notice in the accompanying bill you are giving those clients who have determined not to pay the account an unnecessary extension of credit. Even though the notice is not required in respect of contentious work it may indicate to the court that you have acted fairly in bringing the client's rights to his or her notice at the outset and so help you gain the moral 'high ground'.

Make sure that the notice is on your copy of the bill as well as the client's copy. The District Judge will need to be satisfied that the notice has been validly served and may not accept your bold assertions that you 'are sure it must have been on the top copy' as adequate proof of service if your file copy contains no such notice.

For those solicitors who are unfortunate enough to have to sue their own clients, a form of final letter and draft summons appear at Appendices 6 and 7.

Alternatively, the Law Society now markets a basic debt collection system called *Summons made Simple* for £146.88 including VAT. It is simple to install and operate and has the advantage of lending itself very well to a stand-alone system. We are using it on what was a redundant 286 processing computer. However, you need a laser printer to print out on, and so a printer dedicated to this task will be a further expense.

Even the most basic computerised accounts system now provides for an aged debtors list. This constitutes a computer print-out of those bills that are a month or more (depending on the program) in arrears with their accounts. Once a client has failed to pay after as short a time as a month, you should be chasing them immediately so long as there is no cogent reason why not. At the very least, it should consist of a copy of the bill with a reminder endorsed on it that the account is outstanding. It is important to keep records as to what reminders have been sent out so that you can validly say at the required time that a client has had two or three reminders, as the case may be, and has still failed to pay the account and therefore you are constrained to take stronger measures. There is nothing worse than a client correctly pointing out that he has not had the reminders, at least not as many reminders as you have said. It still does not put the client in the right but it shows that you are capable of making mistakes and makes you appear incompetent.

Apart from the aged debtors list, if you keep a personal bills delivered book and date stamp those bills that are paid, as I have suggested, you will quite readily see gaps appearing where bills are overdue even before the aged debtors list has arrived on your desk. Send out the chasing letters and keep on top of the debtors and where necessary sue those clients who it is clear are determined not to pay. Do not shy away from taking such action. If they are clients who cannot be bothered to pay for the work you have done, then they are clients who are not really worth keeping. If they are clients who are not paying because they do not have the money, then the sooner you are on their trail the better before the other creditors close in. There are always going to be exceptions. There are clients who have fallen on hard times and who already do not have the money. You may be in a position to help them get through a very difficult time by not pressing them for payment and making it clear that you do not wish to add to their worries. These will be very much the exceptions and if you take the view that a client is verging on the point of bankruptcy anyway and you are not going to get your money out of them, then there is nothing to be gained by jumping on them along with the rest of their creditors. There may, however, be something to be gained by making a point of not pressing them and saying you will give them what help you can whilst they are going through a difficult time and keeping in regular touch with them and showing great concern. People in that situation do have a habit of bouncing back at some stage in the future and they may well need you to help set up a second time. Do not, however, make the mistake of rendering them additional legal services on any substantial scale and simply doubling the size of the unpaid bill.

If you have clearly made a mistake in the conduct of the client's affairs and it is for this reason that the client is disputing your bill, then great care should be exercised in deciding whether or not to sue the client. Even if you do decide not to sue you have a duty to advise the client to seek independent legal advice if you think the circumstances would justify a claim against you (see Principle 28.08 of the Guide). If the client's claims are legitimate then a defence and counterclaim will be filed at which point you must notify the Solicitors Indemnity Fund of the claim if it is likely to exceed £500. The SIF may well decide to take over conduct of the whole proceedings and in all probability the end result will be a compromise. If that compromise involves SIF paying out money to the client, then not only will you have failed to recover the fee but you will also have a higher premium to pay when you renew your professional indemnity cover. It does not mean that for every little mistake you make, you can allow the client to refuse unreasonably to pay the bill but it does mean that great care must be exercised in deciding in those circumstances whether or not to issue a summons or whether it would be better to negotiate the best compromise that you can and put the whole matter down to experience.

CHAPTER 10

Holidays and Staffing Requirements

Law Society Regulations

Complying with Law Society regulations as regards the staffing of premises can present substantial problems for small practices. The regulations were designed to ensure that the standards of service and competence which the public are entitled to expect are maintained and it is fair to say that with fewer resources at their disposal smaller practices may be more tempted to cut corners as regards staff than larger practices.

Rule 13 of the Solicitors' Practice Rules 1990 deals with supervision and management of a solicitor's office. The current Rules are set out in *The Guide to the Professional Conduct of Solicitors.*

You should read the Rules in full, as they are important but briefly, Rule 13 states that:

(a) with regard to supervision:

every office that is open to the public shall be attended on each day it is open or open to receive telephone calls from the public, by a solicitor who has a practising certificate and has been admitted for at least three years. This supervisor must spend sufficient time at the office to ensure that things are properly run and that the staff there are adequately supervised.

(b) regarding management:

the office must normally be attended during all hours it is open to the public or open to receive telephone calls from the public by a solicitor with a current practising certificate (i.e. a newly qualified solicitor will do), or a Fellow of the Institute of Legal Executives who has been admitted as a Fellow for not less than three years.

The above is a broad summary of the Rules and there are all sorts of additional exceptions.

The Law Society has made a new Rule 13 on supervision and management. However, at the present time this new rule is not in force. Information regarding commencement will appear in the Professional Standards Bulletins.

In the 1993 Guide's commentary on Principle 3.02 it is accepted that managers are entitled to take normal holidays and that a breach of the Rules does not neccessarily occur just because the manager goes on holiday. This does not mean there is never a need to have a manager whilst you are away. You still have a duty to conduct your clients' affairs properly and to continue to supply a proper professional service. If something goes wrong in your absence and one reason is that your management of the practice was inadequate you may still find yourself in trouble with the SCB in spite of the assistance given to you by paragraph 3 of the commentary.

It all really comes down to common sense. If things are hectic just before you go away and the staff are not sufficiently skilled or experienced to cope you must get someone in who can handle matters despite the expense. It is fair neither to the staff nor the clients to do otherwise. On the other hand, there is no point employing a locum to sit and do nothing for two weeks. With luck, you'll be doing that!

If you are a sole practitioner you are probably going to be, under normal circumstances, both the manager and the supervisor. Principle 3.03 deals specifically with sole practitioners and points out the continuing duty owed to clients whilst you are away. If you are intending to close down for two weeks you must make arrangements to ensure that clients' work will not suffer whilst you are away. This will involve getting things right up to date and putting in place contingency plans in case anything blows up during your absence. This will include temporary arrangements for another solicitor to be able to operate your client account in case a client should demand the return of funds you may be holding.

The rules do not mean that every time you want to nip out and get a sandwich you have to hire a locum to look after the practice. The rules deal with what one might call the 'normal' situation. Under normal circumstances, you must have a qualified solicitor on the premises at all times that the practice is open to the public. Most of the time that will probably be you, or your partner if you have one. What the rules will not allow you to do is to open a branch office and put a trainee solicitor in charge of it and leave it to run itself. Neither will it allow you to have a trainee in the office at all times with the principal popping in and out on the odd occasion to supervise things. If that is the normal situation, then you will be in trouble with Practice Rule 13. If, however, you have to be out of the office for the day on business or for court work, there is no need to go and hire an assistant solicitor simply in order to comply with the rules. It is a question of degree. If you are to be involved in a six-week trial which would require your constant attendance, then you will be reaching the stage where it is becoming 'normal' for you to be out of the office and the practice being run by your trainee solicitor. In that situation, you are going to have to think carefully as to whether you should be taking on additional qualified staff on a temporary basis. Failure to do so may lead you to be found to be in breach of the management requirements of Practice Rule 13. A good rule of thumb is to imagine that there is a terrible disaster with a client and you then have to explain yourself to the Solicitors Complaints Bureau. Explaining why you were out of the office for a couple of days without having made separate arrangements might not be too much of a problem, but you may feel that your excuses were rather thin if you had gone away for four or five weeks, albeit in connection with work rather than pleasure, and had left the practice in the hands of an inexperienced member of staff and something went terribly wrong.

The Locum

The traditional answer to prolonged absence from the office, whether it be for reasons of holiday or illness, has been the locum. Locums may wrongly be thought by some to be third-rate solicitors who are unable to hold down a full-time job. Whilst undoubtedly there are some locums who fit this description, there are a good many very competent individuals who, for one reason or another, are unable or unwilling to work on a full-time basis. Go to a well-known agency and make sure you find out as much as possible about the person to whom you are about to entrust your practice in terms of past history, knowledge and experience. Ensure that the locum has a sufficient level of competence and knowledge of the type of work that you carry out in your practice to be able to do a proper job in your absence. If you do not take these precautions, you may find that they cause a whole series of disasters and you return to a terrible mess. If you are able to obtain a recommendation from another firm as to a particular locum, then so much the better. If possible, try and meet the locum to form your own views.

Sharing Staff

Going away on holiday or being absent from the office for any other reason for a period of more than a few days will mean making arrangements to ensure that there are sufficient administrative staff as well as fee-earning staff. If your spouse works in the practice, then you will be taking two key players out of the game at holiday times. People with children tend to go away during school holiday times and at half terms which is exactly when other parents in other businesses are going away so that the call on temporary secretaries is at its greatest and the quality of temporary secretary available is at its lowest. To a large extent, this cannot be helped. If you have been fortunate enough to share office space with others, you may at least in part be able to answer the problem by making use of their staff. Obviously, you will have to be very diplomatic in your approach to your office colleagues, but you may well find that they are amenable to one or other members of their staff having one of your telephones on their desk which can relieve the pressure enormously. It is a most unpleasant feeling to be on the telephone yourself with two other telephones ringing and no one there to answer them. Even if this only happens two or three times a day, the stress levels go through the ceiling. If, on these isolated occasions, there is a member of someone else's staff who can leap to the rescue and answer the telephone and take a short message, it makes an enormous difference.

Even if the people with whom you share office space are other solicitors, or other professionals, such as accountants, care must still be taken to ensure your client's confidentiality is maintained – and consider whether there is any chance of the other firm acting for clients on the 'other side' to your own clients. If that is likely, you may have to think again about such an arrangement. Confidentiality must be preserved *whoever* you share premises with.

Either instead of asking them to come to your rescue when they are needed or in addition to such an arrangement, you may be able to persuade fellow office workers to enter into a more formal arrangement whereby they put in a couple of hours work for you either during their lunch hour or first thing in the morning or last thing at night. Again, it is absolutely critical that these arrangements are agreed in advance with senior management since it is their staff who are being put upon, but in a great many instances there is no need to call upon them. The mere fact that they can be called upon if the workload gets too great for temporaries or other staff in the office during the holiday period will be a considerable reassurance to them. With that kind of arrangement, it would be more appropriate to agree an hourly rate than simply provide a gratuity.

Shut up Shop?

If you are about to go on holiday, why not simply close down for two weeks? This will avoid staff-sharing arrangements, the cost of a locum and the worry about what is happening whilst you are away. This solution has rather more to commend it than might at first be apparent. Indeed, many of our European counterparts do exactly that. They simply lock the front door and disappear for a couple of weeks. If you are lucky, you may just get an answerphone.

This may well be a suitable solution during the first year when the level of business is probably going to be quite low. If you are going to opt for this solution, you must be mindful of your obligation to provide a proper professional service for your clients. If some problem does crop up on something which was otherwise well under control before you went, you are going to have to answer for it not only to the client but also to the Solicitors Complaints Bureau at a later stage. Clearly, there is much that can be done by way of preventative surgery in anticipating problems that may appear and in trying to head them off. You will nonetheless have to make some kind of contingency arrangement in case the worst happens. The most sensible thing you can do is to have an arrangement with a local practice so that if any real crisis erupts, the client can be referred on to that practice. If you explain your problems to a neighbouring practice and if you have managed to establish some kind of a rapport with someone within that practice, it is surprising how helpful one's professional colleagues can be. There will undoubtedly come a time in the future when in some way or another you can repay them in the same professional way. Again, confidentiality must be protected, and any question of conflict avoided.

You will have to make it clear to your clients that you will be away for two weeks and that other than coping with real emergencies – as opposed to those that are perceived by clients as emergencies – their matter will have to stand still for two weeks. If there is a problem with this, then it is best to sort it out and, if at all possible, carry out what work they would wish you to be doing during that two-week period before you go. The majority of clients are usually fairly understanding. They, too, have holidays and their work stands still for two weeks. You may also like to point out the reality to them that even in large firms, for the most part, anything other than something which gets to screaming pitch is left to pile up on your desk for two weeks. We all like to pretend that there are hundreds of people beavering away on our matters whilst we are away, but during the summer there are not enough people around and all routine items are left to accumulate. There is no reason why the same should not happen in a small firm.

The Watchful Eye Solution

After the first year, it is probably not going to be practicable to close down the firm. For a start, you may well have additional staff and unless you are going to insist that they have their holidays at the same time, you will have to pay them whether you are there or not. If you decide not to employ a locum because you feel that your staff are sensible enough and conscientious enough to be able to get on with work themselves, you are going to have to comply with the Practice Rules on supervision. Clearly, a locum could do this for you, but if you have ruled that out, then you may like to opt for the watchful eye solution. This again involves your professional colleague in a neighbouring firm, who has been admitted for at least three years, helping you out. If there is someone who is willing to take on the responsibility, you can brief them on any problem that is likely to occur. There are usually at least two or three files which will inevitably boil up to one degree or another and with which the staff in situ whilst you are away will have to cope. In addition, your professional colleague will have to agree to come into the office to ensure that all is running smoothly and be prepared to spend as much time there as is necessary to ensure the smooth running of the firm and to deal with any problems. It is also a good idea to try to arrange for them to supervise the opening of your post.

If you were able to get everything up to date before you departed and if your staff are reasonably sensible and competent, then that amount of time may not be very great. Staff often need a certain amount of guidance and direction and it is this steady hand on the tiller which your professional colleague can provide. It should not be necessary for him or her to actually do the work but simply be available to your staff to talk through problems which they encounter and for your colleague to make the decisions on it which you would make. He or she must also be there as a back-up in case a particularly nervous client is unhappy with the advice given by a less experienced member of staff and demands to speak to somebody with greater experience.

In practice, the supervision by your neighbouring colleague should only amount to probably no more than half an hour a day and sometimes not even that, unless a particular problem does explode.

These arrangements will probably involve you making temporary signing arrangements for your client account with your bank. You must realise that you are putting absolute trust in your professional colleague who should be someone at partnership level in the neighbouring firm. It is also probably a good idea when making the signing arrangements with the bank to explain personally to the bank manager what is happening.

So far as office account is concerned, there may well have to be cheques drawn for things like searches. One solution is to leave half a dozen cheques drawn on office account and signed but the remaining details left blank and to endorse the cheque 'not to exceed £50'. This enables the staff to operate office account in a very limited way and the extent to which they are able to dip into office account for the wrong reasons is limited. You may, however, prefer to draw cheques for specific purposes for use if needs be, or better still, to make temporary signing arrangements for your colleague across the road on office account as well as client. Some firms are prepared to let your staff pay for things with cheques on their office account and to settle up with you when you come back from holiday.

Holiday arrangements for some firms, and in particular sole practitioners, are never very easy but holidays are important. If you fail to take them, you will become jaded and run down. Particularly during the first year, it is important to get away. You will probably not realise quite what setting up has taken out of you until you go off on holiday and it is only after two or three days away that you begin to relax and feel an enormous weight disappearing off your shoulders. A recent scanning of the obituary column in the Law Society's *Gazette* revealed that 24 per cent of the solicitors whose deaths were reported died before the age of 50 years. Do not rush to join them. Despite what you may feel to the contrary, the practice can and will survive without you for a week or two. Take your holidays – you will have earned them.

CHAPTER 11

Developing Management Skills

Many people who start their own businesses, and solicitors are no exception, have little or no management experience. Management consists of organising and controlling things and/or people so as to produce the most efficient and hopefully the most profitable result. Whilst a certain amount of knowledge and experience is needed to be able to manage properly, the most important ingredient of management for a solicitor is self-discipline. Whilst there are some people who are more organised than others, most people can manage a business provided they make the time to do so.

If you have been a partner in a firm, then you may have had the opportunity to manage part of the firm, but except in the smallest of firms, management is either spread across all of the partners with individual partners being delegated to carry out certain functions and other partners controlling perhaps the more important areas such as finance and staff, or else it is delegated to a small committee of perhaps three to five partners who will act as the firm's managers for a set period of anything between one and three years.

All partners in firms are theoretically managers, or at least they should be, but there are large numbers of partners who have little or no interest in the management of their own business or prefer to leave it to those who feel they have the aptitude, leaving them to get on with what they feel is the important business of winning clients and servicing them.

If you are starting a business with no previous experience of managing at all how do you develop the necessary management skills to ensure that your business will be successful? There are four basic ways in which you can learn these skills:

Books

With the advent of the Legal Aid Board's franchising exercise, and the introduction of the Law Society's own Practice Management Standards, there has been an enormous emphasis placed on the right and wrong ways to manage a business in the last two years. Whilst there have always been books around on the topic of management, we are now rather spoilt for choice. I would recommend anyone thinking of starting a new firm to read at least one book on the subject.

The Practice Management Standards themselves go quite a long way towards ensuring that a practice is properly managed. My own view is that not all of the Practice Management Standards are appropriate to all firms and many of them are not really appropriate to sole practices, at least in their embryonic stages, but a close eye should be kept on them as the firm develops and progresses to ensure that something which was not particularly appropriate at the outset has become relevant and is not being implemented.

Seminars and Courses

Much the same applies here as applies to books. With the interest in the franchising arrangements and the Practice Management Standards, there has been an upsurge in the number of courses dealing with management. How long this will remain the case is yet to be seen, but I am sure that there will always now be at least one or two courses run per year dealing specifically with managing a practice. If you are in the process of being made redundant and intend to set up your own firm as an answer to your future employment problems, you may have more time available to attend courses than would otherwise be the case. You may even be able to persuade your present employer to pay the cost of a course as a means of assuaging the guilt felt at making you redundant. At least as importantly, even if the employer will not pay for the course, you may be allowed to attend it on full pay. This is worth the course fee several times over. It is likely that once you have actually set up the practice you will find it difficult to take a day out to attend a management course until you have become reasonably well established. Life is just too busy to be able to take the time out even for half a day until you have reached the stage where you have a number of staff who can hold the fort whilst you are off on a course. As the practice changes from simply being you and a secretary, managing a practice effectively becomes ever more important. Different management skills are needed when it comes to managing a two or three-partner practice than was the case when you were on your own, and as you move up into a six or seven-partner firm the skills are different again. By the time you are making these transitions, you should make the time available to attend a course so that you learn from other people's mistakes and benefit from their experiences.

Talking to People

An invaluable means of educating yourself as to how to manage your practice is by talking to other people. These need not necessarily be other solicitors, they might be accountants or non-professional people. Talking to others about how they manage their business and, even better, watching them at first hand, can give you all kinds of ideas which you had never had before. Such opportunities for discussion may present themselves at seminars or courses, local Law Society meetings, or social occasions. If you share office space with other people, then of course you have the perfect opportunity both to observe how other people manage their businesses and also to discuss their way of going about things and your way. You may also have contacts within other firms. Talk to partners in different sized practices and you may find they are surprisingly willing to talk about how their practice is run and what their own thoughts are about the different ways of managing practices.

Experience

There are many things which you can pick up as you go along and managing a practice is certainly one of them. If you are a sole practitioner, then you have very little choice. You are going to be a manager, the only question is are you going to be a good one or a bad one? Lack of management experience is certainly not something which should put you off trying to run your own practice or running it with one or more partners. The two key words are **control** and **organisation**. If you are in control of what you are doing because you take a close interest in what is happening and you make sufficient time to apply that knowledge to your business then you will be able to organise things efficiently. By remaining in control you are more likely to realise, at an early stage, if some aspect of your business is not running smoothly and you will be able to rectify matters more easily. You will of course make mistakes. This does not mean to say that you are a bad manager. You only have to look at major businesses which fail to see that the management has made mistakes. Sometimes these are avoidable and sometimes not. You are certainly going to improve your chances of success if you have the necessary degree of control either on your own or collectively with partners, and if you have sufficient accurate information so as to organise your business in the most profitable and efficient way that you can.

Three Important Areas

To attempt to go into greater depth on how to acquire management skills would mean writing a complete book in itself, as indeed many other people have already done, but I will confine my comments to fairly superficial observations on three key areas.

Managing Staff

The way in which you manage staff will be governed to some extent by employment protection legislation. If you behave badly towards staff, they may consider themselves constructively dismissed and sue you. This does not mean that fear of litigation should produce a situation where the 'tail wags the dog'. You are the boss and it is you who calls the shots. Having said that, the trick is to let the staff know that without actually telling them in so many words. You should try to have staff carry out your instructions by persuasion and suggestion rather than the issuing of orders. If staff have a different solution to the problem from the one that you have put forward, then it will in most cases be worth listening to what they have to say. Rather than stifling any comments or criticism that they may have, you may find that they are able to teach you something occasionally rather than the other way around. There will nevertheless come a point when a decision has to be taken and the contribution from the staff must cease and you make it clear that things are to be done in the way you have decided.

The Law Society's *Solicitors' Office Manual* is intended as a basic kit for firms from which to compile their own office manual. The object of the office manual is to set out as extensively and as exhaustively as possible the firm's policy as to how things should be done. If you decide to follow the Law Society's lead and produce such an office manual, it does place you in the position of being able to provide staff with a copy of the manual as soon as they commence their employment and to the extent that they depart from the procedures laid down in the manual, they will have to justify their actions.

In a small office you are going to be working very closely with your staff and it is very important that people get on with one another and that they have a good relationship with you as their principal. Certainly, over-familiarity can breed contempt, but there is nothing wrong with taking a personal interest in your staff and making them feel that your door is always open to them to discuss problems, be they either of a professional or a personal nature. There will equally be times when it will be necessary for you to make it clear that you are cross with people's failings, but you should never find it necessary to embarrass or humiliate anyone, particularly in front of other people, nor should you be discourteous or rude.

Managing the Finances

There are many books written on specifically how to manage the financial affairs of a business. The basic message is that the figures must add up. They must always add up. The key point is information. You must have good, accurate information as to what money is coming in, what money is going out, and what the level of profit is. With a computerised system, this can be a fairly straightforward procedure. If you do not have a computerised system, then you must either gather the information yourself as you go along or ensure that your book-keeper provides you with the information and you must check it to ensure that it is accurate. You should insist on either manual or computerised reports at least once a month. This information should provide you with a detailed list of outgoings which you will check against your budget figures to see how close to your budget you are keeping. If you are over budget then you must either revise your budget and totally rethink all the figures or look for areas in which to make savings. For example, if by giving salary increases you have gone over your salaries budget, you must either increase your profits by working harder or accept that your profits will be lower because of your generosity to your staff, or you must see if you are under budget on other items which are likely to stay under budget so that the overall figure is still correct.

You must examine the figures carefully since there will be items such as the professional indemnity contribution which will give an inflated figure if it is paid as a lump sum rather than by instalments. A distorted picture may then appear if you take the three months' expenses to date and multiply it by four to produce an annual total. If you have a six-monthly figure of income and outgoings, then you are able to get a much clearer picture as to whether you are likely to achieve your objectives set out at the beginning of the year in your budget. Adjustments at that time may come too late to have any real effect on the yearly figure. It is for this reason that you must take stock of the situation at least once a month.

If your profit costs figures for this month and last month have been disappointing, you must try to decide why this is and whether it is likely to continue. Is it time to cut back the staff? The important thing is that you make a decision even if that decision is that you will do nothing for the time being. What you cannot afford to do is not to take a decision because you are afraid of doing so.

Time-Costing

Time-costing is and always will be regarded as a chore by fee-earning staff and by many principals. It comes as a standard part of many accounts packages and it is probably true to say that most practices cannot get very far today without introducing time-costing at a fairly early stage. Time-costing produces a very substantial amount of information. As well as telling you who in the practice is working hardest, or who according to their time sheets is working hardest which may be quite another matter, it tells you how they are organising their time so that you may spot where time is being inefficiently used and be in a position to correct the errors. It also tells you what type of work is being done and by which people as well as what the cost to the firm of doing the work is so that you can price the rate at which you charge that work to the client. It will give an early warning signal of a fall-off in work to enable you to consider sooner rather than later whether any adjustments need to be made to staffing levels and likewise any increase in work which would require you taking on additional staff to cope.

It is probably true to say that time-costing can be safely dispensed with by a small trader for the first two or three years depending on the speed at which the business grows. In a small office where you are probably literally able to see every one of your staff working, you are very likely to know who is doing what and how they are spending their time. If someone is spending a lot of time on personal telephone calls, you will probably be able to see and hear them doing so. At this stage you are likely to be working longer hours than anyone else and so you will be able to observe at first hand the exact time that people are starting work and leaving and as the sole person to whom they will be reporting, you will be able to see and judge the quality and extent of the work that they produce.

Once the number of fee-earners exceeds three or four, they are beginning to spread themselves out geographically so that you are in a much weaker position to see how they are spending their time and what work they are producing. You may even have to introduce an intermediate tier of management in the form of a senior fee-earner to whom a less experienced fee-earner reports. Once you have reached this stage, you are going to need some form of time-recording

117

system. By the time you have grown to a two-partner firm with supporting fee-earners, time-costing will be a must.

Choosing a system is very important. Since most systems come as an add-on (and many would say an afterthought) to an accounts package it is important to evaluate the time-costing system and not simply to take it because it is offered as part of an accounts package which seems attractive in all other respects. The best means of selection is by recommendation from people who have such a system and by discussing with fellow professionals the merits of that particular system.

The introduction of such a system should be carried out very carefully. You should have meetings with staff to explain why the system is being introduced and the way it will be introduced and to secure their full co-operation. There is no point bringing it in if it is going to cause ill-feeling and suspicion. It must be perceived as an improvement and a step forward rather than a means of keeping tabs on the staff and making them account for every minute of the day. It must be seen as a means by which you can more effectively manage the firm by detecting problems at an early stage and taking the necessary steps to resolve them. It will enable you to identify those areas of the firm that are non or less profitable so that a management decision can be taken to make them more profitable or to avoid them altogether. Thus, the profitability of the firm will increase which means better job security for them.

Making Time to Manage

As discussed earlier, none of the information which you acquire through time-costing or reports generated by accounting systems, nor any of the skills which you have developed will be of any use whatsoever if you do not make the time to manage your business. How you do so is a matter for you. Most partnerships will have partners' meetings once a month. Committees may be appointed who will meet more frequently than that or less frequently depending on their area of responsibility. Two-man partnerships will arrange an ad hoc get together over coffee or lunch or just at some convenient moment during the day to discuss a particular item. A sole trader may use the arrival of a set of reports from his or her book-keeper as a spur to getting out additional financial information and going through the figures to see to what extent he or she is or is not on target. You may decide to make a diary note to look at the figures and you may or may not keep to it. How you make the time to manage does not matter so long as you do. It is essential that you grasp the idea that it is every bit as important to look over the last three months' billing figures as it is to get out a set of particulars of claim on a client's case. There is no point spending 23 hours a day on trying to produce profits for a business if the funds generated are not used sensibly and the effort is misdirected.

CHAPTER 12

Regulatory Bodies

Financial Services Act

There are so many things to think about when you are setting up a new practice that you may make the mistake of giving little or no thought to the question of whether you need to apply for investment business authorisation under the Financial Services Act. Whilst it is true that if you choose not to apply for authorisation, it is one less thing to have to worry about, this should be a conscious decision rather than something which goes by default. Authorisation is not something that is mandatory in order to conduct a solicitors' practice, so should you register or not?

Part of the problem with the Financial Services Act is that much of it has not been tested in court. Until we have the benefit of judicial pronouncements on these matters all we have to go by is the opinions of others who may be better placed than ourselves to express a view, with all the uncertainty that that entails.

It is a criminal offence under section 4 of the Financial Services Act to carry out investment business without being authorised to do so. Interim authorisation was granted to all firms in 1988 as a transitional measure whilst the provisions of the Act were brought into force. That temporary authorisation has long since ceased although apparently there are still firms who believe they have the necessary authorisation to conduct investment business as a result of those provisions. Investment business as defined by the Act is very wide and covers not only giving advice on investments but also dealing in, arranging deals and managing investments and any one or more of these activities requires an investment business certificate if investments as defined by the Act are involved. Stocks and shares, unit trusts and life policies with an investment element are examples of investments caught by the Act. Building society share or deposit or savings accounts are not investments as defined by the Act, nor are National Savings Certificates and Premium Bonds.

As a practising solicitor, obtaining the necessary authorisation is very straightforward. The Law Society will provide you with a form RF2 on which to apply for either a category 1 certificate (non-discrete investment business) or a category 2 (discrete investment business certificate). A category 2 certificate will only be issued to firms with a principal, director or employee who is a 'qualified person'. A 'qualified person' is an individual approved by the Law Society to conduct one or more types of DIB, retail branded/packaged products (for example, life policies), securities/portfolio management or corporate pensions. In order to achieve 'qualified person' status, the individual must have obtained the relevant Law Society qualification or hold an accredited qualification or be able to demonstrate extensive prior experience. The completed form together with the appropriate fee (currently £215 plus £70 per partner) is sent to the Law Society who issues the appropriate investment business certificate. Authorisation is required on an annual basis and the application year currently runs from 1 November of each year.

You will have to comply with the necessary record-keeping provisions of the Rules. There is a very useful starter pack available which not only provides you with the necessary paperwork to complete to ensure that you stay on the right side of the Rules but also tells you what forms to complete and when, and generally how to maintain your records. You may at any time be the subject of a monitoring visit to ensure that you are complying with the terms of the Rules. *Solicitors and Financial Services: a Compliance Handbook* by Peter Camp (published by the Law Society) is very helpful in assisting solicitors to find their way through the maze of rules and regulations. If you choose not to apply for authorisation, you will need to be quite sure that you engage in no activity which would require investment business authorisation. There are perhaps four key areas of work which a solicitor in general practice will want to cover but which he or she would be compelled to steer clear of if they lack the necessary authorisation.

Chapter 26 of *The Guide to the Professional Conduct of Solicitors 1993* contains an overview of investment business and Schedule 1 to the Act is annexed to that chapter. If you are in two minds as to whether to apply for an investment business certificate or not you could do no worse than have a read through the relevant chapter.

Administration of Estates

If a firm is asked to administer an estate which contains stocks and shares or unit trusts, it may be considered to be dealing or arranging deals in investments merely by instructing a stockbroker to sell shares. Advising on what shares or other investments should be sold may be caught by the Rules. Selling investments or exercising rights attached to investments in an estate is likely to amount to dealing in investments whether you do so by means of a stockbroker or not. Further, the fact that the firm may have referred the executors to independent third parties for suitable advice would not alter the position, nor would the fact that no commission is payable to the firm. Recent public share issues, such as gas, water and electricity, may well mean that a greater percentage of the population than ever before own shares and that solicitors may more frequently be faced with estates that have shares in them. In order to avoid the need for authorisation, the firm would need to ensure that it is not conducting investment business. For example, it would have to avoid 'dealing' in investments which may be difficult.

Trusts

As a solicitor, you may be involved in the administration of a trust. This may arise in the course of the administration of an estate where, for example, a minority interest arises in favour of children or grandchildren of the deceased. If you have been appointed an executor under such a trust, it will be almost impossible to avoid the provisions of the Act and the requirement to be authorised, if there are shares in the deceased's estate or in any other situation since the question will arise as to what way the trust money should be invested. Even if you decline to give any advice on the position and your co-executor gets advice elsewhere, you will have to say whether or not you agree with it and by doing so you will be sailing perilously close to the wind. The probability is that you will be the professional and a co-executor will be a lay individual and it may well be the case that your co-executor looks to you to give the necessary instruction to brokers to go ahead with any investments on which they have advised. It is likely this would constitute dealing in or arranging investments and would require authorisation under the Act. Again, the fact that you have not received a fee for any of this, or a commission, and that you have involved third parties to give the advice on a professional basis, does not avoid the requirement for authorisation.

Conveyancing

You will not need an investment business certificate to advise on which building society your client should use for his or her mortgage since mortgages are not 'investments' for the purposes of the Act. If you advise where they should go for their endowment or pension mortgage, and then proceed to make the necessary arrangements and take a commission, you are likely to need authorisation under the Act. You do not need authorisation to give advice on the merits of, say, pension mortgages generally over other kinds of mortgages. The problems start when your advice becomes specific to particular products. What may be less obvious is that simply by discussing the merits of one scheme as against the other and then passing the client on to a broker to make the arrangements and not receiving any of the commission yourself, you are likely to still need authorisation. Perhaps even less obviously, you may be asked by your client as to whether it would be a good idea or not for a life policy to be surrendered, or you are asked to advise on whether a new policy should be taken out. Again, in the widest sense such advice may well constitute 'advising' or 'dealing in investments' and require authorisation under the Act, unless the advice is kept general and reference to individual policies is not made.

Company Take-Overs

One of the more lucrative matters in which you may be instructed as a general practitioner or as a sole practitioner is a company take-over. By the time the client comes to you, the details of the agreement may already have been worked out. If not, you may be asked to negotiate or advise upon the acquisition or disposal of shares in one or other of the companies involved. Such advice may amount to the carrying out of investment business for the purposes of the Act. Useful guidance specifically on this topic is to be found in *The Guide to the Professional Conduct of Solicitors 1993*, Annex 26F.

There is certainly a view which says that to be sure of avoiding the commission of an offence under the Act, you will need to have a greater depth of knowledge of the Act and its workings than you would ordinarily need to operate successfully within the terms of an investment business certificate, and so if you are going to acquire such detailed knowledge you may as well obtain the necessary authorisation under the Act and put it to good use by making money from conducting investment business. Equally, it is also true there are a good many firms who obtain the necessary authorisation purely and simply out of fear of falling foul of the Act and committing offences and who never consciously carry out any form of investment business. If you decide not to register in your early years, you will undoubtedly have to tread very carefully to ensure that you do not infringe the provisions of the Act. It is also clear that by the time you have become well established and certainly by the time you have grown into a two or more partner firm it will be virtually impossible to operate a general practice without being authorised under the Act.

Data Protection Act

Computers have the ability to hold enormous amounts of information (data) and with the proliferation of computers and the data stored on them, it became apparent that a certain amount of control needed to be exercised over those people who stored data and the use to which it was put. The data referred to in the Data Protection Act is information stored on computers and it follows that if you do not store any information on a computer you do not need to be licensed under the Act. If you do store such information, then you will only need a licence if the type of information you store is of a type which requires the storer of the information to be registered. The most likely area of operation which would require a solicitor to be registered under the Act is in relation to personal information on clients, such as their names and addresses and/or information about their businesses. If you hold exactly the same information on a card index system or in an address book, then you do not need a licence under the Act. If you put it on computer, then you do. It may be thought that such provisions were not really intended to catch people who simply wanted to make it easier to obtain their clients' telephone numbers by storing the information on computer and that may well be right, but as things stand at the present time, that is the law. Where the information is stored coincidentally, for example, a client's name and address stored as part of the text of a letter to that client, then you do not need a licence. If you store the information in such a way that you are able to send out a general 'mail shot' to clients, then you would need a licence under the Act.

For solicitors, as with the Financial Services Act authorisation, obtaining the necessary licence is a fairly straightforward business and involves only the completion of an application form and the payment of a fee on an annual basis. Further information is available from the Information Services Officer, Office of Data Protection Registrar, Springfield House, Water Lane, Cheshire, SK9 5AX. Tel: 01652 535777.

Law Society

Rule 14.3 of the Solicitors Indemnity Rules 1992 requires that a solicitor 'shall forthwith give to Solicitors Indemnity Fund Limited notice in writing of:

124

(i) the address of any new practice which he commences or of which he becomes a principal;

(ii) any change in the place or places of business of any practice of which he is or becomes a principal'.

In other words, as soon as you set up you must immediately notify Solicitors Indemnity Fund Limited so that your professional indemnity cover can be arranged. As well as notifying the Fund, you will need to notify the Law Society so that its records are properly maintained. If you are intending to carry out any legal aid work, you will also need to notify the Legal Aid Board which will allocate you a computer number to enable payment to be made for the work you carry out. First of all you will have to find out which legal aid area covers the area in which you intend to trade and unless it is the same area in which you have previously traded, you will need to make a few telephone calls. The letters you will need to write are perfectly straightforward, simply telling the appropriate organisation that as of a particular date you will commence trading under the style of Bloggs & Co. and, in the case of the Legal Aid Board, asking for an account number to be allocated to you.

As discussed in Chapter 2 (see page 13), Rule 11 of the Solicitors' Practice Rules 1990 requires that the name of a firm of solicitors consist only of the name or names of one or more solicitors who are present or former principals 'together with, if desired, other conventional references to the firm and to such person'. For most people, this should not pose a problem. For many, part of the attraction of setting up your own firm is to have your name in lights. If you are buying a practice, you may well wish to retain the goodwill element associated with the name of the old practice. What you are not allowed to do is to set up as, for example 'The London Law Firm'. The firm's name must consist of the names of solicitor principals, either former or present. Special rules apply if you are setting up a multi-national partnership. It may perhaps only be a matter of time before this restriction is removed. Already firms are banding themselves into different associations so as to promote a 'corporate' image with their own common logos and it is becoming increasingly common to see phrases such as 'part of the M5 network of lawyers', etc., on a firm's notepaper, but as the Practice Rules stand at the present time, the position is as stated above.

Do not forget the Law Society's rules on supervision and management of an office contained in Rule 13 of the 1990 Solicitors' Practice Rules, as explained in Chapter 10 (see page 105), and Rule 15 on client care provision

125

concerning complaints-handling and information that must be given to the client as to who is dealing with their matter.

Health and Safety Executive

The Health and Safety Executive operates as an arm of the local authority, generally from the local Town Hall. They have wide powers under a number of Acts. Perhaps the most important ones are the Offices, Shops and Railway Premises Act 1963 and the Health and Safety at Work Act 1974. It is their task to ensure that employees are able to work in a safe environment. Whilst it is probably fair to say that they are perhaps more concerned with an employee who is at risk of having his hand chopped off due to lack of a guard on a piece of machinery in a factory, they are nevertheless keen to ensure that your trainee solicitor will not be electrocuted whilst making the tea using a kettle with defective wiring. It is extremely likely that within the first two years of operation you will receive a routine visit from the Health and Safety Officer. They are fairly thorough and go to some lengths to ensure that even small failures are brought to your attention, without being overly oppressive about it.

Electricity at Work

The Electricity at Work Regulations 1989 came into force on 1 April 1990. These place a duty on employers to assess the work activities which use electricity or which may be affected by it so that any foreseeable risks associated with electricity in the workplace are appreciated and the necessary steps taken to avoid danger or personal injury. In other words, the solicitor employer must look at how electricity is used in his or her office and any dangers that may be posed and take all necessary steps to see that such danger is kept to a minimum. This might cover, for example, appreciating that a dictating machine plugged into a remote socket by means of an extension lead is a bad idea because someone may trip over the flex. This may be another regulation which you may be inclined to ignore when you are first setting up, but if you do, you had better hope that anyone you employ does not have an accident involving electricity since, if such an accident could have been prevented, there may be some very awkward questions to answer. As such potential hazards will include a plug with the wrong size fuse in it which overheats and starts a fire, the only real way to make sure your position is protected is at some stage to have a survey carried out by a qualified electrician who will produce a brief report of what appliances and installations he has inspected and any problems can be identified, or else the report can say that the inspection of the appliance and installation was satisfactory. You should be able to get a quote from a qualified electrician before such an inspection is carried out and it is unlikely to be more than about £50.

First-Aid at Work

The Health and Safety (First-Aid) Regulations 1981 require every employer to make adequate first-aid provision for all employees and to inform employees of such arrangements as exist. Operations which are considered low hazard, such as offices and shops, should have one trained first-aider for every 50 employees. The Act goes on to provide for the display of notices informing employees of the first-aid arrangements. Small establishments, i.e. of less than 50 employees, will not generally need a trained first-aider, but someone must be appointed to take control in the event of an accident or injury and someone has to have responsibility for the first-aid box.

First-Aid Box

Every employer must provide at least one first-aid box clearly identified and marked, preferably by a white cross on a green background. The Regulations provide detailed requirements as to the contents of first-aid boxes. Personally, I feel that unless your practice is in a remote area and you have a lot of employees, the Regulations relating to first-aid boxes are rather excessive, e.g. six individually wrapped triangular bandages. There is no doubt about it that a well-stocked first-aid box is an excellent idea, but if people are sufficiently badly injured that they must have their arm put in a sling immediately, my own choice would be to leave the injured person lying where they are and call an ambulance rather than trying to strap up a dislocated or broken limb.

Reporting of Accidents

The Reporting of Injuries, Diseases and Dangerous Occurrences Regulations 1985, as amended, impose duties on employers to report to the Health and Safety Executive or the local authority certain accidents. These range from fatal accidents at one end through dangerous occurrences, such as explosions, down to accidents causing more than three days' incapacity. The Regulations are fairly complicated but by way of summary, a serious injury such as a fracture must be reported immediately by the quickest practical means, which would normally be telephone, to the relevant enforcing authority. If there is doubt as to whether the incident is reportable or as to which authority is the correct one to notify, you should ask the advice of the Health and Safety Executive. This must be followed up by a written report on Form F2508 to the enforcing authority within seven days of the accident. Accidents causing more than three days' incapacity from work must also be reported on the same form to the enforcing authority within seven days, but immediate telephone notification is unnecessary.

These kinds of incidents must be recorded in an accident book and retained for at least three years from the date the entry was made. Clearly, it is good practice to record any accident and to put as much detail down as possible in case either there is a claim at a later stage or the Health and Safety Executive feels that it is a reportable accident which should have been notified in writing or by telephone.

The Health and Safety Officer

The Health and Safety Officer will also be looking to see that you have the necessary employer's liability insurance and that your certificate of insurance is displayed. Also the statutory notice under the Shops, Offices and Railway Premises Act should be in a place where it can easily be read by your employees in order to bring a summary of its provisions to the attention of your employees so that they know what their rights are under the legislation.

Department of Social Security

This is perhaps one area that may have escaped your notice completely. Perhaps surprisingly the DSS appear to be one of the first regulatory bodies to demonstrate that they are aware of your existence and to pay you a visit. The DSS deal with a variety of matters which affect your business, the most important being the payment of both employees' and employers' contribution. If you have been a partner in general practice and are now setting up on your own, you may perhaps have been only vaguely aware that, in addition to income tax and national insurance contributions paid by employees, the employer has a substantial payment to make by way of the employer's national insurance contribution. Over and above that, you will need to ensure that you are making sufficient contributions yourself as a self-employed person in order to obtain your full benefits in the event of sickness or retirement, and likewise if you employ your

128

spouse in the business, you must make the necessary payments on their account also. An early visit by the DSS should correct any errors or misunderstanding which may have arisen before they get out of hand so that if underpayments have been made any liability that has to be satisfied to bring matters back into line is not too painful to meet. The pitfalls for national insurance contributions are very much the same as for income tax and VAT. The level of contribution will relate not only to the salary that is paid but also to any other benefits that are paid to the employee. If, therefore, you reimburse an employee for all or part of their home telephone bill or for fuel or repair costs in respect of a car where an assistant solicitor has perhaps used their vehicle on the firm's business, it is treated as a benefit-in-kind and will result in an additional payment of employer's contribution. The Rules are comparatively simple to operate once the correct procedures are in place. A routine rapidly develops and the DSS rightly take the view that it is important that the right routine is in place at an early stage. If within the first three months of trading you have not had a visit from the DSS, it is not a bad idea to invite them to inspect your records.

National Insurance Contributions

Employee Class 1 Contributions

Anyone who works for an employer must pay Class 1 national insurance contributions. There is no exemption for casual, temporary or part-time employees except those who earn less than the lower earnings limit, at present £54 per week. The level of contribution is directly related to the level of the employee's earnings and the contributions are paid along with income tax under the PAYE scheme. Both the employer and the employee must make payments of Class 1 contributions. The employer is responsible for payment of both his or her own and the employee's contributions but may deduct the employee's share from his or her pay. If a spouse is employed for the purposes of the other spouse's business, this situation is no different from any other employer/ employee relationship.

Class 2 Employer Contributions

Any individual who has earnings from any business activity, trade, profession or vocation must pay a flat rate Class 2 contribution if he or she is self-employed. This is so unless the self-employed individual is either under 16 or over 65 (women over 60 years) or they are below the small earnings limit for the current tax year (presently £3,030). There are a number of other exceptions which we need not concern ourselves with, apart from possibly where the individual is sick for a complete contribution week. The flat rate contribution is currently £5.35 per week. Payment may be made by direct debit through a bank or through three-monthly instalments. This system of quarterly billing has been introduced to replace the contribution card which was phased out at the end of the tax year 1993/1994, and is undoubtedly more convenient to most self-employed solicitors.

National insurance contributions are rather complicated and troublesome. If you have a cashier, or your spouse has taken on that role, it is important that they understand how the payments system works and there is in place a workable system for collecting the contribution and making the payment along with, in the case of employees, PAYE payments. Accountants are very familiar with the NIC system and if you have a problem which you cannot sort out direct with the DSS an accountant can normally sort the problem out for you and ensure that systems are in place to prevent problems occurring in the future.

PART TWO

Keeping Going - How to Manage the Small Practice

CHAPTER 13

Periodic Reviews

Where are we Going?

You are perhaps by this stage established. You may perhaps still feel rather insecure and be wondering if you are going to be trading next month, but this is all perfectly normal. Small practices naturally feel insecure for at least the first two or three years, and in many cases, much longer. Perhaps the most comforting factor is to look back and see that as a matter of history you have billed X thousand pounds each year since you started and there is no reason why you should bill substantially less than that for the following year, even if sometimes you wonder if you are going to bill anything at all for that month. Insecurity of this type is perfectly normal. The fact remains that if you have managed to survive for that long you are established. All you have to do now is to keep going.

At this time and at intervals of at least two to three years, you should ask yourself where the practice is going. Traditionally, business gurus will say that you should have a three-year and a five-year business plan and should set out targets which you feel are attainable with review dates to see to what extent you have failed or succeeded and what adjustments, if any, are needed to ensure that you stay on course or reach a revised target. Sole or small practices perhaps need not be quite so formalistic. The important thing is that you think about what you are doing rather than just drift.

A Move Up Market?

You may feel that having offered a general service to the public, possibly with a high percentage of legal aid work and having attracted the attention of a number of company clients, it is time to move up market. If you take this decision, it is vital that it is done in conjunction with a marketing plan. Company clients will not simply beat a path to your door to secure your services no matter how good you are. You will need to ensure that you have the necessary degree of flexibility to be able to accommodate any significant increase in work. If you are already working 12 hours a day, you are unlikely to be able to cope with a demanding commercial client. On the other hand, you cannot have lots of spare capacity sitting doing nothing waiting for the clients to arrive. You must have in mind a plan for putting to one side a certain type of work freeing staff of sufficient calibre and expertise to be able to cope with the kind of work you are expecting to win. Your business plan will include costing out the wages of any additional staff you will need to take on. It is difficult to develop your plans in detail as you do not know how many clients you are going to bring in and what level of work they will bring with them, but this does not prevent you from pencilling in a few shapes even though you are unable at this stage to paint the whole canvas. If you have some sort of a plan, you can double the size of it or halve it, as is appropriate. If you have no plan at all, then you have no material to work with.

Marketing Plan

How you go about marketing your practice in order to move up market is a matter for you. The purpose of this chapter is not to tell you what your marketing plan should be but rather to underline the fact that things will not happen unless you have a marketing plan worked out in order to put your business plan into practice. You may decide to do a newsletter to existing clients whose commercial or better quality work you are not presently handling. The plan may include a free preliminary legal advice hotline service. It may involve researching particular areas of law so that you are in a position to pass on your knowledge to others through seminars to which you may invite existing or potential clients whose work you seek to encourage and increase. Any and all of these areas you may need to publicise by means of mail shots. You may decide to target certain individuals or certain businesses by means of the business lunch, the free 'health check', or the lecture to certain elements of their staff on a topic of interest. Consider your product carefully. What is it you are selling? What can you do for the client? Consider carefully your message. How can you convey to the client clearly and persuasively what it is you can do for him or her? Then decide how best you can get the message across, bearing in mind time, cost and effectiveness. How much will all this cost you, when are you best suited to put it all into practice, and how will you cope with the work which results? Set out your timetable, preferably in writing, and if necessary put it all in your diary.

A Move Down Market?

A move up market does not necessarily mean that your profitability will improve. An analysis of where your profits are coming from and who your competitors are may serve to demonstrate that the work that is on the increase is not necessarily business or commercial work and may relate more to general high street type work. Some practices, particularly those located in the more run-down areas of central London, have taken a positive decision to expand into what many other firms have regarded as less profitable work. They have identified certain areas as having a high immigrant and unemployed potential client base and have made themselves experts in immigration and welfare benefits law. They have sought to expand their criminal legal aid work and, having formed the view that their local competitors are not offering a service of particularly good quality, they have rapidly established themselves as the number one providers of that type of work in the area and have moved quickly ahead in profitability terms at a time of recession when those firms who are geared to commercial work have seen a severe downturn in that type of work.

No one can really tell you in which direction you should go. These are business decisions which involve a certain amount of business acumen and a considerable amount of luck. With the right planning and the right amount of determination coupled with sufficient funding, it is likely that you will succeed where others will fail if you set yourself business objectives and plough your energies and your resources into them at a time when other people may well be sitting there waiting for the clients to come to them.

Image

If you are deciding to go for one particular type of work and this involves a considerable change in the nature of the practice either up market or down market you must ask yourself if your image is right. This is really a rethink of the original decisions which you took when you first started out. If you are going more up market and hope to attract business clients, are they going to be impressed by the type of premises you are in? If you are moving down market and are seeking to increase your legally-aided work, will the clients feel intimidated by the type of premises you are in? Should you be relocating to premises that are going to attract passing trade with a shop window so that you can appeal directly to the man in the street? If you are looking for more commercial clients, should you be relocating closer to a commercial centre?

Niche Practices

By this stage of the firm's development, it may become apparent to you that you have a particular expertise in a rather unusual aspect of law and the opportunity may present itself for you to increase your strength in that area and become what is known as a niche practice. Such practices can be extremely successful. You will need to assess exactly where your work is coming from and, as with any other marketing exercise, ensure that you are continually selling your product in that direction. This may well take the form of referrals from other firms who, faced with a problem which is beyond their ordinary field of expertise, immediately think of your practice to which they can safely and confidently refer their client knowing that a competent service will be provided and that the client will return to them after the referral to fulfil their more usual legal service requirements.

The danger is always there with a niche practice that others may develop themselves into your area of specialisation and beat you at your own game and if you have put all your eggs into one basket then you may find yourself in difficulties. Niche practices generally succeed because the particular area chosen is so specialised that to develop a similar degree of specialisation and acquire the same level of concentrated knowledge would be prohibitively expensive and the market is not sufficiently large or the rewards sufficiently attractive to make it a worthwhile exercise. With a small practice whose overheads can be kept low in comparison, you will have a head start on the competition from larger firms and you are in a position to ensure that it is not worth their while competing.

Expand or Stay as We Are?

It should not be taken as axiomatic that expansion is synonymous with progress. It has traditionally been the case that most practitioners have felt that they are somehow failing if the firm is not getting bigger. Whilst it is true to say that a firm should not stagnate by not knowing what it wants to do and making no plans to achieve it, do not make the mistake of thinking that expanding means success and cutting back is failure. Many firms have learnt this lesson the hard way in recent years. The economic successes of the 1980s were put into sharp contrast with the downturn in the economy and the recession of the late 1980s/ early 1990s. Those firms that had expanded with the economy without really thinking why it was happening and where it might be leading, found themselves in great difficulties when the recession began to take hold. The position became unusually dangerous because the recession took hold so gradually. There was no sudden fall off in work which caused alarm bells to ring and which stirred those responsible for managing firms into taking the necessary remedial action. It was felt by many people that it was a temporary state of affairs and that cutting back was an over-reaction. By the time it was realised that the country was in the grip of a deep and severe recession, a great deal of damage had already been caused to many firms, particularly the larger firms, with the consequence that the economic surgery which then became necessary was all the more painful for all concerned.

Larger firms, as a generalisation, can afford to make such mistakes more easily than medium-sized or small firms since they have the additional financial and other economic muscle to be able to survive such bruising experiences. Smaller firms, particularly sole practices, tend to experience an economic 'see-saw' effect. When things go well, they can go extremely well and then when things go wrong they go very badly wrong. A sole practitioner's overheads may, for example, be £50,000 a year. If turnover is £100,000 a year, then he or she has made a gross profit of £50,000. If the firm has a particularly good year and the turnover goes up to £150,000, which is quite a realistic proposition in any one year, the sole practitioner sees the firm's profits, and thus his or her own take home pay, double in one year. If, on the other hand, the turnover drops to £75,000, then the sole practitioner's rewards have been halved. He or she will only be taking home £25,000 that year instead of the £50,000 the previous year. There is no network of partners through which these economic ups and downs are filtered so that the effect is smoothed out. For the sole practitioner, it is either feast or famine. The same is largely true of two-partner firms, although even at that stage the effect is less noticeable unless the partners have agreed that the profit share should be more or less equivalent to the work that they themselves have produced.

Can You Afford Not to Expand?

Some people take the view that in the legal business you cannot afford to stand still. My view is that you can afford to stand still provided you have taken a conscious decision to do so. If you have assessed the pros and cons of expansion and contraction bearing in mind such factors as the rise in overheads, the interest rates, the general economic outlook, the cost of staff and premises as your two major expenses and so on, and you feel that the size you are at is ideal for the current situation and what is likely to be the situation in the next 12 to 24 months then to stay precisely the same size you are at the moment is a perfectly proper and sensible decision to arrive at. It should not be seen as a shirking of responsibility or an over-cautious approach. Many firms took this view during the worst period of the recession and as a result have weathered the storm far better than those who cut back drastically without properly considering why they were doing it or those who took no action until it was too late. It is those firms who have emerged from recession perfectly poised to expand as the economy expands and to take full advantage of the economic upturn. Do not be forced into decisions just because other firms are cutting back or, for that matter, are expanding. Take your own decisions based on accurate management information which you have ensured is available to you and then continually review the position to confirm that your actions were correct.

Merger

The decision to merge one practice with another is perhaps one of the hardest decisions to make. This applies both for multi-partner practices as well as sole practitioners.

Sole Practitioners

For the sole practitioner, it is superficially very attractive to merge his or her practice with another sole practitioner. Being in sole practice can be something of a lonely life and the mantle of responsibility for the practice, its staff and its financial arrangements can weigh very heavily at times. There is the constant worry of what disasters may be befalling the practice whilst the sole practitioner is away through holiday or illness. If you have partners, these responsibilities are shared. There is also the worry as to what happens if he or she has a very bad year. If there is a sudden downturn in a particular area of work which is vital to the practice, it may be dealt a severe body blow and may have difficulty in recovering from it. If there are partners operating in other areas of work, the continued generation of income from those partners provides a vital breathing space to enable areas of the firm which are becoming less profitable to be re-arranged and the necessary corrective measures taken. With a merged practice, all overheads are shared and significant savings can be made. Unfortunately, life is not quite that simple.

Once sole practitioners commence talks on merger, serious obstacles are brought into focus. The most obvious one is perhaps lack of control. As a sole practitioner you and only you are the boss. As soon as there are two of you, you can no longer take decisions without consultation. Your total independence has immediately been lost. Fears creep in as to whether or not you will be compatible with your respective partner on a personal, intellectual and professional level. There is always the danger that as a result of poor health or lack of effort you will be saddled with an unwanted passenger. There is a natural inclination on the part of each sole practitioner eyeing up the other to wonder what will be in it for him or her if he or she amalgamates with the other sole practitioner. For a merger to work, there must be considerable benefits to both sides over and above the ones discussed earlier. For example, one solicitor may have a client base which is not being properly serviced in a particular respect and the other solicitor can supply that service because he or she has the necessary expertise and facilities. An obvious example is where a solicitor has a portfolio of company clients and the solicitor services their conveyancing. They may have expressed a wish that this solicitor should also serve their litigation needs but he or she does not have the necessary ability to do so. Solicitor number two may be a skilled litigator but have no developed ability for conveyancing work. Such practices would have a better chance of succeeding as a merged practice since a merger itself opens up new opportunities which would not otherwise be available. The two partners will not compete against one another for the clients or for the work since they fulfil different functions. There are likely to be fewer problems of trust as the client is more likely to turn to the original solicitor for that area of work where the new partner is unable to service his or her needs. The original partner will probably feel more at ease since the danger of losing that client through a perceived need on the client's part to go to a firm that offers the full range of services instead of only some will have receded.

Take-Overs

Perhaps surprisingly some of the more successful mergers can be as a result of take-overs borne out of rather desperate circumstances so far as one practice is concerned. A practice may see itself floundering for a variety of reasons, be it fall-off of work, a substantial increase in overheads, the loss of an important client, etc., and in desperation may turn to another firm to discuss merger. Merger is in these circumstances something of a euphemism since in reality the second firm will be taking over the first firm. The metamorphosis may be that much more successful since many of the usual fears which would hold back a merger under normal circumstances, whether you will get on with the new firm, whether they will take over your clients, how you will cope with the loss of independence and possible office politics, are all obscured by the more overpowering fear, namely that of imminent bankruptcy. The lack of bargaining position between the two parties means that negotiations for the terms on which the merger will take place proceed much more swiftly and the whole merger process proceeds with fewer difficulties.

Amalgamating with a struggling firm provides the means of taking a substantial step forward quite quickly. An entirely new client base is suddenly before you providing new opportunities for generating more business. The target firm may have desirable premises, an extensive law library and so on.

The dangers involved are considerable. You must consider carefully why the firm became weak and ensure that any problems are corrected. Were the partners or staff incompetent? If so, was this on a professional or a managerial level? New partners who are bad managers can be educated, or persuaded to leave the management side of the practice to those with the necessary expertise. Partners who are professionally incompetent are much more dangerous. If that is how you view them it will be better to offer them salaried partnership or consultancy and to see the merger go off if they refuse.

Loose Associations

Because of the fear surrounding full merger, many people find the idea of a loose association stopping short of amalgamation more attractive. If partnership can be equated to marriage, then loose associations can be equated to cohabitation. Whilst such associations provide the opportunity to get to know a potential partner much better and to see how they operate at first hand, it tends to be the case that if the arrangement works well then people see no reason to change it and clearly if it does not work well then people disengage from the arrangement and feel that they have had a lucky escape.

Sharing Resources

There are considerable advantages in loose associations in terms of the sharing of expenses and assets as well as having a colleague whom you feel you can trust when you need someone to turn to for advice or help, but surprisingly few such arrangements lead to full mergers. It is possible to have a loose association which purports to be a full merger but in reality is not. The practice can be marketed as a merged practice and therefore a partnership with the accounts remaining separate for tax and profit-sharing purposes. In reality, therefore, what you have is two practices run under the same roof as more of a sharing of facilities than anything else. This has many dangers, the obvious one being the liability of each partner to third parties as they are held out as principals in the same practice. If the profit-sharing arrangements are separate, then jealousies can arise where one practice becomes more profitable than the other, or one practice gets into difficulties and looks to the other to help it out. Since there is no proper partnership arrangement between the two partners, it is unreasonable of the weaker partner to expect the stronger one to help out, either in terms of provision of services or finance, but there inevitably develops a false sense of injury on the part of the weaker partner and the situation can become acrimonious. Such kinds of loose associations are best avoided. If you are going to have an association with another firm which is not thinly disguised as a partnership, you should make it abundantly clear from your notepaper that the practices are quite separate. If you are going to operate from the same building and have certain members of staff who in effect work for both firms, it should be clear so far as the member of staff is concerned exactly who the employer is so that if there are employment problems of unfair dismissal or redundancy the legal position is clear. It must also be clear to each member of staff to whom it is they answer, otherwise a rather chaotic state of affairs will arise with some members of staff having several managers, each issuing conflicting sets of instructions.

Upgrading and Improving the Systems

Now that you are established, your thoughts will be turning to the question of whether the various systems you put in, i.e. computers, filing, storage, accounts, telephone, library, etc., are sufficient or whether they should be upgraded. To some extent, these decisions must be taken in conjunction with the earlier decisions as to which direction the firm is going. If you have decided to become a niche practice, then you will be attracting a specific type of client and your premises and supporting systems will need to be geared towards that type of client. This applies to everything from the furniture in the waiting room down to the contents of the library. If your practice is becoming far more specialist and less generalist, you may decide that money would be better spent on acquiring some expensive text books on your particular esoteric specialist subject and that a more generalist precedent encyclopaedia to which you rarely refer can be sold to finance it.

Accounts

If you talk to people in the computer business, especially those in the computer supply business, they will on the whole advise you that after about five years of operation you will probably have to get rid of your present computer system and buy entirely new computer hardware and that you will probably be best advised to upgrade your software at the same time. Even if this advice is not partisan, it is not necessarily true. There are a good many computers which simply stop working after five years and you have no choice. They become expensive to repair and people are less willing to come out to provide the necessary technical assistance to keep them operating to their original specification. The mere fact that you paid only £650 for a computer software accounts package and £750 for a computer on which to run it does not mean to say that after three years you should throw it out and get a better one. When reviewing your computer needs, you should go back to the same drawing board used originally for deciding what type of computer system to buy when you decided to acquire your first computer. It is foolish to think that because you are paying £5,000 for state of the art computer equipment and another £3,000 for an accounts and time-recording package to go on it that you are going to have a better system. The same logic would mean that it is time to trade in your family estate car and buy a Rolls Royce because expensive means better. Plainly, it does not. If what you are seeking to do is to convey the impression of success and wealth and appeal to certain influential and wealthy clients irrespective of the high servicing and running costs, then the Rolls Royce is the right car. If, on the other hand, you need a vehicle that provides an efficient means of comfortable and reliable transportation with more moderate servicing and running costs, with a much lower capital investment, and with sufficient storage capacity to enable you to move an unwanted filing cabinet from the office to home, then it is the estate car that you need.

Another consideration is whether you will need a system which is compatible with someone else's system. The someone else can be your spouse at home, or a set of barristers' chambers which you use frequently. It is rarely a reason in itself for change, but it is something to bear in mind in your choice of system.

A much more compelling reason for heavy investment in a new computer accounts system is the fact that the present system is having trouble handling the number of matters required because of the increase in the number of clients now using the firm. Another reason may be the need for several people to access the accounts information from several different locations and the inability of

142

either the software or the computer system to accommodate that need. If there are no such pressing needs and corresponding failures on the accounts system to fulfil those needs, then do not change the system just for the sake of change. Only do so if you can see that such needs will definitely arise within the next few months.

Storage

Similarly, if you are coping with your storage system well enough at the present time by storing your old files in the office or at home in the shed, continue with the same system. Periodically we all receive mail shots from storage companies extolling the virtues of their air-conditioned storage space and trying to convince you that it is bad management practice to use expensive office space for the storage of files when the cost per square foot of storage space at their sites is much lower. This is entirely correct if you have a specific identifiable need for the space. There must be some sound economic reason why you should be incurring the additional overheads of off-site storage especially when this means that you no longer have instant access to the files as you had when they were stored in the office. As well as the cost of renting the storage space do not overlook the fact that someone will have to travel to the storeroom, retrieve the file, bring it back and then reverse the exercise, all of which costs you money.

Telephones

If you took the right decision to have the correct amount of capacity on your telephone system when you first set up, it will probably be some time before there is a real need to change the present telephone system. The same rules apply. Can the present system cope and will it be able to cope in, say, the next 12 months? Can it be made to cope simply by the addition of extra incoming lines and telephone extensions? If so, why change?

CHAPTER 14

Cornerstones For Future Success

The six rules covered in this chapter will help your practice flourish.

1. Be Nice

The relationship between a solicitor and client is something that merits considerable study. There are as many different types of relationships as there are solicitors and possibly clients. To some, you are merely a means to an end. Business people need solicitors and they need telephonists, managers, cleaners and receptionists. To them, you are just another of the hired help, another cog in the large machine. To other clients, you may be almost a hero figure, the clever and respected person who solved the most worrying and difficult problem they have ever had to come to terms with in their life. You may become a sort of legal Dr Kildare. To other clients, you may be a friend; a trusted confidant whose views are respected on a variety of issues of which the law is but one.

Many members of the public are still frightened of solicitors. Solicitors are not people with whom they come into contact on a regular basis unless they are business people who regularly use legal services. The average man or woman in the street uses a solicitor perhaps once or twice during their lifetime and sometimes not even that. To them, the solicitor is something of an unknown quantity. They will tend to regard the solicitor as someone who has trained for many years and is thus a very knowledgeable and clever individual who, because of his or her long years of training, charges extremely high fees.

This image has been built up over a number of years and to some extent has been enhanced by television and the media. The image is being broken down gradually, but there is still a long way to go. When a client sets foot inside your offices for the first time, you must appreciate that they may have been steeling themselves for a number of days to pluck up the courage to come in and see you. For them it has been something of an achievement even managing to come

144

through the door. If you are immediately able to put them at their ease and to show them that you are someone who is capable of being kind, gentle and understanding as well as tough and strong when needs be, then there may well be a sense of relief on the part of the client that they have found someone with whom they can identify and with whom they can have a comfortable rapport. If you manage to achieve this in your first meeting with your client, you may well have secured yourself a client for life. This 'bonding' process happens with most professional people. Think how many doctors and dentists you have known and how many of them you have felt comfortable with. There needs to be a certain minimum level of understanding and trust between yourself and the professional before you make a mental decision that this is the person you are going to stay with, and provided that level is reached, you will be unlikely to change your professional adviser unless something happens to break that bond. You must, of course, supply the necessary level of skill and expertise to demonstrate that you can fulfil the client's needs, but clients will sometimes stay with a particular professional adviser even though the adviser has clearly made a serious error, simply because they appreciate that everyone is capable of making mistakes. It is this client bonding which will preclude the client from running off to a competitor at the first sign of a problem.

To achieve this relationship, you must be nice to the client. Make them feel important and make it seem a pleasure each time you see them and each time you speak to them on the telephone. Be nice in your letters to them. Show them that you understand the difficulties they face and show them that you care. Keep your conversations with them as light as you can in the circumstances without trivialising their problems. Make them laugh if you can. By following this approach, you may even achieve a state of affairs where clients look forward to coming to see you. Do not undo it all by leaving the client feeling he or she has been charged the full hourly rate for socialising. It is not just a question of using the client's first name and letting them use your first name at an early stage in the relationship. This can, indeed, be totally counter-productive and make it appear that you are being over-familiar with them. I have clients for whom I have acted for nearly 20 years and we are still not on first name terms. Such matters are questions of style and individual taste rather than anything else and the use of first name terms and at what stage depends on what image you wish to project and the type of relationship you wish to promote. Make them feel that they are part of your firm. Make them feel that you want them to come back the next time there is the slightest problem. Even when clients are being rather tiresome and very demanding, you must still be nice to them. Without the clients, there is no firm. They are the ones who pay your wages and your overheads. The customer may not always be right-indeed, the fact that he or she has ended up in something of a mess may mean that he or she is wrong more often than right, but the client is always important and should always be welcomed into your offices.

If you have a letter from a client which infuriates you, or he or she says something on the telephone to upset you, don't write a vitriolic letter telling the client just how ungrateful and obstinate he or she is. Leave it for at least a couple of days. As an alternative, write it as a draft, and then proofread it two days later. You'll probably be shocked at the strength of your own feelings expressed in it. Are you glad now you didn't send it that day? Ask yourself how you would feel if the letter was read out in court. Would it appear professional, or would you cringe as leading counsel reads it out in all its glory? Perhaps one or two changes might be as well after all.

ASK YOURSELF HOW YOU WOULD FEEL IF
THE LETTER TO YOUR CLIENT WERE READ
OUT IN COURT.

2. Be Best

The profession is more competitive now than it has ever been. The Conservative Government of the 1980s specifically encouraged people to shop around for their legal services. They made it their aim to take away solicitors' monopolies of various areas of work and encourage competition between solicitors. They were very successful. Before then, a large proportion of clients did not even ask what the cost of a conveyance was likely to be. Many people considered that to ask about a solicitor's charges or to ask for a quote was tantamount to an insult and was as good as saying that you did not trust the solicitor. Those days are long gone. People now will rarely instruct a solicitor in a conveyancing matter without having obtained at least two or three quotes. A large proportion of people will shop around until they get the lowest quote they can find. If you are to win work and keep it, you must not only be competitive on price but you must demonstrate that you are the best of the solicitors in the area and ideally better than any other solicitors they could have chosen irrespective of area. Everything you do should have quality in mind. You and your staff must answer the telephone faster than any of your competitors. You must be friendlier and more professional than them. The speed of response to the client's problems must be rapid. The amount of effort you put in on the client's behalf must be higher than they expect. They must quickly form the view that your firm is very different to all the other firms they have ever come across. You must be the best. You will not achieve this by words alone. People will not be impressed by you telling them how good your firm is, at least not without specific proof. There is nothing wrong with a moment of self-indulgence with the client when you have completed a particularly good piece of work for them. Equally, there is nothing wrong with telling the client in advance what the philosophy of the firm is, particularly if they are questioning a price differential between your quote and someone else's. You must live up to your promises. Clients will not easily forgive you for saying that you will do something if you then fail to deliver.

3. Be The Fastest

A major criticism of lawyers is that they are slow. In most instances, solicitors today are not at all slow. They can move very quickly when required. It is hard work being the fastest, but that is how to succeed. There have been many occasions when a member of staff has said to me 'This will be alright to go out tomorrow, won't it?' Almost invariably the reply is 'No – let's get it out tonight.' Staff can sometimes feel that you are being unreasonable in this way, but ultimately they tend to respect you for your ideals and enjoy being part of a successful team. There is, generally speaking, no good reason why something should have to wait until tomorrow if it can be done today. The work will be done faster, the firm will be more profitable, the client's problems will be resolved more quickly, the bill can go out earlier. Do not forget your staff's feelings in all of this. If they have worked hard to get something out on time, praise them for it. Being considerate to staff is conducive to a good office environment and thus to productivity.

4. Keep Planning

It is very easy for a firm to lose sight of where it is going. There is, after all, a great deal to be done during the working day. Planning is very much a matter of self-discipline. There must come a time when you stop taking any more phone calls and put things to one side whilst you sit down and think about the firm, what it is doing and where it is going.

Since the client's affairs come first, the obvious thing to do is to put off planning such things until the evening when the phones have stopped ringing and things are a little quieter. So long as you have sufficient self-discipline to do so, then this is the ideal time. Unfortunately, all too often you decide to go home and think about the firm's future another day. If you do that often enough, the firm won't have a future.

- Are we the right size?
- Do we need more staff?
- Do we have too many staff?
- Are they the right kind of staff?
- Should we be breaking into new areas?
- Do we need to buy new equipment?
- Do we need a new marketing initiative, and if so, what?
- Is it time to refurbish the waiting room?

It is no good thinking about these things superficially. You must go through the pros and cons and take some firm decisions. Having taken the decisions, you must put them into practice. If you make the time to do the planning and then spend the time thinking things through and then taking decisions but never act on them, then the whole process has been a total waste of very valuable time. Make the time, do the planning, take the decisions and then action them.

5. Keep Monitoring

Small firms, by their nature, tend to worry a lot. We all wonder if we are going to be in business next month and the month after, particularly after a disappointing set of figures. It is usually when that happens that we get out the records and the reports that our systems have produced and start going through them to try to give ourselves some sense of security. There is nothing wrong with that except the timing. It is not only during the good months and the bad months that you need to keep checking to see where you are, but to do it on a continuous basis. There is no hard and fast rule of every month or every two months or whatever, simply at regular intervals. You must be the judge of how regular those intervals will be, but the situation needs to be seen in the context of a year and then to compare one year with another. In this way, you will be able to see what has happened to the firm and whether you are going in the right direction. You may be able to highlight particular problems and do something about them.

- Are the staffing costs too high?

- Is someone not pulling their weight?

- Is a particular kind of work not sufficiently profitable?

- Does someone take longer than everyone else to do the same job and needs training?

- Is there a fee-earner who is not pulling his or her weight?

- How should you handle the problem?

- Does another fee-earner need an assistant?

- Are there too many people in general office or not enough?

- Do we need more secretaries?

- Has conveyancing work increased or decreased? What should we be doing about it?

Managing a firm is like driving a car. You can only afford to take your eye off the road for a few seconds at a time. You must constantly adjust here and there to ensure you are on course.

6. Keep Marketing

Marketing should, even for a small firm – and some would say particularly for a small firm – be an almost constant operation. Advertisements in directories, etc., go some way to placing yourself and your firm in front of the public and potentially new clients on an almost constant basis, but all too often people think that once they have renewed their advertisement in Yellow Pages, they have done their marketing for the year. Placing advertisements in the media is only one form of marketing. Some additional ways to market the practice are covered in Chapter 18, but the secret is to keep marketing. You should constantly be thinking about how you can win more clients. You should monitor the results of any marketing initiatives that you have at the present time. It is also a useful exercise to look back at new business and see where it came from and to see if there is a lesson to be learnt.

Last year I targeted a particular individual in a particular company. Whilst it was very pleasant to renew an old acquaintance and we had an extremely pleasant lunch, I made no secret of the fact that I was looking for their work. I was in luck. They were less than impressed by the solicitors they were using and they were replacements for another firm with whom they were dissatisfied. They tried me out on small debt collecting work and the first three rules discussed in this chapter were put into immediate operation. We were nice, we were best and we were fastest. More debt collection work followed. One of them turned into a two-day county court trial with costs running into a number of thousands of pounds. Private client work for other members of the company followed. My business lunch took me out of the office for some three hours – time I had to make up for by working even later that day. The lunch itself cost a good deal less than an advertisement in Yellow Pages, but it has resulted in business running into several thousands of pounds. Should I be having more business lunches and placing fewer advertisements? The answer is immaterial to the point being made. The point is: keep marketing. Your marketing plan may consist of several different types of marketing, but it is an on-going almost day-to-day affair, not a couple of ads placed and that's that out of the way.

CHAPTER 15

Preventative Medicine

What Happens if I Die?

It is all too easy to brush out of sight the problems that will be left behind when a sole practitioner dies with the supercilious comment that you will not be here to worry about it. There will be a good many other people who will be here to worry about it, including your immediate family and your clients. If you are a partner in a two or three-partner firm, then a very considerable burden will fall upon them also.

In *The Guide to the Professional Conduct of Solicitors 1993* Principle 3.04 states that a sole principal should make a will containing adequate provision for the running of the practice after his or her death. There is no system in place to ensure that this guidance by the Law Society is followed and there are doubtless many sole principals whose practices degenerate into chaos on the principal's death. The Guide strongly advises that one of the executors of the will should be a solicitor. It will be appreciated that in most sole practices the sole operator of the client account will be the principal and on his or her death client account is paralysed. It does not take much imagination to perceive the severe problems that would arise for clients in a busy conveyancing practice where clients were about to complete and the sole principal dies. Many hundreds of thousands of pounds of mortgagees' and clients' money could be locked up in client account for, at the very least, many days if not actually weeks or months if there is no solicitor executor able to operate the account. An executor's authority to deal with the estate derives from the will itself but not so an administrator of an intestate estate who, strictly speaking, has no power to act until such time as a grant of letters of administration has formally been given. The Guide acknowledges this situation but nevertheless goes on to say that in these circumstances prospective administrators are encouraged to nominate a manager for the practice before the grant is obtained. The Guide tacitly appears to accept that technically the administrators would be meddling in the estate if they take this action before obtaining a formal grant, but given the very unsatisfactory state of affairs that has arisen, it appears that the administrator's intervention prior to the formal grant is seen as the lesser of two evils. It is wrong of a sole principal to put what will probably be their immediate family in such a difficult situation at a time when they may be overcome with grief when the very simple step of making an elementary will naming at least one executor who is a solicitor would have done so much to simplify matters.

The Guide goes on to set out the various other steps that can be taken, including those by the Law Society itself, to sort out the practice of a sole principal including, if needs be, an application to the court for a grant in favour of a nominee of the Law Society which in most instances will be in connection with an intervention by the Law Society to enable the practice to be wound up.

In most cases, the only practical solution will be to wind up the practice of a sole practitioner. It may well be that the practice has a sale value, but if it is to be sold, steps must be taken immediately to ensure that the practice continues to be properly run by the appointment of a manager to enable the business to be run as a going concern until a purchaser can be found. It is vital that the practice is put up for sale as quickly as possible after death before the client base starts to drift away. A good many legal staff recruitment agencies also arrange the sales of practices of both living and dead principals and, for that matter, will act as matchmakers for practices seeking merger. A copy of the relevant sections of the Guide appears at Appendix 13.

The Deceased's Family

An immediate consequence of the death of the principal will be that income from the practice by way of drawings ceases, at least in the short term until such time as a manager has been appointed. Every principal should ensure that sufficient insurance and pension arrangements are in place by the time of their death so that their spouses and families will be able to survive financially without them. It can be a salutory exercise to sit down and go through the family budget and then to see what funds there are available to satisfy the outgoings if you were dead. It is a reasonably straightforward, if a little time-consuming, exercise to work out what the proceeds of the various policies would be and to see if there would be enough money to go round. If there is not, then you may need to make extra provision by means of pension or life policies to make up any shortfall. You may find your spouse unwilling to discuss such matters, but it can also be a useful exercise to sit down together and try to think yourself through such a scenario. If your spouse is working part time or not working at all, how easy would it be to arrange a child minder and what would the cost be? What kind of an income would be produced if your spouse then worked full time? Would a sale of the family home be inevitable or advisable? Whilst it may be painful and a little demoralising to discuss such matters, these facts will need to be faced one day and a little pre-planning may go a very long way.

The reverse situation should not be ignored. For the sole principal to try to run a practice after his or her spouse's death and possibly look after a young family at the same time, the burden will be a very heavy one. Making sure that the loss of one's spouse is counter-balanced to some extent by insurance and/or pension arrangements is just as important if the survivor is the sole practitioner. It is all too easy to fall into the trap of making sure that the sole principal is covered in insurance and then to find that he or she is the one who survives and it is the other half of the team who is struck down and there is little or no insurance cover.

Why not leave a complete set of instructions? It will probably take no more than about two hours to set out precisely what your spouse should do on your death so far as the practice is concerned. You can cater for everything from drafting your own specimen letter announcing your death to your clients to which trusted members of your profession or other close friends your spouse can turn to for help and advice on how to deal with the situation. You can go as far as dictating the strategy for the sale of the practice if you wish. You could nominate a particular agency through whom the practice should be marketed and say that you would like efforts to be made for, say, a period of six weeks for a buyer to be found, but that if no buyer is found within that time then a further letter, dictated by you, should be sent to all the clients advising them that the firms that had assisted you with the running of the practice in the past would be your choice of solicitor for them now, but that, of course, it is entirely up to those clients who they choose as their new solicitor. Your nearest and dearest may not be disposed to follow your blue print for the disposal of your practice, but at least it will give them a few ideas and suggestions as to what to do at a time when they may be devoid of any ideas themselves.

Two or More Partner Firms

The blow of losing a partner in a two or three-partner firm can be crushing. The importance of a particular individual to a firm is never more appreciated than the time when they are no longer there. Only then is their full importance realised.

Clients will need reassurance that the work carried out by that partner will still be dealt with competently. There may be obligations to the family of the deceased partner under the terms of a partnership agreement. The outflow of funds to comply with such obligations may leave the remaining partner or partners short of the necessary financial resources to take on an assistant solicitor or principal from elsewhere of sufficient calibre to replace the deceased partner. The answer to this problem lies in insurance. It is vital that small practices insure their partners. The premiums can be paid by the practice as an expense. If the partner retires without the policy operating, the capital value of the policy can belong to the partner, if that is what is agreed by the rest of the partners. The firm may decide that the sum paid out on the maturity of the policy is in part payment of that partner's capital account. If proper insurance arrangements are made, the surviving partner or partners are free to spend what would have gone by way of that partner's draw in recruiting a senior solicitor to take his or her place. Such a replacement may well have high hopes of achieving partnership at an early stage themselves and so care must be taken in choosing the successor. Any immediate problems can be catered for by means of a senior locum. If you have consultants on two or three days a week, this may be the time to try to persuade them, with a suitable financial inducement, to come out of retirement for a short time in order to fill the gap. If they can see that it is a real emergency and that it is a one-off opportunity for them to make some cash, you may find that they are only too pleased to help out.

How to be Ill and Still Trade

The way in which you tackle the problem of illness will depend to a large extent on what type of illness afflicts you and how long it is likely to take you to recover. It will also depend on how many staff you have. Planning for illness is every bit as much a part of managing a practice as any other aspect. The important thing is to have a contingency plan. At least for the immediate future the one person unable to take decisions will be you, or at least you must assume so, and take a 'worst case' position. If it turns out that you are well enough to give instructions as to how to cope, then so much the better. However, you may be in hospital unconscious as a result of a road traffic accident or you may have had a stroke. In this situation you have got to assume that you will be out of commission for at least two to three months. If not actually undergoing treatment, you will need considerable time to recuperate afterwards. There is no alternative in this situation but to conscript an experienced practitioner.

The ideal person would be a consultant from another firm with whom you may have a good relationship. The relationship may be because the firm is local to you or it may be that you have a contact in another firm and they have someone who may perhaps have been a partner and is now working two or three days a week. That firm may be prepared to release their consultant for a period of two to three months so that a 'safe pair of hands' is running your practice whilst you are incapacitated. A proper commercial fee must be arranged with the firm concerned. They will probably be large enough to absorb the work which the consultant would have been carrying out himself or herself and he or she will have sufficient knowledge and expertise to be able to cope with such a situation and will also have the necessary support systems, such as access to partners of his or her own firm, to discuss particular problems which you feel are beyond him or her.

The effect on the clients should not be underestimated. If they hear that their solicitor has had a stroke and will be away from the practice for an indeterminate period of time, something akin to panic will set in and they will need the reassurance of having someone who is obviously experienced and confident in charge, quite apart from Law Society regulations which also require that proper arrangements are in place. Whether the Law Society or the Solicitors Complaints Bureau are likely to impose disciplinary proceedings on a solicitor recovering from a stroke for having failed to make proper arrangements for the practice whilst he or she was ill is not really the point. You owe it to your clients and to your staff to ensure that proper arrangements are in place and you cannot make those arrangements from a hospital bed. They must be thought about in advance and a contingency plan made.

If you are unable to make such arrangements for the loan of someone's consultant you, or more probably, someone trying to cope in your absence, will very likely be forced into engaging a locum. A locum will be a fairly expensive way of answering the problem but there are no cheap ways. It is unrealistic to expect a friend in another practice to split their time between running your practice and their own. They will be unable to do both properly and whilst they may be able to carry out some emergency surgery within your practice to keep things afloat, they are always going to put their own practice before yours. It will also mean that half the time that clients wish to speak to a senior solicitor they will be unable to do so. Whether it be true or not, people will rapidly take the view that their affairs are being neglected. You do not want to return from your convalescence to find your practice has evaporated and the years of hard work in building the practice have been wasted.

Enduring Power of Attorney

People tend to think that only the elderly need to consider making an enduring power of attorney. An enduring power of attorney must be executed before the onset of mental incapacity. Such mental difficulties are not the sole prerogative of the elderly and can strike down even the young. In the same way that death will paralyse a solicitor's client account if there is no one else able to operate it, the same will also be true for a solicitor who becomes mentally incapable of dealing with his or her practice. By executing an enduring power of attorney while he or she has all their faculties, the sole practitioner will ensure that there is someone in a position to manage the practice in a professional way either until it can be sold or until it can be run down in an orderly fashion. There may be premises to be sold. There will be considerable difficulties in the way of such a sale if the solicitor concerned does not have the mental capacity to dispose of a lease. It may require an application to the Court of Protection in the absence of such an enduring power of attorney with the consequential delays and additional expense.

How to Cope with Burglaries and Fires

Next to illness, death and bankruptcy, probably the biggest fear for small practices are burglaries and, worst still, fires. Insurance policies for small businesses will often cover many of the immediate financial consequences. Policies may pay for the reinstatement of the premises and the loss of equipment, furniture, and books, etc. Depending on the kind of policy, there may be cover for loss of profits whilst the business is being reinstated. What it cannot properly cover is the disruption to the business and the inability to conduct the clients' affairs properly. It will also not cover satisfactorily the loss of precedent libraries and so on unless very specialised insurance cover is obtained. The answer to the latter point is duplication.

The key to a practice is its financial structure. By duplicating the financial information, you will have a complete client list and full details of all financial transactions for each client, including how much client money you are holding and how much money they owe you. If you are running a time-recording system as part of your accounts package, you will also be in a position to know how much unbilled work has been carried out for each client. Many clients may sympathise with your predicament and may agree to such work being billed at that point in order to ease your cash flow problems.

A huge amount of information is contained within clients' financial ledgers. For example, if you need to obtain a copy of a writ or a divorce petition that has been issued and you do not know the action or case number, the court may well be able to provide you with a duplicate if you can tell them when it was issued. The issue fee will be shown on the client's ledger. Without knowing either the action number or case number, the court would normally refuse to attempt to locate such a document because of the vast amount of work involved in trying to find your pleading amongst the thousands issued. Having located that pleading, then you have immediately located all other documents filed with the court and ascertained the name and address of the opposing solicitors. A letter to them will undoubtedly result in a complete copy of the inter-solicitor correspondence and discovered documents and also your own client's name and address! Within a fairly short space of time, you will be able to duplicate most if not all of what was on the original file either from the court, the opposing solicitors or your own client. Without the original financial information from the client ledger, you may well be dependent on the client or the opposing solicitors contacting you. This may take a number of weeks. Letters may go astray due to the fact that you have had to relocate from one office to another in the case of a serious fire.

The one important set of information and documentation that you will not be able to reproduce from the client or from the court or from opposing solicitors will be the financial information relating to your client. If you are able to make any progress at all from these sources, it will be painfully slow and will be incomplete. It will be an enormous task to try to get all the figures to add up. This heartache can be saved simply by backing up your computer information on at least a weekly basis and taking the copy disk home. Strangely, many secretaries/ accounts clerks appear very reluctant to do this. They are quite used to backing up information and leaving it in a disk holder in the office but show great resistance to the idea that they should either take that set of disks home or make an additional set to keep at home. Even pointing out to them that the exercise will be wasted if the office catches fire or if someone steals the computer and takes the disks along with them, seems to cut no ice. It is also common for people to agree to take an extra set of disks home in this way but then unilaterally to stop doing it. You may have what little satisfaction there is in saying 'I told you so' when disaster strikes, but it will be of small comfort and of no practical use whatsoever. You must insist that the information is backed up and removed from the office so that the information, more or less up to date, can be reproduced in the event that the original information is destroyed by fire or is stolen. The disks removed from site should include the software program for the accounts package itself. Do not forget that your duty to your clients to keep their information confidential extends to financial information and applies just as much to information stored at home as elsewhere. Suitable safeguards should be put in place at home to ensure your client's affairs remain secret.

You should also remove from site your major precedent library. All commercially purchased software should be backed up and a duplicate kept away from the office. As you create your own precedents or store drafts on disk to await a client's approval of, say, an affidavit or a will, these should also be backed up on to other disks and taken home. The amount of information that can be stored on modern day floppy disks is enormous. The task of making such copies and of taking them away from the office is minute compared to the quantity of information which you have put out of harm's way. It does not make any kind of sense to do otherwise. Again, back-up copies are confidential material and suitable safeguards to ensure they stay that way must be put in place.

In the last five years, we have had about four or five burglaries. On each occasion the only thing that was taken was cash and postage stamps. Fortunately, we never keep more than £100 of cash on the premises at any time. Having grown tired of losing the £30 or £40 that happened to be in the cash tin every time the offenders struck, we now take the petty cash home with us out of office hours. Other solicitors in the area have not been quite so fortunate and have had expensive computers and fax machines stolen. It is tempting to think that you have nothing worth taking but apart from anything else, burglars can cause considerable destruction once they have gained access. The usual crime prevention rules apply. Do everything you can to keep them out and you will not have gone too far into the future before you will need to carry out a thorough review of your security arrangements. This may well entail putting in a burglar alarm system and possibly a video camera placed fairly obviously where potential thieves will see it, but placed where they cannot attack it. A visit from the crime prevention officer of your local police station is always worthwhile, and can be extremely enlightening, pointing out hazards and entry points that you had never even considered before.

Again, duplication is the key. Whilst the loss of a computer in itself can be mitigated by your insurance arrangements, a burglar may well have carried off all the information stored on your hard disk. If you are not backing your information up at regular intervals onto floppy disks and ideally removing those from site at least in duplicate form, the burglar may well have inadvertently stolen many hours of your and your typist's work which will have to be repeated.

Most sole practitioners will have some sort of office capacity at home as well as in their office, assuming that they do not work entirely from home. As well as providing the ability to work from home out of hours and when the need to get the client's work done in a hurry so requires, it also means that you have additional computer hardware and telephone and dictating facilities should those in the office be lost due to a fire. If you have the necessary computer information on your duplicate set of disks, the recovery period is very much shorter. You will be able to write to your clients, courts, other solicitors, etc., virtually immediately to tell them what has happened and to enlist their help in reproducing the files that have been lost. It is almost worth having a second base for this reason alone, but I suspect most people will have the facility anyway for the reasons given. If not, there is nothing for it but to rush out and buy another computer, reload your software and data and get going again.

CHAPTER 16

How will we Structure the Firm?

Partner Staff Ratios

In this context, the staff being discussed are fee-earning staff. All fee-earning staff and partners will need adequate support in terms of secretaries, receptionists, outdoor clerks, messengers, etc., and it is important to put in place and maintain a correct balance between having sufficient support staff for the fee-earners and yet not having people sitting around idly. Most small firms will not be able to afford the services of a practice manager and the management of the firm will be split between the partners until such time as the practice grows to at least five or six equity partners, unless you wish to engage the services of a retired solicitor who has good management skills, on a part-time basis. A good practice manager is going to cost £20,000 to £30,000 a year and small practices cannot afford such an expensive luxury. The money is better spent on a good assistant solicitor if that sort of cash is available.

I have known some quite prestigious if rather old-fashioned firms in the City and the West End which give the appearance of being medium-sized to large in terms of being 10 or 15 partners strong who in fact hide a dark secret. All partners on the notepaper are equity partners and they have no assistant solicitors. Worse still, all partners are more or less the same age, except perhaps for one or two. Such a partner/staff ratio is akin to a hand grenade with the pin out of it. It is only a matter of time before the firm super novas and will probably cease to exist. All partners are likely to want to retire at about the same time or will become ill as they become older and their health deteriorates. All partners will want to have their capital out of the firm at about the same time. A great many of the important players in the client base are of a similar age to the partners who attend to their business needs and are also likely to retire within a year or two of the solicitor concerned. It is only a question of time before two-thirds of the partners will have retired, their contacts within the client companies will also retire and will probably be replaced by younger men and women who have little or no association or loyalty with anyone else within the firm and will have little trouble in persuading other people within their companies to go to other solicitors. The remaining partners will find themselves very few in number with a sudden and massive fall-off in work, with several partners clamouring for repayment of their capital at the same time and with the overheads of the firm continuing unabated.

Such problems are the result of bad management and planning. Those charged with the management of the firm should have one eye to their own successors as well as keeping several other eyes looking into the future. Those who have demonstrated a talent both for legal work and winning and retaining clients should be seen as the assets of the firm that they are and should be wedded to the firm by means of partnership. Such gaps in the structure should be openly recognised and suitable calibre replacements should be sought so that there is a good spread of talent coming through with individuals being groomed for partnership.

Supervision

Until such time as fee-earners get to the stage where they can work with virtually no supervision, by which time they should normally be serious contenders for partnership, they will need supervising to a greater or lesser extent. Partners have their own workload and there is a limit to the extent to which they can supervise. No partner should be expected to supervise the work of more than three fee-earners. He or she will be unable to cope with rendering a proper service to their own client base and to check properly through work which the other fee-earners are producing. Such partners may also have administrative jobs within the firm which will also take up their time. There comes a limit when even the ablest and most hard-working partners can no longer cope.

It is possible to delegate all or part of the supervision of a fee-earner to a senior assistant solicitor, but again, such a senior assistant, if able and required to supervise others, will be on the brink of partnership anyway.

Salaried Partners

Salaried partnership is something of a mixed blessing. The salaried partner is, from a legal point of view, held out to the world as a partner of a firm and is thus ostensibly liable for the firm's debts. It is extremely rare for firms to show salaried partners in that capacity on the notepaper. To an outsider, no distinction is drawn between salaried partners and equity partners. Indeed, some firms may go to great lengths to conceal such information, both from clients and from other firms of solicitors. In fact, salaried partners are employees just like other employees. They will have a contract of employment and be liable to be dismissed. They do not share in the profits of the firm unless there is a bonus scheme in operation but do benefit by the fact that they draw a salary every month irrespective of the firm's fortunes. This has not been strictly true in some cases due to the exigencies of the recession when staff in all types of businesses have been asked to take a cut in pay to help the firm survive. Salaried partners have in many instances gone along with such proposals rather than see the firm try to make savings in other ways, such as by making certain staff redundant and running the risk that they may be the one to draw the short straw. During the recession, it has been common not only for partners to be expected to take no draw for a month or half their usual draw, but also to inject additional capital into the firm. Accordingly, not only have they not been paid, but they have sustained a loss for all the hard effort they have put into the firm for that month, and in some cases, over a period of several months. This is not normally the fate of the salaried partner.

Salaried partnership is seen as a stepping stone to full partnership. As a small practice, should you be making people salaried partners? There is a school of thought which says that salaried partnership is something of a deception. It is a means of keeping quiet a member of staff who is fairly useful but not so useful that you wish to be saddled with him or her for the rest of your professional life, and whilst they may perform a useful function, you do not see them as deserving of a substantial slice of the profits. It is dishonest to use salaried partnership as a means of retaining a member of staff who is important to the firm but whom you do not regard as having the qualities necessary ever to become a full partner unless you tell such an individual frankly that you are prepared to make them a salaried partner and to give them the status of partnership but that you are most unlikely ever to offer them full equity partnership.

Such news may come as a considerable disappointment but can perhaps be softened by pointing out the advantages, as outlined above, enjoyed by salaried partners. You may make it perfectly plain to them that you have no wish to see them leave the firm but you felt it only right and proper to tell them how you felt about the situation. You may also care to point out that it is difficult to form a view about how someone will perform at partnership level in advance and that they may yet develop qualities and talents which have hitherto escaped you and that no such decision is irreversible but that they should be under no illusion as to what your present views are. So long as this is said and meant sincerely, then it is perfectly fair and reasonable to put forward such views. People do behave differently when brought into partnership, even at salaried partnership level, and you should be prepared to change your opinions of people if the situation warrants such change of heart. A useful summary of what salaried partnership is and its pros and cons can be found in the *The Young Solicitors' Partnership Guide* in Chapter 2 (published by the Law Society).

Consultants

Consultants are usually former partners and often have a valuable part to play in a firm. They may have spent 20 or 30 years with a practice and as well as having a wealth of experience and knowledge, they have a considerable client following. The sudden loss of a partner can have a detrimental effect on the client base. By offering a partner a consultancy with a firm, a transitional phase is provided which enables the client base to be passed on to the succeeding partners as the consultant introduces the succeeding partners to his or her clients or strengthens the bonds that have already been made. Clients gain considerable reassurance from knowing that, although not perhaps quite so available as before, and with a much lower profile, there will still be a familiar and trusted face dealing with at least part of their affairs. This reassurance is invaluable until such time as partners have gained the confidence of the consultant's clients and, as well as providing a settling-in period for the succeeding partners, it gives a 'bowing out' period in which the consultant can slowly withdraw from full-time practice, perhaps dropping down to four days a week, then three, then two and ultimately retiring full time if that is what the continuing partners want.

Retaining Consultants

There is also considerable goodwill attached to most consultants and the respect attached to a consultant's name will continue to reflect upon the firm whilst that name still appears on the notepaper, albeit a little lower down and under a different heading.

Unlike salaried partners, consultants are not held out as principals. There is a clear distinction to be made between partners of any kind and consultants. Nevertheless, they are employees and can be sacked. Most consultants will have a consultancy agreement which is a form of contract of employment. A specimen consultancy agreement appears in Appendix 2.

When a firm is purchased by new partners, it is a very common arrangement for the seller of the practice to negotiate a consultancy with the new firm as part of the overall package. Equally, on mergers of firms, the stronger of the two merging practices will probably not wish to retain all those persons in the weaker firm who were partners and who may well not have the enthusiasm and drive which their younger counterparts possess. As senior members of the practice, it may well be the case that they have been drawing substantial proportions of the profits which may not be proportionate to the effort expended in the practice, which in itself may be the reason why the weaker firm has found itself in a position where it makes good economic sense to merge with a stronger practice. In these conditions, a consultancy with the merged firm is often the answer. Some consultants can go on for years. Initially, it is probably a good idea that a consultancy agreement should last no more than three years. In some cases, it will be desirable to make it five years. It is generally a bad idea for any fixed term contract to last any longer than five years for a consultant although there is no reason why it should not then become a 'rolling' agreement so that it continues from year to year until terminated by a notice provision by either side, normally of either six months or one year. Most consultants will not wish to go on for ever and after many years of loyal service to a firm they are entitled to enjoy their retirement. There are, however, some consultants who will not recognise that the time has come for them to hang up their briefcase and a notice provision may need to be operated. Such considerations will undoubtedly form part of a firm's overall business plan. In most instances, after three years of diminishing chargeable hours spent with the firm, the continuing partners will have absorbed the goodwill element of the consultant's client base and will probably be looking to bring the arrangement to an end. There will always be those exceptional people who will continue to be a considerable asset to the firm beyond that period of time, but these people will be rather unique.

Partnership Agreements

I wonder how many solicitors have actually made a will? It is much the same sort of question as how many self-employed life assurance salesmen have taken out one of the policies that they sell or have put in place a pension plan. As solicitors, our thoughts will inevitably at some stage turn towards the question of a partnership agreement once we have partners. Is there any need? The Partnership Act of 1890 was once described by one House of Lords member as a 'model piece of legislation'. The mere fact that the partnership agreement is still the one that was passed in 1890 and has not been amended out of sight like so many other pieces of legislation, is a good indicator of the fact that like many products of the Victorian era it was made to last. The Act can always be excluded by agreement, either in whole or in part, but where partnership agreements do not provide an answer, the Act is usually there to step in to fill the gap. The question therefore arises, is there any need for a partnership agreement at all between solicitors? In general, the only time when you need to refer to a partnership agreement is when things are going wrong. If everybody behaves reasonably and sensibly, solutions automatically emerge. It is only when people start to behave dishonourably or unreasonably that there is any need to look to the terms of any contract, including that of a partnership agreement.

Like any other contract, if you are going to bother to have one it is crucial that it works. You must agree on the fundamental points, such as profit share, dissolution, expulsion, and interest on capital introduced. Having agreed on the salient points, you should then commit them to writing in such a way as to leave no room for doubt and no room for manoeuvre for those seeking to avoid the terms which they had previously agreed in an attempt to wriggle out of the commitments they have made. If your agreement has been properly drawn, it should mean that you will not finish up in court. The only occasions when people go to court are when they think they have a chance. If the agreement is in unambiguous terms and is properly drafted, it should leave no room for doubt as to who will win or who will lose, no matter how reasonable or otherwise the agreement may be. If the agreement provides an answer in clear, unequivocal terms, then there is no point going to court because the court will only reach the obvious conclusion. No partnership agreement at all is better than a badly drafted one, but a properly drafted agreement is always the preferred option. If the agreement is badly drafted, it will be capable of several different interpretations and each party will fancy their chances before a court. Such an agreement is a blueprint for a lawsuit. A suggested form of partnership agreement appears in Appendix 1. In the light of the foregoing observations, I would like to disclaim any responsibility if anyone enters into such form of agreement but nevertheless ends up in court. The suggested form of partnership agreement is intended as a starting point and may need modification depending on your particular circumstances. You may need to instruct another firm of solicitors to draw up your deed or to modify the suggested one. As you can see, the only thing that I am better at drafting than partnership agreements is exclusion clauses!

Further information on equity partnership agreements can be found in Chapter 4 of *The Young Solicitors' Partnership Guide* (published by the Law Society).

CHAPTER 17
Coping With Getting Bigger

If all has gone according to plan, you may be sitting in your office one day and suddenly realise that you are no longer the firm. From the day that you set up in practice until this moment, you have been indispensable. The entire practice has revolved around you and without you there would have been no practice. The clients came purely because of you and your name and the advertisements you had placed and because of the way you had managed the firm. Suddenly, it dawns upon you that this is no longer the case. Clients are giving the firm instructions because of the helpful way in which your assistant dealt with them previously. You may have a trainee solicitor who attends Citizens Advice Bureaux evening surgeries and has developed his or her own client following. You begin to realise that if your assistant solicitor left next week he or she is quite likely to take half a dozen clients with them. The firm is no longer just you – it is a separate entity and has almost taken on a persona of its own. You might even be able to go away on holiday for two weeks and be fairly certain that the firm will still exist when you return!

When you reach this stage, it is time for a few changes. The first of these changes is the psychological adjustment needed and to be able to view this new state of affairs as a positive development which takes a lot of pressure off you, as opposed to having lost something, since strangely, this can be the case. There is almost a desire to take a few steps backwards because of the feeling that the firm is getting out of control. It is no longer just a question of getting the work done at what is often breakneck speed and keeping the clients happy. Members of staff have grown in importance and their loss could be a severe setback to the firm.

For a solicitor who has never been in a position of management within a firm before, these problems can seem quite overpowering at times. Where does the line of sympathy and understanding towards members of staff end and strong management and a firm hand begin? Only the experience of different kinds of situations and making mistakes can teach you the finer points of how to handle staff and how to manage. One thing you should always keep at the back of your mind is that staff are always replaceable. It is undoubtedly the case that some staff feel that they are irreplaceable and often some principals begin to feel that a member of staff is irreplaceable. There is no such thing as an indispensable member of staff. Your staff are there to make your life easier.

When the point is reached where they cease to do that, they must be given their marching orders. It may be painful psychologically and it may be painful financially, but when staff become a burden for whatever reason and start to become a problem, then it is time for a change. It may perhaps be a little unkind to say that within a matter of a few months it is almost as if they had never been there, but the firm will continue on without them no matter how unlikely that may seem at the time.

Staff Morale

Part of the essence of managing a firm well is to be able to cater for the idiosyncrasies of individual members of staff and to try to maintain stability. Rapid turnover of staff is bad for morale and is bad for the service that is delivered to the clients. Continuity of staff helps to develop a happy family atmosphere which also rubs off onto the clients.

Next to the clients themselves, the greatest asset of the firm (apart from you!) is the staff. Choose your staff carefully and do not be rushed into taking someone on because there is a gap to fill and you are tired of interviewing. Having said that, with a small practice it is often the case that you cannot compete with the wages of larger and more established practices and you sometimes do have to compromise between the calibre of staff you would like to have and the calibre of staff you can afford. Nevertheless, there are minimum levels to be set and you should be looking for honesty and integrity above all else, together with commitment and personality. Sheer ability is probably the least of the qualities needed for the individual to fit in well with your practice. Their educational and professional qualifications will, hopefully, ensure a certain minimum level of ability. The fact that the individual does not have grade As and first class honours at each level does not mean to say that they would not do well within your practice. Indeed, if someone is particularly well qualified, they may be taking your job as a stop-gap measure before moving on to bigger and better things, as they may perceive them to be, at the first available opportunity. Someone with their sights set a little lower may prove a more loyal and committed member of staff. In my view, it is more often the case than not that the better qualified applicants do not necessarily make the better fee-earner. They may be so wrapped up in the theoretical side of their work that they take their eye off the need to get the work done and bill it.

Training

Having found what you consider to be the right kind of applicant for your position, they will need to be given a degree of training by you if only in the way that the firm operates and the firm's general ethos. After spending the time necessary to settle the applicant in and to have them working productively, you will then need to work at ensuring that they stay for a long time. You may need to be more thoughtful and considerate than had been the case in earlier days. You need to be sensitive to the way in which staff interact with one another. Petty squabbles, particularly in a relatively small office, can soon appear and can get out of hand. You may need a firm but thoughtful hand in resolving them. At the same time, you must always ensure that the tail never wags the dog. There can be discussion and points of view exchanged, but at the end of the day there is only so far you can allow the member of staff's views to go before it is time to say that this is the way it will be, simply because that is what you have decided.

Monitoring Systems

The days may be gone when you could sit in your office and physically see and hear everything that was going on around you. You may have moved premises or taken on extra space. Although you should still be seeing all the incoming and outgoing post and be able to keep quite a careful eye on things in that way, inevitably your grip on the firm will be considerably less by now than it had been when you first started. Now is the time to put in place proper and effective monitoring systems.

The Law Society's Practice Management Standards contain helpful advice on how to put these systems in place. One should not be too dogmatic about these things. Some systems that are appropriate for some practices will not be appropriate to others. Much depends on size and volume of work and also on considerations such as physical location of supervisors and fee-earners and support staff. The important thing is that there comes a time when you take a long, hard look at the degree of control you have over what is happening and what you need to put in place to ensure that any loss of control is regained. The

Practice Management Standards and the *Solicitors' Office Manual* can go a long way to putting forward suggestions to achieve this. Here are just a few suggestions to get you thinking

Centralised Diary

By issuing an instruction to all members of staff that they will not only diarise court hearings, time-limits, deadlines and even, if necessary, appointments with clients and conferences with counsel in their own diaries but also in a centralised diary (probably one for each department would be sufficient), you will benefit in two ways. Firstly, you can ensure that appointments and time-limits are not missed. This produces an added benefit if someone is away ill unexpectedly. Secondly, it gives an extremely good idea of how busy everyone is. The regularity with which the entries are made will show how meticulous a particular individual is. By keeping a close eye on the centralised diary, it may rapidly become apparent that certain people are somewhat less than enthusiastic about what they see as unnecessary bureaucracy. This will immediately identify them to you as people on whom you will need to keep a close eye. If they are going to cut this kind of corner, they may well be of a mind to cut other corners. Your level of supervision over such people will necessarily increase.

Perhaps a further bonus of the centralised diary is that it gives a good idea of how busy the department is. The fewer entries in the diary, the more cause for concern and the earlier on you will be able to detect a fall-off in business and start to look for causes and also for solutions.

Time Reports

Because of the pressures on a small practice in the early years, the time-recording side of an accounts package may have been ignored. It is only worth operating a time-recording system if it is going to be used as a proper management tool. If an accounts department or a secretary produces time reports which sit on your desk for a number of weeks until filed away after a cursory glance, it is a waste of good paper. The time will come when your practice becomes sufficiently large that even if you have been able to ignore time-costing up until that point, you will no longer be able to run your practice satisfactorily without it.

As well as telling you how much you should be charging for the work you carry out in order to make a profit and persuading taxing masters that they ought to allow your bill in full, time-recording also tells you who has too much work within the department, who has too little and who is working profitably. A downturn in work can be identified at an early stage, as can increases in work. Work in progress can be accurately monitored and can assist with cash flow forecasting. Those types of work which are unprofitable can be spotted and either phased out or reduced and those areas of work which are profitable can be targeted for special attention to capitalise on, so as to maximise the available profits. If your software program produces an unbilled time report, you can chase those people who are bad at getting out their bills.

Weekly Meetings

Whether you have staff or department meetings once a week, once a fortnight or once a month, it does not really matter too much. You are presumably operating an 'open door' policy so that people who have problems before scheduled meetings can come to you with them for guidance, but a weekly, fortnightly or monthly meeting (possibly even a combination) can help to formulate policies of one kind or another. Such meetings should be kept as brief as possible. Tying up several fee-earners for an hour or two is extremely costly in lost billable time. Conscientious members of staff will regard attendance at such meetings as a chore unless it is clear that they are benefiting the department as a whole. You may well be able to keep your meetings as short as 15 minutes. They should be kept moving and persons invited to contribute to an agenda before the meeting. They should be chaired by someone who will keep the meeting moving so that there is not prolonged discussion on something which only affects one person and is not relevant to the whole department. Such matters can be discussed individually, either with you or with someone else who may be responsible for the department on a one-to-one basis outside of such a meeting.

File Lists

Your software program on your computer may be capable of producing a list of files that each fee-earner has under his or her control. If not, fee-earners concerned should be required to produce such lists and these should be updated at least monthly. It may be that the matter ledger listing system of a time-recording program can fulfil this function, but if you are not running a computerised time-recording system or the system you have is incapable of producing such a list, then a separate manual list may need to be produced. Whilst pure numbers of files under an individual's control may not give an entirely accurate picture of how busy someone is, it is nevertheless quite a good guide. In any event, by discussing file lists with fee-earners, you will soon get an idea of which files are weighty matters and which have remained dormant for some time and you will be able to take this into account when assessing who has spare capacity and who is not pulling their weight.

Sickness and Holiday Book

Someone fulfilling an administrative function with the firm, i.e. not a fee-earner, should be tasked with keeping a sickness and holiday book. The firm may be small enough so that an individual's physical absence from the office can easily be noticed. If only half a dozen of you work there, it will be fairly obvious when someone does not work. However, you may be at the stage where this no longer applies, in which case you will need some kind of reporting system so that a person's absence when noticed by their colleagues can be notified to the individual responsible for keeping the records. A periodic review of the statistics gathered in this way can be quite revealing. If a person is repeatedly absent through illness, there must be some very good reason why their services should not be dispensed with. They are either malingering, in which case, after suitable warnings they should be fired, or they are too ill to do the job. Either way, such absences are a drain on even large firms, and with a small firm are quite intolerable. You will need to tread carefully for purposes of unfair dismissal. It is especially important to monitor the performance of those persons with less than two years' service where terminating their employment is very much easier since it does not carry the same kind of risks so far as unfair dismissal and redundancy are concerned. Bear in mind also that all part-time workers now have the full protection of the Employment Protection (Consolidation) Act once they have completed two years employment. Generally speaking, people are either hard-working or slackers. It is rare to find someone who works hard and has a good attendance record for two years and then decides they are safe as they have the protection of the Employment Protection Act and can afford to take things easy.

Holiday Request Slips

If your staff have increased in number, it is very easy to lose track completely of who is going on holiday and when. The answer is the holiday request slip. Do not allow staff to catch you when you are only half thinking about what they are saying and ask if they can have next Tuesday off. Make it a universal rule that anyone who wishes to have even half a day's holiday must complete a holiday request slip which comes to you or to their head of department, and once the slip has been dealt with, one copy of it goes back to the employee and the other copy goes to whoever is responsible for collecting the data centrally. An additional advantage is that if people start having arguments with you over whether or not they have used up the whole of their holiday entitlement for that year, you can go back to the raw data, i.e. the holiday request slips and the sickness and holiday book, and add up the amount of holiday taken. It may well be that they have genuinely forgotten about a half day or day here or there. If you do not have the data to fall back on, it will be difficult to refuse the member of staff's request for time off and you may find you have granted them a week's more holiday than had been agreed upon.

Photocopying Slips

It may seem like a rather pedantic point, but insisting on each member of staff completing a photocopying slip before taking copies can save the firm a great deal of money. You may have made arrangements for a member of general staff to do the copying on behalf of the fee-earners. Even if you have not and individuals carry out their own photocopying, they should still complete a slip and anyone seen copying who has not made out the appropriate slip should be taken to task. The number of copies should then be recorded on the slip which is then placed on the correspondence tag of each file so that when a bill is prepared the number of copies made can be totalled. Courts have made it clear that photocopying should not be added as a separate item to a solicitor's bill and should be treated as part of the normal overheads of the office unless the number of copies produced is exceptional. One is tempted to say that such pronouncements from the Court of Appeal demonstrate perfectly how easy it is to spend other people's money for them, and before making such pronouncements, the Court of Appeal ought to try their hand at running a solicitor's office for a week or two. Nevertheless, there is a point to be made, namely that it is bad practice to charge people £5 or £10 on the bill for photocopying charges. You will probably find, by enforcing a fairly strict regime for the completion of photocopying slips and their placement on the correspondence tag, that over the course of a year's work on the file the amount of copies produced is substantial. If the copying charges thus collated result in a charge to the client of £25 or £30, then in my view it is perfectly proper to add those on to the bill as a separate item. Clients rarely challenge such items where it is clear that it is not part of a general sundries item. Furthermore, if either the client or the court on a taxation challenges the figure, it does mean that you are in a position to justify it by stating precisely how many copies have been made, and producing the slips for examination, if requested.

Monthly Billing Targets

Virtually all commercial organisations, including professionals such as accountants and surveyors, have monthly billing targets. Members of staff are left in no doubt that they are expected to achieve a certain level of billing each month and will be required to provide some compelling reasons as to why they have failed to achieve that target if that proves to be the case. To the extent that this is not universal practice amongst solicitors, we are the exception. There are all kinds of reasons given as to why this cannot be achieved, for example, a lot of work may have been carried out but the job is not complete and it cannot be billed until it is complete, or that there is a long-running case which has not come to trial yet, and so on. The fact remains that profit costs are the life blood of the firm. Without the costs coming in, the firm will slide gently into oblivion. There is nothing wrong in a solicitor's practice with the supervisor assessing what level of costs a fee-earner should produce and applying pressure each month on the fee-earner to see that they keep to the billing figure. If it proves that the targets are unattainable, then they will need to be adjusted. The fact that it is not as easy to set billing targets for solicitors and their staff as it might be for a car salesman does not mean to say that it should not be attempted.

Bonus Incentives

Hand in hand with monthly billing targets can go staff bonuses. This can be a bonus for a department which achieves a certain figure, or to an individual or possibly to both. Allowances will have to be made for work which is less profitable or for fee-earners who are also expected to carry out certain administrative tasks. One must be careful with bonuses since there may be accusations of unfairness where a certain individual's targets are perceived to be easier than others, and if targets are set too low and are easily reached resulting in large bonus payments to fee-earners and the targets are then raised to more realistic levels, you will be accused of moving the goal posts, which of course, is exactly what you are doing. If you feel that this kind of performance-related pay has difficulties and dangers attached, you may prefer to have a bonus system in relation to new work which is introduced. Members of staff will quite naturally point work in the direction of the firm where appropriate, but the fact that they may receive a bonus for work that they have introduced may make them press that little bit harder once there is a suggestion from a friend or relation that there is some legal work in the offing. It is important to make a record when such work is introduced so that there can be no doubt as to whether the work qualifies for a bonus or not and should be paid as a percentage of profit costs once the bill has actually been paid.

Career Paths

You will need to bear in mind each member of staff's hopes and aspirations for their progression through the firm. Trainee solicitors will be thinking about whether or not to remain with the firm on qualification, even if you are not. If they are retained by the firm on qualification, their thoughts will at some stage turn to the question of partnership. Inexperienced office juniors will not wish to stay as office juniors for the whole of their lives. Some will be more ambitious than others, but few people will see standing in front of the photocopier eight hours a day as a fulfilling vocation. If you do not anticipate their future needs, the first you may learn of their dissatisfaction is when a month's notice of their intention to leave the firm arrives on your desk. Many people's attitude to such things is that as and when the office junior leaves, a new one is simply employed. This overlooks the fact that the individual concerned is someone whom you know. You have had the opportunity to observe them over the period of time they have been with the firm. You have been able to assess their qualities and their limitations. If you have planned ahead, you may have been able to see a way in which you can use their services better and groom them to fulfil an emerging need that is developing within the firm. If you fail to map out these career paths for your members of staff, there will be a lack of continuity within the firm and you may be paying substantially more in recruitment fees or advertising than need be the case.

Staff Parties

Some firms view expenditure on staff parties, or for that matter on anything to do with staff welfare, as money down the drain. In my view, they are an extremely cheap and effective means of promoting unity within a firm. They are best held at the end of the week and should be arranged by the staff themselves with a set level of contribution from the firm and the opportunity of members of staff to contribute themselves by bringing a bottle or a plate of sandwiches or whatever. There is no reason why they should not be held on a regular basis, such as every two or three months, and should be attended for at least an hour or so by a

174

partner. Gatherings of this nature do an enormous amount to show that an employee's services are valued and to break down barriers between principals and employees and between one employee and another employee. It should also be made clear in advance that staff are expected to behave sensibly at such functions and that over-indulgence with drink will not be held to be an excuse for bad behaviour. It should also be made clear that staff are expected to clear up after such functions and that the debris will not be left to the cleaning staff to deal with.

Office Manual

If you do not have an office manual by this stage, perhaps now might be the time to put one together. Apart from anything else, it may be useful when dealing with any unfair dismissal applications which may come your way. If office procedures and policy are clearly set out in an office manual and an employee repeatedly goes against what is laid down in the office manual, it may stand you in good stead for dealing with an unfair dismissal application brought by a disgruntled former employee. The manual itself may provide you with an aide-mémoire for the installation of such systems as may not already be in operation. The Law Society's *Solicitors' Office Manual* is intended to form the basis of an in-house produced manual, and is an excellent starting point.

A Change of Funding

It is a fact of economic life that as a firm expands, its requirement for working capital accelerates. The more staff you have, the bigger your wages bill, the more PAYE to be paid at the end of each month, the bigger the stationery bill, the bigger the telephone bill, the more search and court fees there are to be paid, etc.

Whilst you are small and the working capital requirement is comparatively modest, you may be able to fund this yourself. This becomes progressively more difficult as the firm expands. It is for this reason that most businesses, and that includes most firms of solicitors, of any size, ultimately have to rely on banks for the funding of their working capital.

As discussed in Chapter 3, overreliance upon banks can prove costly. They have a nasty tendency to want their money back when you can least afford to repay it. In addition, you are at the mercy of the bank rate, so that if the banks suddenly decide to quadruple the interest rate, the cost of borrowing goes through the roof.

Another nasty habit that banks have is of suddenly requiring either additional security to be provided by the principals of the business or a substantial injection of capital from partners' own resources. Principals of businesses, solicitors included, are often prone to wax lyrical about how sound their business is and whilst there may be short-term difficulties, the long-term outlook is very promising. It can be at this point that bankers will in effect tell the principals to 'put their money where their mouth is'. If the principals wish to have the continued support of their bankers, then they must find some cash to put in themselves so that they are not only playing with the bank's money but with their own life savings. If you have no life savings to play with, this can prove something of a problem.

Nevertheless, it may be that you have no choice. Unless you are single-handedly, i.e. both yourself and your partners, going to finance the firm from your own capital resources, which may mean not being able to enjoy the fruits of your labours quite so much, you will have little choice but to find some of the capital needed by the firm from bank borrowing.

Getting the Balance Right

At one time the teaching was that anyone who financed the working capital primarily out of their own resources was a mug. Many of the recipients of that advice are now living under assumed names in different parts of South America. My own view is that for firms of three or four partners and 10 to 20 members of staff, a 50/50 relationship is probably about right. In other words, if your total working capital can be split equally between bank funding and contributions by partners, then it is a reasonable compromise. Alternatively, you may prefer to err on the side of caution and to ascertain two figures, the first being the absolute minimum amount of working capital with which the firm could operate on the one hand and a more realistic working capital figure on the other hand. If the partners contribute the first figure and then borrow the difference to make up the second figure, then you should have a fairly safe operation. If the bank suddenly decides to withdraw its support, the firm can keep going without making any drastic changes. It may need to operate even more efficiently by taking a firmer line on credit control, increase its output and make a few cutbacks, but it is not suddenly going to have to dispense with half of its labour force and move to smaller premises.

One policy decision which will have to be taken is as to whether the funds contributed by partners will carry interest. This is something of an old chestnut and can be quite a contentious issue. My own feeling is that probably the better course is not to have interest on capital, which serves as a great encouragement to have an equalisation of capital between partners. If you do pay interest on partners' capital, you generally find that certain partners who have been with the firm longer amass substantial capital accounts and a large slice of the firm's profits go in paying a healthy rate of interest on to the capital accounts of the partners concerned. This then causes widespread dissension between generally the younger partners on the one hand, and the longer-serving partners on the other hand who are those people with more capital in the firm, and there is the feeling that you are spending most of your professional life in paying out the more senior partners who have lost much of their sharpness and drive and are contributing far less in real terms to the firm than the younger partners who are doing all the work and seeing very few of the rewards.

If partners are not being paid interest on their capital, the capital accounts will rise much more slowly or not at all, depending on the policy adopted in relation to the retention of profits within the firm and there will be greater pressure for younger partners to put more money into the firm and for the older partners to take the money out. All in all, this makes for a much healthier working environment and stops a potentially dangerous and explosive situation building up when the younger partners are tempted to rebel against what they see as a wholly inequitable system whereby those who take out the most contribute the least.

CHAPTER 18

Marketing Your Practice

Planning a Marketing Campaign

The hardest thing about a marketing campaign is actually getting around to planning it. The smaller the firm, the more difficult it is. It is difficult enough trying to cope with the clients' work, managing the practice, recruiting staff and the thousand and one things that have to be done during the normal working week, without also having to make time to plan a marketing campaign and then to execute it. It is something that everybody agrees is a good idea and should be done and is something which can always be put off until next week. As a result, it tends to be something that we finally get around to when business is slack.

Marketing is something which should be done more or less continuously. Once one marketing campaign is over or the returns appear to be diminishing, the next campaign should start to take shape on the drawing board.

Targeting

The best way to approach a marketing campaign is to treat yourself as just another salesman with your product being your legal services. Solicitors are simply purveyors of legal services. What is your product and who are you trying to sell it to? You will instantly see that instead of having one range of products, you have several. This may cause you to split your marketing campaign into several different ones. It may also result in certain different individuals within the firm having responsibility for different marketing campaigns, each concentrating on their own area of expertise. So the first question is, are you selling the whole firm or just certain aspects of it?

Let us suppose that there is an expertise within the firm in employment law. If there is no such expertise, then it is always possible to develop one. You read everything you can on employment law and you attend a few courses, basic general ones at first, moving on to narrower in-depth ones as your knowledge increases. Then you start looking for the work. Having acquired a degree of expertise, you can now start your marketing campaign. Your product is your expertise and knowledge and ability in employment matters. This will cover areas of unfair dismissal, sexual and racial discrimination in the workplace, redundancy, the construction, interpretation and drafting of employment contracts and dealing with hearings before Industrial Tribunals. It may also go further and cover such areas as health and safety at work. Having identified your product, you now need to target your potential clients. The first place to start is your existing client base. Which clients are likely to need help and advice in those areas you have identified in which you have a degree of expertise? A list of targets amongst the existing client base will then be drawn up.

Who else could you sell to? There may be local businesses for whom you are not presently acting but who may have an unfulfilled need in these areas or who may be dissatisfied with their current advisors and already be half looking for someone more suitable to fulfil that need. More names for the list. It is important to ensure that the person within the organisation you will be contacting is in a 'buying position'. It is no good taking the sales manager of a company out to lunch if all decisions relating to legal matters are taken by the managing director. You may have to do a little phoning around and talk to one or two telephonists or secretaries in order to identify who it is who makes these decisions.

A word of warning – Rule 3 of the Solicitors' Publicity Code 1990 prohibits unsolicited visits or telephone calls except to current or former clients or existing or potential professional connections. The relevant Rule appears in Appendix 12.

Timing

With a product such as legal services, timing the start of the campaign is not particularly crucial in most instances. The campaign can be started at any time unless, of course, you are approaching the summer holiday period when most of the people you will need to speak to will be away. Timing is nevertheless important from the point of view of setting yourself a timetable for each phase.

- How long will it take you to comb your existing client base and prepare lists of names and addresses?

- How long will it take to do the same with local businesses?

179

- How long will it take you to phone around to find out who makes the decision on which firm of solicitors to use for which work?
- How long will it take to carry out the campaign itself?
- How long will it take to analyse the results so that you know how successful you have been and what lessons are to be learnt for the future?

All of this should be mapped out in advance so that the campaign is properly co-ordinated and it actually gets executed. The easiest way is to write the whole thing out and then to make diary entries for the beginning and end of each phase and possibly a mid point date as a reminder. The person whose responsibility it is to carry out each task and who will oversee things and chase up the progress of each phase must be clearly identified. There must be no instances of, 'I thought you were doing that.'

SOMETIMES PUTTING THE CLIENT SECOND IS LIKE ROBBING BANKS - IT GETS EASIER THE MORE OFTEN YOU DO IT.

Executing

Strangely enough, this is probably the part where most people fall down. Having done much of the work in terms of targeting and mapping out the timing, when it comes to execution there is a psychological barrier that needs to be broken. It is possibly because solicitors as a breed are rather shy and conservative and pushing ourselves forward and telling people how good we are does not come easily. We do, after all, have little or no training in it, unless like me, you have had a few years in selling before coming into the profession. We are not natural salesmen and it might perhaps be true that until the recent, almost unprecedented trading difficulties, we have not felt the need. Make no mistake – gone are the days when we can sit back with the brass plate on the wall and wait for the clients to form an orderly queue outside our doors. We must go out and find them and then convert them into clients. The simple message, therefore, on the question of executing the marketing plan is – get on with it. You will have your timetable drawn up – stick to it. You may have to commit the unholiest of sins and put off the clients' work until tomorrow whilst you spend today, or at least part of it, on your marketing exercise. There will probably have to be several such sins committed over the next few weeks. Like robbing banks, the first one is the most difficult and then it gets easier with every succeeding one.

Analysing

Probably not as hard as executing, analysing is still something which people are a little reluctant to carry out. A careful analysis of cost and time and the resultant benefits is very important as is comparing one type of campaign with another. Only by this careful analysis will mistakes be recognised and those methods which are successful screened in and the less successful screened out.

A spin-off benefit of analysing the campaign results is the recognition of the fact that marketing works and has tangible benefits. The measurement of the precise level of success is the sharpest spur to planning and executing a further campaign at a later date. When possibly some months later you are trying to find the necessary energy to plan another marketing campaign, you are able to look back at how many new clients the last campaign produced and the level of additional profit costs billed to date that would not have been there had there been no campaign. Suddenly you find the incentive to stay in the office that bit longer to pencil out your next campaign!

Ten Suggested Marketing Tools

1. Mail shots

These are both time-consuming and expensive. The advent of the word-processor and 'mailmerge' computer software packages have made them faster and cheaper. It is particularly important to ensure that the mail shots are going to the right target audience. If they are going to be of no interest at all to the recipient, the mail shot will go straight into the bin without hardly a glance and your time and money will have been wasted. The message must at least be read. This means that the message must be attractive and gets to the point early on and is at least going to prompt the recipient into a buying decision. If the recipient gets as far as reading right the way through the mail shot and then pauses for a few moments to consider whether to take up the offer or not, then the exercise has at least had limited success. If enough of the recipients fall into this category, then at least a small percentage will decide to act on the mail shot and an even smaller percentage will go as far as engaging you to do something for them. Again, the letter must be addressed to the person able to take the buying decision. The mail shot may be a prelude to some further action, the most likely thing being a telephone call to follow up the mail shot to see if the recipient is interested in taking things further, but this will only be permissible if the call is to a current or former client or to another solicitor, or to an existing or potential professional connection. Rule 3 of the Solicitors' Publicity Code 1990 allows telephone calls to people in these categories but not otherwise, (see Appendix 12). The letter may be designed to set up a meeting and the mail shot may state that you will be telephoning to see what level of interest there is in such a meeting.

There have been some very innovative mail shots recently by solicitors marketing to other solicitors. These have included initiatives such as offering specialist advice in areas such as employment law, welfare law and the like in an attempt to sell the products that they have produced in preparing for a legal aid franchise and which will avoid solicitors having to duplicate the effort that they themselves have put in. I have also received mail shots from solicitors who buy and sell land in other countries. They have recognised that they have a narrow area of expertise which the average solicitor is unlikely to have but yet may well be asked for advice from clients on the subject. Unable to satisfy the clients' needs themselves, there is a good chance that they will pass the client on to the firm with that expertise, and if so, the mail shot in that event has worked.

2. Talks and Seminars

You may be fortunate enough to be able to supplement your earnings in general practice by being invited to lecture or give talks by professional providers of legal education. Undoubtedly, such public appearances enhance the reputation of the lecturer and his or her firm. There is, however, no need to wait to be asked. There is nothing to stop you from contacting a large organisation and offering to come along and give a talk on a subject which may be of interest to them. This can be anything from a talk to the local rugby club on civil and criminal liability following a suit arising out of injuries that they may cause during a game, to a talk to a group of doctors and nurses at the local hospital on the possible dangers of administering first-aid to the victims of road traffic accidents who subsequently allege negligence.

You will be regarded by your audience as an expert on these matters simply by reason of standing in front of them for 20 minutes and holding forth on the topic. You must therefore make sure that you have a reasonable knowledge of your subject and have done your homework in advance. You will need to know a little more than precisely what is in the notes in front of you as there will be questions from your audience at the end of your talk and inane waffling in an attempt to avoid admitting that you have no idea what the answer is, rarely impresses. Do not allow the fact that you are not an expert to put you off giving such talks. You are imparting a good deal of knowledge to people which they will find useful if you have hit upon the right subject and have tried to make it interesting.

Remember, the whole point of the exercise is marketing. There is no point in walking away from such a talk leaving your audience in the dark as to who you are and where they can contact you. There is always the ceremonial distribution of business cards, but why not contrive a 'handout' such as a summary of the talk, a specimen statement of claim, a list of judicial authorities or whatever, making sure that the firm's name and address are suitably displayed? The one thing that such talks and seminars do is to bring you into contact with fresh potential clients in a very favourable scenario. You are there as someone who knows their stuff when it comes to legal work and they have the opportunity of seeing you performing at first hand. At least as importantly, they have the opportunity to talk to a real live solicitor and to see what kind of person you are, all at no expense. If you have impressed on both fronts, and there is no reason why you should not, given that you have had the opportunity to do as much preparation as you want prior to placing yourself in front of your audience, some of your audience may come to you when they need legal services. It may well be that the services they need have nothing at all to do with the topic you have pronounced upon, but if it is good fee-paying work, that does not matter.

3. Free Advice Surgeries

A marketing initiative which is always popular with the general public is a free advice surgery. Generally speaking, this will have to be carried out during the evening or at a weekend. The reason for this is, firstly, you may be too busy during the day and such matters should not really be allowed to get in the way of other clients' work, and secondly, clients attending such advice surgeries will find it far easier to come along after work or at the weekends. Such sessions can be rather expensive in terms of resources as it is important that the sessions should not be counter-productive. If people come in expecting free advice and are then made to wait for an hour, they will not be very impressed with the practice. On the contrary, they will go away feeling rather hurt. If people are to be seen promptly, then the individual advice sessions must necessarily be kept short, no more than 15 minutes maximum, and you will need at least two if not more legal advisors conducting the interviews. You may well be able to persuade people to give up their time to carry out these advice sessions without any form of additional payment. They may find the concept of pro bono work in their own time socially fulfilling and may also feel that by giving up their time in this way they are making a real contribution to the firm's progress and ultimately their own job security.

Beware of 'blackmailing' staff into feeling they must take part in these exercises if they are to have a future with the firm. The wish to take part must come from the heart and not out of fear.

In addition, you may well find that you need to have at least one other person to act as a receptionist and provider of cups of tea. There is nothing like a free cup of tea for promoting an image of friendliness.

Such advice sessions are not intended to be an instant solution to people's problems and it is important that their expectations are not raised to think otherwise. What you can do in 10 or 15 minutes is assess whether the client has a problem which lawyers can help solve, and if they are not eligible for legal aid, whether it is worth their while committing resources by means of lawyers in an attempt to solve it. Once again, it provides the opportunity for interaction between the solicitor and a client. It is from such situations that long-term solicitor/client relationships can arise. You will need to give some thought to how to publicise the event and the information given out should include a description of what is offered, i.e. 15 minutes' free advice, so that people do not come expecting you to devote the whole evening to them.

4. Citizens' Advice Bureaux

The CAB provide a very valuable outlet for many people's worries and frustrations. Inevitably, the advice which a proportion of CAB clients need is of a legal nature. The CAB are scrupulously non-partisan. They will not recommend any particular firm but what they can do is to advise their clients of the names and addresses of local firms and who to speak to within those firms. They can also tell clients of the particular areas in which the firms operate and of any specialisms. A high proportion of CAB clients can only pursue solutions to their problems with the assistance of legal aid. Very many of them qualify for legal aid. Particularly if your practice accepts legal aid work, you should constantly ensure that your lines of communication with the CAB are good so that they are aware that you still deal with legal aid matters and are aware of any changes within your practice. They will often run legal advice sessions in the evenings for clients who clearly need legal advice and you may well be invited to attend such advice sessions. Having obtained an initial view from you at such a session, the client may wish to engage you to deal with the problem since, again, the barrier between solicitor and potential client has been broken down and the fear of coming to the solicitor's office will not be so intense now that they have already met you.

5. The Business Lunch

There was a time when the business lunch was the main form of marketing, particularly when the costs of such entrepreneurial dinners were tax deductible. Sadly, this is no longer the case. The strange thing is that if you take a member of staff out to lunch, then it is tax deductible under the heading of 'staff welfare'. However, taking a potential client out to lunch in the hope of increasing business which ultimately will increase the amount of taxes that you pay, is not tax deductible. Perhaps the thinking is that the business lunch is still such a useful marketing tool that it would survive despite the removal of tax relief. The business lunch is useful, both for breaking new ground and also as a means of consolidating existing ground.

185

The business lunch should not be treated as a gastronomical bribe. People who are in a 'buying position' are not so stupid as to feel obligated to use your services simply because you have spent a lot of money in wreaking havoc with an elaborate menu of a high class restaurant. Whilst there may be the odd naive individual, on the whole such people are businessmen first and bon viveurs second. By all means make it abundantly clear that the object of the lunch is to acquire their business, but the occasion should be seen as an opportunity to ascertain from the potential client what their prospective needs are and how you may be in a position to fulfil those needs at least as efficiently if not more efficiently, and more cost-effectively (never use the word cheap!) than is the case at the present time.

Before the lunch, you must go back to basics and decide precisely what image you wish to project and this must be borne in mind throughout the lunch. There is no point in selling yourself as a cheap (oops, I mean cost-effective) practice if what the client is primarily after is quality and speed of service. You should be concentrating on the fact that because you are hungry for work you will try that much harder to conduct the client's business whilst maintaining high standards and providing a quality service. The fact that you may happen to be less expensive than their existing provider of legal services can then be seen as an added bonus rather than that being the whole point of changing firms. Indeed, it may well be the case that you are no less expensive than the competitor. The chances are that if the prospective clients are coming to see you, they may be less than content with their current firm and are keeping an eye open for a suitable replacement.

When changing firms, there is always a 'fear area' which must be overcome. The person taking the decision may be doing so by placing themselves out on a limb. If you are appointed and your performance is less than adequate and legally speaking you fall flat on your face, then your appointer does likewise. The safe thing is, therefore, for them not to appoint you unless the level of dissatisfaction with their existing provider of legal services is very high. What you need to do is to reassure the prospective clients that your commitment to the work will be unstinting and that you will not betray the confidence that they place in you by giving you the instructions. The key is to persuade them to instruct you in a small way whilst not necessarily terminating the instructions to the other firm. This will give you the opportunity to demonstrate the level of service that you can provide. If you are given such an opportunity, it is desperately important that you do not waste it. You should equally be aware of overkill. The idea is to impress, not to play the part of a fawning sycophant for whom the client's every wish is your command. You must win the client's respect by providing a cost-efficient and, above all, professional service.

The lunch itself should not consist of one long sales pitch which will have the result of boring the client to death. Neither should the time be spent purely in idle chitchat without getting the message across. There is a delicate balance between the two extremes. As with all other types of marketing, the lunch must be with someone who is in a buying position. There is no point in taking a junior executive to lunch if it is a superior who is in a position to say yes or no to the idea of your firm being appointed as their solicitors. No matter how well you sell yourself to the junior executive, no one will ever sell your firm as well as you will.

Above all else, beware of drinking too much and making a fool of yourself. If at all in doubt, do not drink alcohol during the meal. You may run the risk of being accused of not entering into the spirit of things, but that is a far better crime to be accused of than making an idiot of yourself because you have misjudged your ability to handle drink. It will also mean that you will be in no fit state to work during the rest of the afternoon. If it takes you two hours to sober up, then it has increased the cost of a lunch from possibly £80 to £280 due to lost chargeable hours.

Beware the client who asks you out to lunch. Whilst it is flattering to the ego, almost certainly the purpose of the lunch is to obtain free legal advice. From the client's point of view, this provides an opportunity to pick your brains for some two hours for £50 instead of £200, half of which the client spends on himself or herself! There is no reason why you should not go along with the idea, but be under no illusions as to what most people have in mind when they invite a solicitor out to lunch, unless perhaps it is to say thank you for a particularly good piece of work you have done for them.

6. Joining Organisations

The more organisations of which you are a member, the more people with whom you will come into contact. Each person that you meet is a potential client. If they know you on a social or professional level, then there may come a time when they have a requirement for legal services, or possibly they have a friend who does, and you may be in line for a recommendation. The classic organisation is the golf club. I would never suggest to anyone that they join such an organisation purely for business purposes, but it is a fact of life that an enormous amount of business is carried out on the country's golf courses. There are hundreds of organisations you can join, either sports clubs or they may be connected with social activities of other kinds, such as the local Chamber of Commerce, Parent/Teacher Associations of schools and committees of one kind or another. With each organisation that you join, you will meet new people, make new contacts and provide the opportunity for such people to become clients. The opportunity may present itself for you to join a charitable organisation. I have always considered it repugnant that people should join such organisations with anything other than the welfare of others in mind. People who do otherwise, in my experience, are rapidly recognised for what they are. On the other hand, someone who gives of their time freely for the benefit of their fellow men may well find that their efforts are rewarded, not only in terms of the thanks from those whom they may have helped but with the respect of other like-minded individuals, and with that respect may come the opportunity to serve them in a professional way as well as in a purely altruistic way.

7. Banks, Building Societies and Accountants

Each of these organisations have one thing in common. They are considered respectable and trustworthy. As a result, if a bank manager or building society manager suggests to an individual that he or she uses a certain firm of solicitors, that recommendation goes a long way to securing the individual as a client. In some cases, the recommendation is not made purely for unselfish reasons. Rightly or wrongly, banks and building societies often recommend people to use those firms of solicitors with whom they have an existing connection, namely, the large sums of money that the solicitors have deposited with them. This arrangement whereby the solicitor helps the bank or building society and they help the solicitors is euphemistically known as 'reciprocal business'. There is nothing wrong with reciprocal business so long as it is all done for the right reasons. If you offer a poor service to persons referred by banks or building societies, then they will not recommend you to their customers no matter how much money you might deposit with them. As commercial organisations themselves who have been brought up in an atmosphere of competition and selling, they are generally happy for you to sell to them and indeed may respect those firms who try to sell to them over and above those who do not bother. They may regard the latter as complacent and be more inclined to direct work to those firms who are perceived as being eager for work and eager to please both them and the clients they refer to that firm. Accordingly, such organisations should be a feature of your marketing campaign. It may be that the business lunch is a suitable approach, but equally, a busy bank manager may not want to give up two or three hours and may be just as happy, if not more so, with a 20-minute interview at his offices so that you can get to know him or her, explain the kind of work that you do and give them the opportunity to make up their own mind as to whether they feel you are the kind of solicitor to whom they can confidently recommend their customers.

Banks and Building Societies

It is quite surprising how often bank managers and building society managers will say that they do not really know or have any kind of a relationship with solicitors in the locality and how they welcome the opportunity to enjoy such a rapport. The senior personnel of such organisations do have a rather unfortunate habit of moving around quite a lot. It is not unusual to find that the manager with whom you have spent two years cultivating a relationship suddenly moves to a branch miles away and you have to start all over again with someone new. So long as you are aware of what is happening and continue your marketing campaign, then you can carry on where you left off, albeit a little further down the field. What tends to happen is that the contacts are neglected until it suddenly dawns upon you that you have had no referrals for five or six months and you then discover that not only has your contact taken over as the manager of the local branch in Port Stanley, Falkland Islands, but that his replacement has just been seen having lunch with the senior partner of the firm down the road.

Accountants

Not only do accountants have a reputation of honesty and professionalism, they are also regarded as having the 'ear' of their business clients. They are considered men of affairs whose advice in business matters is not to be disregarded lightly. Solicitors in days gone by were regarded in at least as much standing, if not more, and it is a sad indictment of our profession that we have allowed ourselves to be usurped by fellow professionals. The Law Society is doing much in terms of improving the image of solicitors by marketing techniques and of raising the standards of the profession by means of the Practice Management Standards, but there is a lot of lost ground to make up. Accountants fit into the same category for these purposes as banks and building societies, namely, that it is often the case that they welcome the opportunity to be able, with confidence, to place a client in a safe pair of hands. They see this as simply another part of the total service that they are able to offer their business clients. If you can win the trust and confidence of a firm of accountants with the result that they feel able to recommend their clients to use your services, you will have secured a valuable source of referrals.

As fellow professionals, accountants approach business and the management of their own firms in the same way as solicitors, except that by and large they do it rather better. They know all about marketing techniques, business lunches, seminars, mail shots and the rest and you are unlikely to impress by the business lunch type approach. A totally direct and open form of marketing may be far more successful. You may have more success by suggesting a meeting whereby you could discuss in what ways your two firms could co-operate for their mutual benefit. Again, you will have to win their respect and vice versa. It would be wrong of you to refer your clients to them when they need the services of an accountant if you were not convinced that the firm was competent and it would be in the client's best interests to use them. By the same token, the accountants will need to be satisfied that you are the right firm for their clients. These relationships are not easy to build up, but if you succeed, then it can work very successfully to everyone's benefit, not least the client's benefit.

8. Newsletters

A newsletter is an opportunity to place your firm's existence and an image which you wish to convey in front of both existing and potential clients. It will need to tell its audience of recent changes in the law and give examples of how those changes might affect the reader. Putting together a newsletter is a suprisingly time-consuming business. In addition to the compilation of the newsletter itself, there is then the composition of the list of persons to receive it. The advent of computer databases and software programs that can easily handle mailing lists represent an enormous step forward in bringing such marketing tools within the grasp of even the humblest of practices, but it is nevertheless a substantial undertaking. Even if you have a client database and the necessary software on your computer, the software may not be easily programmable to enable you to sift through it and select only certain clients. There is no point in sending a newsletter which deals primarily with commercial matters to a divorce client unless that client is also a business person. A comparatively easy method of achieving the same end is by buying the Law Society's own newsletter which can be customised with your firm's own logo. Accountants have this particular marketing tool highly refined. They are able to produce a very polished product which looks very much as if it has been personally produced by the firm in question for comparatively low cost. Ideally, each firm would like to produce their own newsletter so that they can take full credit for its content and govern precisely what is included in it, but it may be difficult to devote sufficient time to do this exercise justice on a regular basis and cope with everything else in the daily routine of practice.

If you do go in for a newsletter, it is sensible to include some kind of disclaimer. This should not be phrased in such a way as to give the impression that you are not prepared to take responsibility for your own articles since they may well be wrong, but it should state that each situation is different and only general advice and guidance can be given in a newsletter and any clients who feel that they have specific problems related to the item in the newsletter should seek professional advice rather than relying on the contents of the newsletter, the advice preferably being given by you, of course!

9. Newspaper Column

If your local newspaper does not run a legal column, why not offer to write one for them? They might even pay you a modest £10 or so for it. A fortnightly column is more sustainable than a weekly one. It is amazing how copy deadline for even a fortnightly column will creep up on you before you know it. Once you have thought of an interesting and informative topic, it will take you about three-quarters of an hour to write. It must have direct relevance to the ordinary member of the public, or else people will not bother to read it. The article should state that you are a local solicitor and give a contact telephone number, but if the article looks too much like a commercial for your practice, it will not be read in a favourable light and will be counter-productive. Something of the order of 'Mr Bloggs is a solicitor practising locally in Any Town. Should you wish to speak him, you can contact him on 0181-111 2233' is perfectly acceptable and does not detract from your professional image.

10. Entertainment

Used sensibly, this can be a very powerful marketing tool. The bigger firms tend to go a little over the top with entertainment. They will have their golf days and their evenings at the theatre, the dinner dance, the box at Ascot and corporate hospitality tent at Twickenham. If you are not careful, you will create a state of affairs where a client accepts an invitation to that type of event because he or she feels flattered and because it is free, only to find that it is rather more of an imposition on their time than they had at first imagined and then they attend merely out of courtesy as they have left it too late to cancel. A ridiculous situation is then produced whereby they are attending only out of a sense of duty and to preserve good manners and you are giving up the whole of a Saturday or most of a Sunday evening thinking how you would rather be at home with your family and wondering how you are going to meet the expense of putting on the event and thinking how there must be an easier way of earning a living.

Make it Enjoyable

If you go in for this kind of marketing, then the event must be a thoroughly enjoyable one which preferably does not take up too much time and is sufficiently expensive to flatter your guests without anyone feeling that you are trying to buy their custom. A simple cocktail party for two or three hours, either at your offices or at home, can prove quite an enjoyable occasion. People will have the chance to meet new contacts amongst your other guests and may well feel honoured at the fact that you have included them on your guest list. The event does not take too long to organise and is not too costly. If people can drift in and out during the two or three-hour session, then it has not become a chore. They can drop in when it suits them without being tied to a deadline and can leave as soon as they become bored. It is important that you make the flexibility of the evening clear to your guests so as to take the pressure off them, both in terms of having to attend and the length of time they need to spend there. It is important to select your guests with care. Including some people who are friends or acquaintances of others who have not been invited can lead to the latter feeling left out. If needs be, have two such events and tell the second group that you have had to organise things that way in order to make the gatherings manageable. Take your lead from President Clinton who organised his celebratory election party by two such events so as not to offend some of his supporters whilst at the same time as rewarding the others. By means of such methods, the President was, on this occasion, able to please all of the people for much of the time.

In the summer a barbeque can often be a popular event. Like the cocktail party, you can quite successfully declare open house and let people drop in for an hour or two between certain times. If you pick the right day and you have a garden big enough for activities such as table tennis, badminton and so on, it can prove to be a very successful day and at comparatively low cost and without an enormous amount of organisation. The price that might be paid is of having to have a constant supply of food from the barbeque when you have no accurate picture of the numbers you will have to cater for, or when they will arrive.

Some firms with the necessary space available have been able to include their own games room for entertaining clients. Rather than inviting clients out for a full business lunch, they have invited them over for beer and sandwiches at lunch time coupled with a game of snooker or table tennis. An excellent idea if you have space available, even if you do have to let the client win every once in a while. Similarly, a bridge evening with clients and their other halves can prove enjoyable unless those concerned are likely to take the game too seriously.

How about a quiz evening? If your own staff are willing to make time available for a couple of hours in the evening to make up a team, perhaps with an additional client on their side here and there with other clients and their staff or friends making up two or three other teams, a very pleasant evening can be spent. All of these kinds of events demonstrate that you understand the need to market your practice and are prepared to make time available to do so and will enable people to get to know you better, affording you the opportunity to make new contacts with those people who have not met you before and reinforcing the ties that exist with those who are already clients of the practice.

CHAPTER 19

Good Luck

Well, you have read the book, do you have the nerve to boldy go where only a few have gone before? Many people consider setting up in practice on their own or starting a new firm with one or two others, but only a small proportion of those who consider it actually go through with it. If you do decide to take that great leap into the unknown then, if nothing else, it will be an enormously valuable experience. You will be a better person and quite possibly a better solicitor for it. Only those people who have taken that step fully appreciate the size of the undertaking and the considerable achievement and satisfaction of making a success of a practice that they have started themselves. It must be fairly close to the feeling someone gets who has built their own home. Building a practice is not nearly so clear cut. You are never quite sure when you have finished. Indeed, do you ever finish? There must come a point in time when the man who has built his own home feels confident that it is not going to fall down. It takes a long time before someone who has built their own practice manages to banish the phantoms of bankruptcy and failure from their everyday thoughts. There is no set time for the sole practitioner to put away lists of expenses and billing figures and to abstain from the frenzied addition of the figures in a frantic attempt to convince him or herself that the practice is still solvent. Indeed, such exercises should be part of regular routine. The only difference is the reduction in intensity of the blind panic in which the calculations take place.

Be assured of two things. Firstly, it is normal to feel that way, not just for a few months but for a few years. The constant nagging doubt is a spectre called failure. No one likes to fail and and the ever-present fear in the early years is that the practice will crumble and you will have to undergo the ignomy of admitting to your friends and colleagues that you could not make a go of it and have had to look for a job. Do not let this put you off. You won't fail. Those practices that fold normally do so as a result of being too successful as solicitors, but which lack proper management and fail after a number of years to take corrective action in time. Anyway, you gave it a go whilst your friends didn't.

Secondly, the fear and the doubt will pass. As one year builds on another, history is on your side. If you made it through last year, why should you not make it through this year, or the year after? With proper planning and management, you will keep the risks as small as possible and in as many different compartments as possible. Even if something does go wrong, the chances are that a quick damage limitation exercise will have the ship back on an even keel. There is no need to be afraid of failure if your failures are little ones and, as the boss of the firm, it is part of your job to anticipate the dangers and failures and to make sure that the risks you run are acceptable risks and that if the cards do not go your way, then the result is something of a minor inconvenience rather than a catastrophic event.

Probably one of the biggest disadvantages of being in a small practice is that of isolation. In a larger firm, there is much greater interaction with other firms. Your partners will have friends who are partners in other practices of different sizes and types. Even if they do not know you, almost certainly your assistant solicitors, legal executives and your secretaries will have contacts within other firms. From these various contacts, you will get feedback as to how everyone else is doing. When you find that everyone else is in just a big a mess as you are, you begin to relax. Whether you should do or not is immaterial. Misery loves company. If things are going wrong for everyone else and you are doing no more badly than anyone else, then you feel it is not really your fault.

As a sole practitioner or partner in a small firm, your lines of communication with other firms are very much more restricted and when things begin to go wrong you tend to fear the worst and think it is the beginning of the end. Because there is no one or very few people with whom you can share your problems and talk over your difficulties, you may well begin to panic. Your morale is likely to drop and before you know where you are, you are thinking of running down the shutters and handing in the keys to the landlord. Quite by chance you may be lucky enough to have a conversation with someone in another firm, or perhaps one of your larger clients who is starting to use you as a shoulder to cry on, explains how their fee income has dropped by 50 per cent in the past month, which in itself was 30 per cent down on the previous month and how they are going to have to lay off 30 staff and have a 'crunch' meeting with the bank next week that everyone is dreading. Suddenly, you feel normal. It is not that you are making a mess of things – it is just that market forces are operating against you. You may resist the temptation to tell your friend that you have just had to sack the cleaner and buy a new mop and bucket for yourself and that you have just managed to duck out of your crunch meeting with your bank manager and have put it off for a further three weeks in case the client gets the wrong idea.

With a bit of luck, the next phone call might produce what seems to be a promising client. Suddenly you feel perhaps you might persevere with the practice for another month. Next minute you look out of the window and the sun is shining and things really don't seem quite as bad as they did a little while ago. You will have your failures but undoubtedly you will have your successes too. If you decide to start a new practice, you will be in for exciting times. Good luck and fasten your seat belt. If this book has done anything to ease the birth pangs involved in the delivery of your new practice into the turbulent world of clients, landlords, tax inspectors and similar irredeemable reprobates, then my labours in writing this book will have been most amply rewarded.

APPENDICES

Specimen Deed of Partnership

THIS DEED OF PARTNERSHIP is made the Twenty-third day of November One Thousand Nine Hundred and **B E T W E E N RAYMOND GREED** (hereinafter called '**Mr. Greed**') of the first part **ANDREW PLEASANT** (hereinafter called '**Mr. Pleasant**') of the second part **JOHN STRANGE** (hereinafter called '**Mr. Strange**') of the third part and **CHRISTOPHER DEVIOUS** (hereinafter called '**Mr. Devious**') of the fourth part (and which persons are in this deed referred to as '**the Partners**')

WHEREAS:
(1)   The Partners (with other persons who have retired from partnership) [1] practised as Solicitors in partnership together at 1 Crooks Corner London WC2 under the firm name and style of **GREED & CO.** until the Thirtieth day of September One Thousand Nine Hundred and Ninety Five and the Partners have agreed to practise as Solicitors in partnership from the First day of October One Thousand Nine Hundred and Ninety Five
(2)   The Partners have agreed to enter into this deed to record the terms on which they practise in partnership as Solicitors from the First day of October One Thousand Nine Hundred and Ninety Five.

NOW THIS DEED WITNESSETH as follows:
1.   **THE** Partners hereby agree to carry on the profession of Solicitors in partnership under the name of '**Greed Strange & Partners**'

2(1)   **THE** Partnership shall begin on the First day of October One Thousand Nine Hundred and Ninety Five

2(2)   **THE** offices of the partnership shall be at 1 Crooks Corner London WC2 and at such other place or places as the Partners may from time to time agree

3. **THE** following property shall be deemed to be assets of the partnership and shall belong to the Partners in the proportions in which they shall from time to time share profits, that is to say:-

3(1) The freehold office premises 1 Crooks Corner London WC2

3(2) Goodwill of the partnership business

4(1) **THE** capital required for carrying on the partnership business shall be contributed from time to time by the Partners in shares to be agreed between them from time to time (but with the intention that ultimately it shall be contributed by the Partners equally)

4(2) **CAPITAL** contributed by the Partners shall not carry interest unless otherwise agreed [2]

5. **THE** Bankers of the partnership are Solid Bank PLC or as may otherwise by appointed by the Partners

6. **ALL** partnership monies not required for current expenses and securities for money shall as and when received be paid into the partnership Bank to the credit of the partnership accounts and all monies and securities received by the partnership or by any Partner on behalf of any client or third person shall forthwith be paid to such client or third person or (as the case may require) shall forthwith be paid into a separate client account with the said Bank and all cheques on any such accounts shall be drawn in the partnership name and may be so drawn by any Partner or person duly authorised by the Partners. Proper books of accounts and entries shall be kept and made by the Partners at any premises at which the partnership business shall be carried on and each Partner shall duly and punctually make full and proper entries of all business transacted by him on account of the partnership in accordance with such Rules as may be prescribed from time to time by the Law Society

7. **EACH** Partner shall devote the whole of his time and attention to the partnership business and no Partner shall without the consent of all the other Partners engage in any other business or hold any office or appointment PROVIDED ALWAYS that the emoluments from all offices and appointments held by any Partner during the partnership shall belong to the partnership

8. **EACH** Partner shall be entitled to four weeks holiday in each year

9. **IF** any Partner shall:-

(1) become bankrupt or insolvent or compound or make any arrangement with his creditors or

(2) grossly neglect the partnership business or

(3) commit or permit any serious wilful breach of the provisions hereof or

(4) be struck off the Roll of Solicitors

then and in any such case the other Partners may give to such Partner written notice requiring him to retire forthwith and upon receipt of such notice that Partner shall for the purpose of all the provisions hereof relating to the retirement of a Partner from the partnership be deemed to have retired from the partnership accordingly subject to such amendments as are necessary in consequence of such retiring Partner not retiring on the Thirtieth day of April in a year and provided also that the payment for goodwill under clause 17(1)(c) of this deed shall not apply

10. A Partner may be required to retire from the partnership upon being given not less than 12 months' written notice to that effect by all the other Partners (such notice to expire on the Thirtieth day of April of any year). The payment for goodwill under clause 17(1)(c) of this deed shall not apply unless the Partner has reached the age of 60 years by the expiration of the notice requiring his retirement [3]

11. **NO** Partner shall without the written consent of the other Partners:-

(1) enter into a contract with a trainee solicitor and any premium received in respect of a trainee shall belong to the partnership

(2) pledge the credit of the partnership except in the normal course of partnership business or give credit to or conduct any business for any person company or firm after being forbidden in writing to do so by all the other Partners

(3) engage directly or indirectly in any business or profession other than that of the partnership

(4) engage or (except for gross misconduct) dismiss any clerk servant or other employee of the partnership

(5) use any of the money goods or other partnership property except in the normal course of partnership business and for the benefit of the partnership

(6) enter into or agree to enter into any contract for any goods or services exceeding the value of One Hundred Pounds (£100) on behalf of the partnership

(7)   enter into any bond or become bail surety or security with or for any person or do or knowingly cause or permit or suffer partnership property or any part to be seized distrained upon or otherwise attached or executed upon

(8)   assign mortgage or charge his share of the partnership or any part of such share or make any other person a Partner in the partnership

12.   **EACH** Partner shall at all time duly and punctually pay his private debts whether present or future and keep the Partners and partnership property indemnified therefrom

13.   **ON** the Thirtieth day of April in every year or such other date as may be agreed a general account and balance sheet shall be taken and be made by Messrs Dodgey Accounting & Co. of 1 The Alleyway Fleecem Surrey Chartered Accountants (or by such other Chartered Accountants as may be agreed between the Partners) of all assets and liabilities of the partnership and of all the dealings and transactions of the partnership during the preceding twelve months and of all matters usually included in the accounts of a solicitor's practice and in taking such account a fair evaluation shall be made of all items requiring valuation and such account and balance sheet shall when signed by the Partners be binding on them save that if any manifest error shall be found therein and brought by any Partner to the attention of the other Partners within three calendar months after such signature the error shall be corrected

14(1)   **THE** profits of the partnership appearing in the yearly accounts shall be shared among the Partners in such proportions as they shall from time to time agree (provided that any one dissentient Partner shall be required to concur with the agreement reached by all the other Partners)

14(2)   **EACH** Partner may during the continuance of the partnership draw out of the partnership account at the Bank a monthly sum to be agreed with the other Partners on account of his share of profits PROVIDED THAT if when the said yearly account is taken at the end of the year it shall appear that any Partner has drawn any sum in excess of his share of the profits he shall forthwith repay such excess into the partnership accounts

15(1)   **IN** the case of the death of a Partner the surviving Partner or Partners shall as from the date of such death succeed to all of the assets of the partnership (including the goodwill) and the surviving Partner or Partners shall undertake all the debts liabilities and other obligations of the partnership and shall pay to the personal representatives of the deceased Partner the following sums (and no others) at the times set out below:-

(a) within three months of the completion of the partnership accounts for the financial year current at the date of death a sum equal to the share of profits he would have earned in the months up to the date of death had he survived to the end of such year divided by twelve and multiplied by the number of months the deceased Partner survived in that year less his drawings and his share of the partnership's liability for Income Tax [4]

(b) by eight equal half-yearly instalments commencing six months after the date of death of the deceased Partner the amount of any capital sum standing to the credit of such deceased Partner in the books of account of the partnership together with the amount of any sum standing to the credit of the Current Account of such deceased Partner in the books of account of the partnership at the end of the financial year immediately prior to the financial year in which such deceased Partner dies PROVIDING nevertheless as follows:-

(i) that any sums received by the surviving Partner or Partners from any Insurance Policy which the surviving Partner or Partners have or may have effected on the life of such deceased Partner shall be paid forthwith to the personal representatives of such deceased Partner as part or full payment of the sum due under sub-clause 15(1)(b) (but provided further that if the sum received by the surviving Partner or Partners under such Insurance Policy should exceed the sum due under this sub-clause the surplus after payment as aforesaid shall belong to the surviving Partner or Partners

(ii) in the case of the death of a Partner named in the Schedule hereto the amount payable to the personal representatives of the deceased Partner shall be reduced by the sum set opposite his name in the Schedule hereto (being the nominal value of the Endowment Policy of Assurance effected or intended to be effected by him on his own life) whether or not such Policy shall in fact have been effected and whether or not the same shall have remained in full force and effect down to the date of the deceased Partner's death [5]

(iii) pending payment to the personal representatives of such deceased Partner the net sum payable and from time to time remaining due shall carry interest at the rate of one per cent per annum over the base lending rate fixed by Solid Bank PLC (with a minimum of five per cent) at the time such interest is payable and such interest shall be payable half-yearly at the times here before appointed by sub-clause (1)(b) of this clause

(2) As between two or more surviving Partners they shall be and become entitled to the assets of such deceased Partner in such shares as they shall agree (provided that any one dissentient Partner shall be required to concur with the agreement reached by all the other Partners) and the share of profits previously enjoyed by such deceased Partner shall be apportioned between such surviving Partners in like manner

16.[6] **IN** the case of the death of a Partner the surviving Partner or Partners may in their absolute discretion if they think fit (but without being under any legal obligation so to do) make an ex gratia payment of a sum equivalent to one-third of the sum of the deceased Partner's share of profits in the preceding three completed years prior to his death such payment to be made to such dependant or dependants of the deceased Partner as the surviving Partner or Partners shall in their absolute discretion think fit and such payment shall be provided by the continuing Partners in the proportions in which they acquire the assets of such deceased Partner

17(1) **ANY** one Partner may upon giving at least twelve months' notice in writing to that effect to the other Partners expiring on the Thirtieth day of April in any year retire from the partnership and upon his retirement the remaining Partner or Partners shall as and from the date of such retirement succeed to all the assets of the partnership (including the goodwill thereof) and the remaining Partner or Partners shall undertake all the debts liabilities and obligations of the partnership and shall pay to the retiring Partner (or as he may direct) the following sums at the times stated below (but no other payment whatsoever) that is to say:-

(a) by eight equal half-yearly instalments commencing six months after the date of such retirement the amount of any capital sum standing to the credit of such retiring Partner in the books of account of the partnership together with the amount of any sum standing to the credit of the Current Account of such retiring Partner in the books of account of the partnership at the end of the financial year immediately prior to the financial year at which end such retiring Partner retires PROVIDING nevertheless that pending payment to such retiring Partner the net sum payable and from time to time remaining due shall carry interest at the rate of one per cent per annum over the base lending rate fixed by Solid Bank PLC (with a minimum of five per cent) at the time such interest is payable and such interest shall be payable half-yearly at the times hereinbefore appointed by sub-clause (1)(a) of this clause

(b) within three months of the completion of the yearly accounts for the financial year ending at the date of his retirement a sum equal to the proportion of the retiring Partner's share of the profits for such year (but deducting from such sum the amount of the retiring Partner's drawings during that year and his share of the partnership's liability for Income Tax) PROVIDED nevertheless that in the case of the retirement of a Partner named in the Schedule hereto the amounts payable to such retiring Partner under sub-clause (1)(c) of this clause shall be reduced by the sum set opposite his name in the Schedule hereto (being the nominal value of the Endowment Policy of Assurance effected by him on his own life) whether or not such Policy shall in fact have remained in full force and effect down to the date of such Partner's retirement

(c)   in the event that the retiring Partner has reached the age of 60 by the expiration of his notice to retire from partnership by eight half-yearly instalments commencing six months after the date of such retirement a payment for goodwill of a sum equivalent to one-third of the sum of such retiring Partner's share of profits in the preceding three completed years prior to his retirement [7]

(2)   As between two or more of the remaining Partners they shall be and become entitled to the share of partnership assets of such retiring Partner in such shares as they shall agree (provided that any one dissentient Partner shall be required to concur with the agreement reached by all the other Partners) and the share of profits previously enjoyed by such retiring Partner shall be apportioned between the remaining Partners in like manner and the amount payable to the retiring Partner under paragraph (c) of the foregoing sub-clause of this clause shall also be apportioned between the remaining Partners in like manner

18.   UPON the retirement (from the Partnership howsoever occasioned) or death of any Partner he or his personal representatives shall if so requested in writing by the continuing or surviving Partner or Partners join with him or them in giving Her Majesty's Inspector of Taxes a notice under Section 154(2) of the Income and Corporation Taxes Act 1970 or any statutory replacement or modification thereof for the time being in force and the Partner so retiring or the personal representatives of such deceased Partner shall be indemnified by the continuing or surviving Partner or Partners against any Income Tax which may be payable by him or them as a result of giving such notice in excess of the Income Tax which would have been payable if no such notice had been given

19.   ANY Partner retiring from the partnership and receiving a payment for goodwill hereby covenants with the other Partners and each of them that he (the retiring Partner) will not in England or Wales practise privately as a Solicitor either by himself or as the Partner or employee of any other person or firm for a period of three years from the date of such retirement PROVIDED that nothing

herein contained shall preclude him from acting for his relatives or any client for whom he shall have acted solely in an honorary capacity [8]

20.   **ALL** disputes and questions whatsoever which shall either during the partnership or afterwards arise between the Partners or their respective representatives or between any Partners or Partner and the representatives of any other Partner concerning this deed or the construction or application thereof or any clause herein contained or any account valuation or division of assets debts or liabilities to be made hereunder or the rights duties or liabilites of any person under this deed shall be referred to a single arbitrator agreed upon between the parties or failing agreement by the President of the Law Society and be subject to the Arbitration Acts 1950-1979 or any statutory modification thereof

IN WITNESS whereof the parties hereto have set their hands and seals the day and year first above written

THE SCHEDULE above referred to

Name of Partner	Name of Life Company	No. of Policy	Nominal Value
Mr. Greed	Fat Insurance Co. Ltd	CP33456	£30,000
Mr. Pleasant	Nice Life Insurance Co. Ltd	A5639083	£30,000
Mr. Strange	The Wierd Life Assurance Co.	C3423543	£30,000
Mr. Devious	Subtle Life Insurance Co.	C312456	£30,000

SIGNED SEALED and DELIVERED)
by the said **RAYMOND GREED** in the) ....
presence of:-)

SIGNED SEALED and DELIVERED)
by the said **ANDREW PLEASANT** in the) ....
presence of:-)

SIGNED SEALED and DELIVERED)
by the said **JOHN STRANGE** in the) ....
presence of:-)

SIGNED SEALED and DELIVERED)
by the said **CHRISTOPHER DEVIOUS** in) ....
the presence of:-)

Notes:

(1)   If appropriate.

(2)   Or 'shall carry interest at ___ per cent above the base lending rate of the partnership's Bankers prescribed from time to time'.

(3)   This clause is an expulsion clause. The Partner concerned need have committed no wrong and may simply have alienated himself from his fellow Partners. Careful thought should be given before including a clause of this kind in an agreement.

(4)   The purpose of the clause is to give the deceased's estate a share of profit averaged out over the year rather than just the months up until death to avoid an artificially high figure if the months to death were exceptionally good or a low figure if exceptionally poor.

(5)   If this clause is included, its effect can be draconian. It is designed to ensure that Partners take out life policies for the benefit of their fellow Partners and see to it that the premiums are maintained since if not, the payment to the next of kin of the sums due under the deed is reduced by the sum which the policy would have yielded.

(6)   Strictly speaking, such a clause is otiose, as it gives rise to no legal obligations. It may, however, provide comfort to some Partners who would like the deed to be more generous on death. It also provides a means of escape if at the time of death the Partnership is having a lean time, as the payments are discretionary.

(7)   The purpose of this formula is to take the average of three years' profits so that the goodwill payment is neither artificially inflated nor depressed by an unusually good or bad year.

(8)   Whether this clause will stand the test of reasonableness for restraint of trade purposes will depend to some extent on the age of the retiring Partner and the size of the goodwill payment. You may prefer to (a) make the covenant less onerous and (b) set out the restrictions in separate clauses to reduce the risk of the whole clause being struck down and the reasonable parts being thrown out along with the unreasonable.

APPENDIX 2

Specimen Consultant's Agreement

THIS AGREEMENT [1] is made the   day of   1995

B E T W E E N :
(1)   **GREED & CO.** of 1 Crooks Green, London, WC2 (**'the Partnership'**) and
(2)   **RONALD EVERGREEN** of 50 Long Road Enfield EN4 9PT (**'the Consultant'**)

1.   DEFINITIONS

In this Agreement the following expressions shall unless the context otherwise requires have the following meanings:-

'the Termination Date'   the date of termination of this Agreement howsoever occasioned

'the Consultant's Duties'   the duties of the Consultant as specified in the First Schedule

2.   TERM

The Partnership shall retain the services of the Consultant and the Consultant shall carry out the Consultant's duties from the date of this Agreement until the expiration of two years from such date [2]

3.   REMUNERATION

The Consultant shall be paid a Consultancy Fee of £120 (together with Value Added Tax) in respect of each day spent in the performance of the Consultant's duties payable on receipt of an appropriate invoice which shall be rendered at the end of each month

4.   EXPENSES

The Company shall repay to the Consultant all travelling hotel and other out-of-pocket expenses reasonably and necessarily incurred by the Consultant in the performance of the Consultant's Duties upon suitable evidence of such expenditure being provided to the Partnership

5.   PERFORMANCE OF DUTIES

5.1   The Consultant shall perform the Consultant's Duties in a good, efficient and proper manner consistent with the standards expected of a professional person

5.2   Subject to clause 5.4, the Consultant shall be expected to work for such period as the Partnership reasonably considers necessary to devote to the Partnership for the proper performance of the Consultant's Duties

5.3   The Consultant shall:-

5.3.1   be required to work for not less than 150 working days each year
5.3.2   not be required to work:-
5.3.2.1 during any holiday absence
5.3.2.2 in the case of illness or accident in which case he shall notify the Partnership immediately and shall provide such evidence as to his illness or accident as the Partnership shall reasonably require

5.4   For the purposes of this clause, the Consultant shall in addition to the usual bank or public holidays be entitled to be absent for the purpose of holidays for five weeks in each calendar year commencing 1st January to be taken at such times as may reasonably be agreed between the parties [3]

6.   SELF-EMPLOYED STATUS [4]

The Consultant is engaged as a self-employed contractor. He is not and shall not be deemed to be an employee of the Partnership for any purpose whatsoever. The termination of this Agreement by the Partnership or the expiry of its term without renewal shall not in any circumstances constitute or be deemed to constitute a dismissal for any purposes

7.   AUTHORITY

The Consultant shall not hold himself out as having power to nor shall he purport to bind the Partnership in any way whatsoever

8.   CONFIDENTIALITY

The Consultant shall not whether during the continuance of this Agreement or thereafter except in the proper course of his duties or as required by law use or divulge to any person, firm or company whatsoever and shall use his best endeavours to prevent the use or disclosure of any information concerning the businesses or finances of the Partnership, transactions or affairs of the Partnership or the names of or secrets of the clients of the Partnership which have or may come to his knowledge during the continuation of this Agreement

9.   OUTSIDE INTERESTS

The Consultant shall not during the continuance of this Agreement be directly or indirectly interested or concerned (other than as a holder for investment purposes only of securities not exceeding 5 per cent in nominal value of the securities of that class) in any capacity or manner whatsoever and whether as principal or agent in any company trade or business without the written permission of the Partnership which shall not be unreasonably withheld

10.   TERMINATION BY EVENTS OF DEFAULT

The Partnership may at any time and without prejudice to any rights or claims it may have against the Consultant by notice in writing terminate this Agreement forthwith and without any liability to pay any remuneration compensation or damages if at any time the Consultant shall:-

10.1   be guilty of serious misconduct, commit a material breach of any of the terms of this Agreement or wilfully neglect to perform or (other than as a result of illness accident or other such incapacity) prove to be incapable of performing the Consultant's Duties; or

10.2   become bankrupt or compound with his creditors or have any judgment against him which shall remain unsatisfied for more than one month or suffer execution against his effects; or

10.3   commit any act of fraud or dishonesty (whether or not connected with the performance of the Consultant's Duties); or

10.4   be prevented as a result of illness, accident or other such incapacity from performing the Consultant's Duties for any period in excess of six consecutive months;

211

10.5 be struck off the Roll of Solicitors or be suspended from practice;

10.6 be guilty of any conduct which brings or is likely to bring the Partnership into disrepute in the eyes of the profession or its clients

11. CONSULTANT'S OBLIGATIONS UPON TERMINATION

On the Termination Date the Consultant shall forthwith deliver to the Partnership all records, documents, accounts, letters and papers of every description (whether originals or copies) within his possession or control relating to the affairs and business of the Partnership and any other property belonging to the Partnership [5]

12. NOTICES
Any notice:-

12.1 shall be in writing;

12.2 to be given to the Partnership shall be sufficiently served if either delivered personally to or sent by first class post to its usual trading address for the time being

12.3 to be given to the Consultant shall be sufficiently served if delivered to him personally or sent by first class post to his usual or last known address

12.4 if posted shall be deemed to have been served at the time when in the ordinary course of post such notice would have been received

13. SURVIVAL OF COVENANTS ON TERMINATION

Notwithstanding the termination of this Agreement it shall remain in full force and effect insofar as the obligations of the Consultant that are expressed to operate or to have effect thereafter or are of a continuing nature are concerned and may be enforced against the Consultant accordingly

14. GENERAL

The provisions of the First and Second Schedules hereto form part of this Agreement which contains the whole of the terms agreed in respect of the Consultant's appointment as from the Commencement Date and is in substitution for any previous agreement or arrangement between the Consultant and the Partnership and shall only be capable of being varied by a supplemental agreement in writing signed by or on behalf of the parties hereto

Signed by   ....
on behalf of the Partnership

and by the Consultant   ....

THE FIRST SCHEDULE
The Consultant's Duties [6]

1. To provide advice and assistance to the Partnership in connection with any matters relating to the business of the Partnership which the Partnership may refer to him

2. To conduct the affairs of those clients of the Partnership as shall be referred to him by the Partnership PROVIDED ALWAYS that such matters shall be within the reasonable sphere of competence and experience of the Consultant

THE SECOND SCHEDULE
Restrictive Covenants [7]

1. The parties hereto agree and acknowledge as follows:-

1.1 it is reasonable and necessary for the protection of the goodwill and trade connections of the Partnership that the Consultant should be restrained in the terms of the covenants hereinafter set out from making available or using for the benefit of himself or a competitor or potential competitor information which he has obtained and is likely to obtain in the course of his engagement as a Consultant to the Partnership; and

1.2   after 12 months from the Termination Date the making available or use as aforesaid of the information will be less damaging to the goodwill and trade connections of the business by virtue of all or some parts of the information becoming redundant, non-confidential or out of date

2.   The Consultant accordingly covenants with the Partnership that in view of the circumstances referred to in clause 1 of this Schedule he will not without the prior written consent of the Partnership (such consent to be withheld only so far as may be reasonably necessary to protect the legitimate interests of the Partnership directly or indirectly):-

2.1   at any time during a period of 12 months from the date of termination of this agreement by whatever means:-
2.1.1   be engaged or concerned or interested or participate in or carry on business as or practise as a solicitor anywhere in England or Wales
2.1.2   solicit or entice in relation to a business which may in any way be in competition with the Partnership the custom of any person who at the date hereof or at any time during the period of 12 months prior to the date of termination of the agreement has been a client of the Partnership

3.   The Consultant hereby acknowledges and agrees with the Partnership that:-

3.1   each of the sub-paragraphs contained in paragraph 2 of this Schedule constitutes an entirely separate, severable and independent covenant by and restriction on him;

3.2   the duration, extent and application of each of the restrictions contained in paragraph 2 are no greater than is necessary for the protection of the goodwill and trade connections of the Partnership

3.3   if any restriction contained in paragraph 2 shall be found void but would be valid if some part were deleted, such restriction shall apply with such deletion as may be necessary to make it valid and effective

3.4   each of the covenants set out in paragraph 2 of this Schedule shall (without prejudice to any other rights or remedies of the Partnership) be enforceable by the Partnership against the Consultant by interlocutory injunction

Notes:

(1) The agreement is for a self-employed Consultant. You or the consultant may prefer the consultant to be an employee depending on the Consultant's personal circumstances. The Consultant may need to obtain an accountant's advice as to which status is preferable.

(2) This provides for a fixed term of two years. A longer term may be specified, or it can be converted into a 'rolling' agreement by adding, 'and thereafter shall continue until determined by either party serving at least six months' notice of termination on the other, unless otherwise determined in accordance with the terms of this agreement".

(3) If the terms agreed include provision of a motor car paid for by the Partnership it would be convenient to add in the terms as to who pays what. Current tax legislation may make this fiscally unattractive, since if self-employed, the Consultant can deduct the cost of providing his own car from his tax bill as an expense.

(4) See note (1).

(5) If the Consultant's terms include provision of a car, include here a clause for its return in a good and clean condition.

(6) The precise terms will need to be agreed with the Consultant, but it is in the Partnership's interests to have the clause reasonably wide. Alternatively, have one clause describing a narrow area which both parties expect to cover the area in which the Consultant is expected to be employed and then a saving clause such as, '2. such other duties as the Consultant may reasonably be expected to carry out taking into account his particular skills and areas of experience'.

(7) The extent to which it is reasonable to require a Consultant to give restrictive covenants at all is debatable. It will depend on the age of the Consultant whether he or she was formerly a partner in the firm and for how long and the likelihood of him or her being able to set up a competing practice and the level of damage thus inflicted. Bear in mind the clause as drafted precludes the Consultant from earning a living for a year and a court will require to be satisfied this is reasonable on the facts before allowing it to stand. It may be safer to restrict the proximity to the firm's offices in which the Consultant may practise rather than an absolute ban.

Explanatory Notes on New Practices from SIF

These notes are for help and guidance only and in no manner supersede the Solicitors Indemnity Rules in force from time to time.

1. NEW PRACTICE

A new practice is a practice which is set up entirely from scratch without succeeding to any part of another firm's client base.

As the practice has no gross fee income it is not possible either to assess its contribution or its deductible by reference to actual gross fees as would be the case with established practices, which have to return annually details of gross fees, accounting periods, principals, staffing levels, and other information during the month of March in a Gross Fees Certificate.

The contribution payable by a new practice commencing between the 1st September and the 28th day of February is the minimum payable plus value added tax at the date of commencement. A new practice commencing between the 1st March and the 31st August pays a contribution of one half of the minimum plus value added tax at the date of commencement.

The contribution can either be paid in one lump sum or in the appropriate number of equal monthly instalments by direct debit (not exceeding ten) the first payment to be made on the 1st day of the month following inception of cover and the last on 1st August.

The deductible (otherwise called a self-insured excess) applicable to all claims notified to Solicitors Indemnity Fund for the current year is 1% of gross fees notified for the purpose of contribution calculation, subject to a minimum standard deductible of £3,000 and a maximum deductible of £150,000, irrespective of the number of principals in the firm. A new practice is deemed to have gross fees of £100,000 per principal for calculating the amount of the deductible which will still be subject to the minimum and maximum mentioned above. The deductible is additionally subject to an aggregate limitation on the amount a practice can be asked to pay in respect of claims notified in an indemnity year. Currently the aggregate provision is 3 times the standard deductible.

Thus, a new practice which has a deductible of £3,000 (the minimum standard deductible) will have a total aggregate liability for deductibles under the Rules of £3,000 x 3 = £9,000. By way of example, assume this firm notifies four claims in the indemnity year which are settled for £5,000, £4,000, £2,000 and £7,000 respectively. The firm would be called upon to pay £3,000 on the first two claims, the whole amount of the third claim as it falls totally within the deductible, but only £1,000 on the fourth claim.

The first claim uses up £3,000 of the deductible as does the second, but the third uses up only another £2,000. These payments total £8,000 leaving £1,000 of the aggregate deductible to be paid on the fourth claim. Any further claims would be met in full without the firm being asked to make any contribution by way of deductible.

The deductible and the aggregate can be varied upon payment of additional contribution if desired. The full range of options is open to all new practices. As these are subject to a minimum contribution the option of totally deleting the deductible is usually the most cost effective.

2. SUCCESSION

When a principal leaves a practice taking with him part of the client base of his former firm, however small, two successions for the purposes of the Solicitors Indemnity Rules occur. The first succession is that of the leaving principal to a proportion of his former firm and the second succession is that of the remaining principals to the balance of the former firm. Successions will also occur when a practice disposes, whether for value or not of part of the existing practice, e.g. on the sale of a branch office to another solicitor whether he be a principal or not.

A merger is a succession where one practice succeeds to the whole or part of two or more predecessor practices. The principles governing the calculation and payment of contribution and the calculation of deductible are the same as for any other practice.

All successor practices are required to complete a Notice of Succession containing certain of the information required in the annual Gross Fees Certificate.

Practices involved in successions after delivery of a Gross Fees Certificate but before the commencement of the indemnity year should complete the Notice of Succession together with a fresh Gross Fees Certificate to enable an accurate contribution calculation to be made.

Apart from details of principals, names and addresses of the practice and the name and address of any predecessor practices, i.e. the practices to whose client base the successor practice has succeeded in part or in whole, S.I.F. need to know, most importantly, the proportions of the predecessor practices to which there has been a succession.

There are two basic methods of determining the proportions. The easiest way is to agree between the principals the percentages of the predecessor practice's business to which each successor practice succeeds. The second way is for each successor practice to return a gross fee figure rather than leaving S.I.F. to apply a percentage to the predecessor practice's declared gross fees used in the contribution calculation. This approach is more often adopted when branch offices are involved in the succession.

Whichever method is adopted please note that S.I.F. can only accept percentages or figures which add up to the whole of the predecessor practices' gross fees. Any potential or actual loss of clients arising from the dissolution and succession must be ignored for this purpose. In the event of a disagreement between the principals on the proportions involved, the issue will have to be referred to the Law Society which has powers under the Solicitors Indemnity Rules to make a determination.

3. THE CALCULATION OF SUCCESSOR PRACTICES' BASIC CONTRIBUTION

(i) In the current year

The basic contribution paid by all predecessor practices covers all successor practices until the 31st August next (the end of the indemnity year).

If the basic contribution has been paid in full any apportionment must be a matter between the principals in the practices concerned. S.I.F. does not give refunds to any predecessor practices nor does it claim additional basic contributions from any successor practices for the balance of the year.

If any predecessor practice has opted for payment by instalments then the Rules stipulate that when a practice ceases during the indemnity year (with or without) successors in part or in whole the amount of any monthly instalments outstanding due and to be paid during the year shall be payable in full immediately prior to cessation. However, S.I.F. will not seek the full amount due so long as:

(a)   the principals in the ceased practice continue to pay the original direct debits or

(b)   the principals in any successor practices continue to pay by direct debit the outstanding amount due from the ceased practice.

Again, this is a matter to be settled by the principals in the practices. All that S.I.F. requires is one or more direct debits for the balance of the contribution payable by the predecessor practice or alternatively, the outstanding balance in full.

Two or more practices which merge totally will be asked to pay in full, continue their existing direct debit mandates or provide a fresh one.

(ii) Thereafter

The contribution payable on the 1st September immediately following the succession will, of necessity, be based upon the gross fees for the predecessor practice. It cannot be calculated against a successor practice's gross fees until that practice has had a 12-month accounting period expiring on or before the 31st March immediately preceding the commencement of an indemnity year.

The proportions, referred to in note 2, will need to be applied against the predecessor practice's gross fees when making the annual return in the Gross Fees Certificate. Detailed notes are issued annually to assist in completion of the Certificate. Mention is made of it at this stage to ensure that successor practices are aware that any decision over the proportions into which a practice has divided has a longer term relevance than might initially be appreciated.

Merged practices need to supply details of all predecessor practices' gross fee income in the annual gross fees return. Although there will be no difficulty in providing apportionments (except in the case of partial mergers) some problems may be encountered due to the use of different accounting periods by the predecessor practices, but S.I.F. will be able to offer advice.

4. THE CALCULATION OF THE SUCCESSOR PRACTICE'S DEDUCTIBLE

The deductible applicable to claims notified to S.I.F. on or after the 1st September last is 1% of the gross fees notified for the purpose of contribution calculation, subject to a minimum deductible of £3,000 and a maximum deductible of £150,000 irrespective of the number of principals in the firm. In addition the deductible is subject to an aggregate limitation on the amount a practice is asked to pay in respect of claims notified in an indemnity year of 3 times the standard deductible applicable to that firm.

The gross fees notionally assigned to each successor practice as agreed between the principals in the practices concerned will form the basis of each successor practice's deductible in respect of claims notified after the succession.

When a succession occurs there is an immediate need to determine the deductible applicable to each successor practice. In order to do this S.I.F. should be advised as soon as possible of the proportions in which the predecessor practice divided. How this can be done is discussed in Note 2 above. If percentages are used S.I.F. will then apply those percentages to the gross fees used in the contribution calculation of the predecessor practice as at the 1st September last. The gross fees thus notionally assigned to the successor practices will then form the basis of their own deductible contribution in respect of claims notified after the date of the succession. If gross fee figures are submitted then the deductible will be calculated against those figures.

When the succession arises from a merger the practice's deductible will be calculated on the combined gross fees of all predecessor practices.

5.   DEDUCTIBLE AMENDMENT

Both the deductible and the aggregate referred to above can be varied upon payment of additional contribution if desired and the detailed deductible and amendment option notes describe the various permutations.

Successor practices will have the options of:-

(a)   continuing or cancelling the predecessor practice's deductible amendment or

(b)   effecting their own new deductible amendment.

Please discuss individual requirements with one of our Practice Advisors.

6.   EVIDENCE OF INDEMNITY*

Evidences of Indemnity are only required for submission to the Law Society upon application for the issue of a Practising Certificate in November each year. When a succession occurs after the issue of the Practising Certificate then there is no need to submit a further copy to the Law Society.

However, when the succession takes place before the 1st November then the principals in the successor practices need to present evidence of the changes to the Law Society. In most cases, rather than issuing a revised Evidence of Indemnity, S.I.F. will issue a confirmatory letter stating that as from a given date the named principals are practising at a given address under a given style.

Such letter will be issued only after the contribution due for the predecessor practice has been paid in full or direct debit mandate forms for the full amount of the contribution payable have been received from the successor practices.

January 1993

*The procedure has since changed and Evidences of Indemnity are no longer issued. Confirmation of payment of the indemnity contribution is provided by S.I.F. direct to the Law Society.

Specimen Business Plan

Information required	Example plan
1. Name:	M.S.J. Smith Esq.
2. Practising as:	Martin Smith & Co.
3. Business address:	17-21 Shenley Road Borehamwood, Herts WD6 1AD.
4. Partnership/Sole trader:	Sole trader.
5. Services offered:	The full range of contentious and non-contentious services normally associated with a 'High Street' type of practice. Whilst it is intended that the practice will be registered under the Financial Services Act to carry out Investment Business, it is not expected that this will be a major area of operation for the first two years.
6. Business start date:	Proposed start date: 1st December 1995.
7. Business objectives:	To establish a wide client base incorporating both private and business clients and to provide a wide range of legal services to satisfy the needs of both. It is anticipated that the client base will initially consist of clients associated with a previous practice and thus outside the locality, with the balance shifting as the new practice becomes known. It is intended to offer a service to legally aided clients as well as private paying clients and to develop this particularly in the field of family law.

8. Capital to be provided: £25,000 to be introduced by M.S.J. Smith.

9. Staff:	Position	Name, Age and Qualifications (if known)	Start Date	Salary £
1.	Part-time Secretary and Book-keeper	Mrs Rachel Smith	01/12/95	5,000.00
2.	Trainee Solicitor	Michael Pulford	01/03/96	12,000.00

Services offered and potential market	**Example plan**
Services offered: Brief details of the services you are to provide should be given together with proposed charging structure (details of individual hourly rates and/or fixed fees).	(see Note 1)
Your market and potential: Indicate your likely clients, where they will come from and their potential.	(see Note 1)
Other competitors: Ascertain who they are likely to be and if possible their strengths and weaknesses together with estimated charges to clients.	(see Note 1)

Fee income and break-even figure:

	£
Fee income level projected in first year:	42,000

Fee income break-even figure.
(This is equivalent to total overheads
of the practice).

Total overheads	43,545

Note 1: With a solicitors' practice, this information need not be overly detailed. Bank managers will have a reasonably clear idea of what solicitors do. Show just enough information to demonstrate you have thought about the problems you are likely to face and are not expecting just to put your sign on the door and work to come flooding in.

MONTHLY PROFIT AND LOSS ACCOUNT FORECAST

NOTES ON BUDGETED FIGURES

General Comments

The budgeted monthly profit and loss account forecast is given purely as a guide and is not intended to account for every eventuality in respect of your practice. Every practice is unique and there are almost certain to be additional items which will need to be included in your forecast and some in the example which you may not need.

The profit and loss account forecast is drawn up on an accruals basis. This means, for example, that rent which is shown in the cash flow forecast as paid on the usual quarter days, is paid in advance for the coming three-month period and, therefore, the cost in respect thereof is spread over those three months. Other items, however, are accounted for as the expenditure is incurred and such items may include motor expenses, periodicals and sundries.

In the forecast, it has been assumed that the practice is VAT registered and, therefore, budgeted fee income and overhead costs are shown net of VAT. If the practice is below the VAT threshold, currently £45,000 and decides not to register for VAT then VAT will not be applied to fees charged out, but will also not be recoverable on any expenditure incurred which has VAT thereon. These overhead expenses would then need to be shown in the profit and loss account inclusive of VAT.

Fee Income

1. Estimating fees chargeable throughout the first year, and the timing of the fees, are likely to be the most difficult figures to forecast. Consideration will need to be given to how quickly you expect to start undertaking chargeable work, the length of time that work is likely to take, the actual amount of work involved and when you are likely to be able to charge, possibly on account of final fees. This will depend on the circumstances relating to each individual practice.

In the example, fees are budgeted based on the fee income during the first year of a now well established practice. As will be seen, initial fees chargeable are low, with peaks and troughs arising thereafter throughout the year, depending upon the timing and completion of the work.

Other Income

2. *Interest received*

Large sums of money may well be held on clients' call accounts and interest received by the practice thereon. This interest is usually received twice yearly, in June and December, and is reflected accordingly in the budget on a receipts basis.

Overheads

3. *Salaries and Employment Costs*

Employment of staff will need to be given careful thought, particularly in relation to the projected level of fee income. In the example staff costs have been calculated, as follows:

	Monthly £
a. First three months:	
Part-time secretary at £5,000 per annum:	
Gross £5,000 ÷ 12	417
Employer's N.I. at 3.6%	15
	432

b. After three months:

It is assumed that due to the increase in work load, the part-time secretary's hours need to be increased and one fee-earner is taken on. The figures throughout the remaining nine months will then be:

	£
Part-time secretary now at £7,500 per annum:	
Gross £7,500 ÷ 12	625
Employer's N.I. at 5.6%	35
	660
Fee-earner at £12,000 per annum:	
Gross £12,000 ÷ 12	1,000
Employer's N.I. at 10.2%	102
	1,762

The employer's national insurance rate varies according to gross pay and this needs to be considered in the calculations.

4. Rent and Rates

The offices are rented from a firm of accountants, who have spare space, and rent and rates of £1,620 are invoiced and payable on the usual quarter days in advance. However, for the purposes of the profit and loss account this needs to be spread over the applicable three month period, giving a budgeted profit and loss account charge of £540 per month.

5. Property Insurance

This is assumed to be payable once a year in advance, but in the profit and loss account is spread throughout the year. Insurance can often be paid in instalments throughout the year, although a charge may be made for this option.

6. Light and Heat

Electricity and gas charges are often billed quarterly in arrears. The likely charge for each quarter needs to be spread over the appropriate three months and it needs to be borne in mind that charges are likely to be higher for the winter months compared with the summer months.

7. Property Repairs

The occurrence of repairs will depend upon the condition of the property occupied and any budgeted figures will need to take this into account.

8. Equipment Rental

Photocopier rental of £450 is assumed to be payable quarterly in advance and is, therefore, spread over the applicable months. In addition, depending upon the type of agreement, there may be a maintenance charge payable depending upon machine usage.

9. Equipment Maintenance

This will depend upon the condition of the equipment purchased and whether it is covered by guarantees, but this does need to be considered. The charge shown here is only in respect of the service contract for the fax of £192 annually.

10. Printing, Postage and Stationery

There will be some hefty expenditure incurred initially on set up, which in the example is made up as follows:

	£
a. Cost of setting up and printing 1,000 letter heads	150
b. Additional stationery:	
Copy paper	
File covers and correspondence files	
Accounts notebooks	
Copy paper for word processor	
Typewriter ribbons, envelopes, pens, etc.	160
c. Document exchange joining fee	150*
d. Postage stamps (three months' worth)	185
e. Law stationery forms (wide range of commonly used forms sufficient for three/six months)	350

* Since the business plan was prepared the joining fee has been increased to £200.

f. 50 interview/attendance note pads   90

g. Manual accounts system   500

Total (Part of £1,610 shown in December)   1,585

Throughout the year there will be odd bits and pieces of stationery required month by month. Every once in a while, items such as letter heads will need to be re-ordered.

11. Law Library and Books

On set up, there is likely to be substantial expenditure incurred, depending upon what you feel is essential as far as your own library is concerned. Thereafter, the expenditure may be minimal month by month, but again this will depend upon what you think you require.

12. Periodicals

Expenditure on newspapers and magazines, etc, is really optional rather than necessary. You may wish to provide some reading in your reception area for your clients whilst they are waiting to see you.

13. Advertising

As little or as much can be spent on advertising as you feel is required. It may be that you will want a concerted advertising campaign in the first month or two, thereafter you will just take a small advertising box in the local press each month, and from time to time depending on how the work is coming in have a more determined effort. For the long term you will need a properly thought out campaign involving entries in yearly directories.

14. Telephone

There will be initial connection charges to account for in setting up the telephone line and system. In the example £440 is assumed for this. Thereafter, the usual quarterly rental and call charges are likely to increase as the practice expands.

15. Motor Expenses

Motor road fund tax and insurance is assumed to be accounted for in the first month. There will then be monthly running expenses, particularly fuel and oil, and depending upon the age and condition of the vehicle servicing and repair costs from time to time.

16. Accountancy

It has been assumed that a fee of £2,400 will be chargeable for preparation of the first year's accounts and reporting on those accounts in accordance with the Solicitors' Accounts Rules.

17. Subscriptions

Membership of the Law Society is free of charge. No other subscriptions have been assumed in this example.

18. Professional Indemnity

An amount of £504 is assumed to be payable in advance as contribution to Solicitors Indemnity Fund in respect of the first year but see Appendix 3 for the basis of assessment of the contribution for a new practice and the importance of ascertaining what this will be at an early stage.

19. Bad Debts

It is assumed that the collection of fees charged is well controlled, often with funds being provided by the client and held on clients' call account before the work is actually undertaken. However, there is bound to be some experience of bad debts and a notional amount of £50 per month has been provided in the second six months of the year.

20. Sundry Expenses

There are bound to be items not budgeted for above which crop up from time to time and it is usual to provide a figure month by month for such eventualities. The amount provided will depend upon how detailed you have already been in breaking down your overhead expenditure.

21. Depreciation

It is assumed that the furniture and office equipment are acquired on commencement of the practice and that no further assets are acquired or any assets disposed of during the rest of the first year. The motor vehicle is assumed to be owned by the proprietor and brought into the practice at its market value.

Details of the assets on set up are shown on the attached schedule together with depreciation rates and the calculations thereof.

Depreciation policy is a matter to be determined by each practice and would often be determined in discussions with the firm's accountants. The rates given in the example are therefore not necessarily the right rates to use for your practice, but are merely an example of rates that could be used in suitable circumstances.

22. Net Profit (Loss)

After much careful consideration being given in order to produce the above figures, the forecast will now show month by month whether you will be making a profit or a loss, together with an overall figure for the first year.

The example shows that the practice has in fact come out with a small loss of £720 for the year. The actual figure in respect of the practice on which this budget is based showed a somewhat larger loss for the first year, but is now well established and has since been trading profitably. You should, therefore, not become too concerned if the first year shows a small loss or little profit, as there are inevitable one-off set-up costs to be accounted for in the first year anyway. The most important thing is to be objective in your forecasts and realistic about the figures used, especially in respect of the budgeted fee income.

230

FIXED ASSETS

Office furniture:

No.	Description	£
4	4-drawer filing cabinet	480
5	Desks (second-hand)	300
2	Secretaries'/typists' chairs	60
1	Principal's chair	180
2	Client chairs	100
2	Fee-earners' chairs	170
2	Storage cupboards for stationery	300

Total   1,590

Depreciation

Suggested rate: 10% on cost

Depreciation first year £1,590 x 10%   159

Monthly budgeted figure £159 ÷ 12   13

Office equipment:

No.	Description	£
2	Electric typewriters	700
1	Word-processing system: Monitor with hard disk, keyboard, bubble jet printer and windows software	1,200
1	Fax machine	1,600
4	Dictating machines/transcribers with ancillary equipment (microphone/foot pedals/headsets, etc.)	1,406

Total   4,906

Depreciation

Suggested rate: 20% on cost

Depreciation first year £4,906 x 20%   981

Monthly budgeted figure £981 ÷ 12   82

Motor vehicle:

No.	Description	£
1	Second-hand Volkswagen Golf 4 door GL	
	Reg. No: K198 NJH	10,000

Depreciation

Suggested rate: 25% on cost -

Depreciation first year £10,000 x 25%   2,500

Monthly budgeted figure £2,500 ÷ 12   208

MONTHLY CASH FLOW FORECAST

NOTES ON BUDGETED FIGURES

General Comments

Having produced a monthly profit and loss account forecast the next stage is to produce a monthly cash flow forecast.

The figures shown in the cash flow forecast, although related to the figures given in the profit and loss account forecast, will not be related to each other on a month by month basis. This is due to the timing of cash inflows and outflows usually being quite different to fee invoices raised and expenses invoices received as shown in the profit and loss account forecast.

Various assumptions have to be made in producing the cash flow forecast and for the purposes of the example given those assumptions have been greatly simplified. For example, all fee income shown in the profit and loss account forecast is assumed to be collected together with the applicable VAT thereon, one month later. In reality, some of the fees may be collected during the month billed, some may be collected one, two or three, etc., months later.

VAT has been added to the fee income collected and similarly, where applicable, added to the overhead expenditure incurred.

Fee Income (including VAT)

1. As already mentioned above, fee income is assumed to be collected in the following month (i.e. one month later) after billing. No cash is assumed to be received in respect of the fee income although in practice you may receive some cash. The table below shows how the collection of fee income, as debtors, is calculated from the fee income figures forecast in the profit and loss account:

Profit and Loss Account Month	Net Debtors £	Cash Received VAT re Debtors at 17.5% £	Total £	Cash flow Month
0	-	-	-	1
1	1,000	175.00	1,175.00	2
2	2,000	350.00	2,350.00	3
3	2,750	481.25	3,231.25	4
4	2,000	350.00	2,350.00	5
5	5,500	962.50	6,462.50	6
6	6,750	1,181.25	7,931.25	7
7	4,000	700.00	4,700.00	8
8	6,500	1,137.50	7,637.50	9
9	3,350	586.25	3,936.25	10
10	3,000	525.00	3,525.00	11
11	3,500	612.50	4,112.50	12
12	1,650	288.75	1,938.75	Y/E Debtors
	42,000	7,350.00	49,350.00	

Other receipts
2. *Capital introduced*

It is assumed in this example that £25,000 of the proprietor's own capital is introduced into the business as cash.

It is also assumed that the proprietor already owned the motor vehicle introduced into the business. This has a market value of £10,000 and the proprietor will be given credit for the value of this vehicle in his capital account on the balance sheet. Therefore, the balance sheet will show total capital introduced of £35,000, being cash introduced of £25,000 and the market value of the motor vehicle introduced being £10,000.

3.   Loans received

It may be, if you are unable to introduce sufficient cash of your own in order to set the business up, you need to borrow money possibly from a bank, perhaps a relative or friend or some other lending source.

4.   Disposals of assets

No fixed assets have been disposed of in this example, during the first year, but any cash received in respect of any such disposals would need to be shown here.

5.   Interest received

Interest is assumed to be received twice yearly, in June and December, in respect of monies held on client call accounts.

Payments

6.   Drawings

It is assumed that the proprietor draws a regular monthly sum of £1,500. However, in practice this may not be achievable and the proprietor's drawings will fluctuate from month to month, depending upon the practice cash flow month by month.

An essential exercise to carry out is to review your own personal expenditure and commitments in order to establish the level of drawings you require on a monthly basis to fund your personal life style. This will be a vital consideration to bear in mind in considering the viability of your proposed business.

7&8. Salaries (Net) and PAYE/NIC

Salaries are usually paid at or towards the end of the month during which the staff are employed. The calculations detailed below give net pay and PAYE / NIC payable, assuming a single personal allowance of £3,445 and assuming 1994/95 tax and national insurance contribution rates:

a. First three months:

			Monthly £
Gross salary	A		417.00
Less: Personal Allowance Monthly £3,445 ÷ 12			287.08
Taxable Pay			129.92
PAYE	C		25.80
NIC: Employee's	D		21.94
	B		47.74
Net Pay A - B			369.26
Employer's NIC	E		15.01

Summary:	Net Pay A - B	369.26
	PAYE / NIC C + D + E	62.75
	Total Employer's Cost A + E	432.01

b. After three months:

		Monthly £	Monthly £
Gross salary per month	A	625.00	1,000.00
Less: Personal Allowances £3,445 ÷ 12		287.08	287.08
Taxable Pay		337.92	712.92
PAYE	C	71.75	165.50
NIC: Employee's	D	42.74	80.34
	B	114.49	245.84
Net Pay A - B		510.51	754.16
Employer's NIC	E	35.00	102.10

Summary:	Net Pay A - B	1,264.67
	PAYE / NIC C + D + E	497.43
	Total Employer's Cost A + E	1,762.10

For PAYE purposes the tax year is divided into 12 months ending on the 5th of each month. PAYE and NIC is due in respect of each month then ended by the 19th of that month, i.e. two weeks later. Therefore, for example, PAYE and NIC in respect of the salary paid in December is due by 19 January. Net pay and PAYE and NIC will be paid out as follows:

Cash flow Month	Net Pay £	PAYE & NIC £	Total £
Dec	369	-	
Jan	369	63	
Feb	369	63	
Mar	1,265	63	
Apr	1,265	497	
May	1,265	497	
June	1,265	497	
July	1,265	497	
Aug	1,265	497	
Sept	1,265	497	
Oct	1,265	497	
Nov	1,265	497	
Y/E Creditor	-	497	
	12,492	4,662	17,154

9. Fixed assets

Fixed assets are assumed to be bought and paid for in the first month, as follows:

	£
As per fixed assets schedule:	
a. Office furniture	1,590
b. Office equipment	4,906
	6,496
V.A.T. @ 17.5%	1,137
Total	7,633

As already mentioned, it is assumed that the motor vehicle was owned by the proprietor and that this was introduced into the business at market value, therefore giving rise to no effect on the cash flow forecast.

10. Rent and Rates

Rent and rates of £1,620 are assumed to be paid on the usual quarter days, with an additional amount of £450 being paid for the first 25 days of December.

11. Property insurance

This is assumed to be payable once a year in advance in the first month.

12. Light and Heat

It is assumed that light and heat is payable quarterly in arrears, with VAT being accounted for thereon, as follows:

	Net £	VAT £	Total £
February	135.00	23.62	158.62
May	110.00	19.25	129.25
August	90.00	15.75	105.75
November	105.00	18.38	123.38
	440.00	77.00	517.00

13. Property repairs

These are assumed to be payable one month after the invoice is received, as follows:

	Net £	VAT £	Total £
April	100.00	17.50	117.50
August	100.00	17.50	117.50
	200.00	35.00	235.00

14. Equipment rental

The rental of £450 net in respect of the photocopier is assumed to be payable quarterly in advance, as follows:

	Net £	VAT £	Total £
December	450.00	78.75	528.75
March	450.00	78.75	528.75
June	450.00	78.75	528.75
September	450.00	78.75	528.75
	1,800.00	315.00	2,115.00

15. Equipment maintenance

A charge of £192 annually in respect of the service contract for the fax is payable yearly in advance, as follows:

	Net	VAT	Total
	£	£	£
December	192.00	33.60	225.60

16. Printing, postage and stationery

With the exception of postage which is paid at the time, it is assumed that printing and stationery is payable one month after receipt of invoice, as follows:

	Net	VAT	Total	Memo Postage (Non VATable)
Dec	185.00	-	185.00	185.00
Jan	1,475.00	249.38	1,724.38	50.00
Feb	65.00	2.63	67.63	50.00
Mar	65.00	2.62	67.62	50.00
Apr	215.00	28.87	243.87	50.00
May	65.00	2.63	67.63	50.00
June	65.00	2.62	67.62	50.00
July	65.00	2.63	67.63	50.00
Aug	215.00	28.88	243.88	50.00
Sept	65.00	2.62	67.62	50.00
Oct	65.00	2.63	67.63	50.00
Nov	65.00	2.62	67.62	50.00
Y/E Creditor	165.00	28.87	193.87	
	2,775.00	357.00	3,132.00	735.00

17. Law Library and Books

Publications for the Law Library and books are assumed to be payable one month after the invoice is received. It should be noted that no VAT is chargeable on publications and books.

18. Advertising

Advertising is assumed to be payable one month after the invoice is received, as follows:

Cashflow Month	Net £	VAT £	Total £
Dec	-	-	-
Jan	250.00	43.75	293.75
Feb	200.00	35.00	235.00
Mar	50.00	8.75	58.75
Apr	50.00	8.75	58.75
May	50.00	8.75	58.75
June	200.00	35.00	235.00
July	50.00	8.75	58.75
Aug	50.00	8.75	58.75
Sept	50.00	8.75	58.75
Oct	50.00	8.75	58.75
Nov	200.00	35.00	235.00
Y/E Creditor	50.00	8.75	58.75
	1,250.00	218.75	1,468.75

19. Telephone

The initial connection charges of £440.00 plus VAT are assumed to be invoiced and payable in December.

Thereafter, the usual quarterly rental and call charges are assumed to be invoiced quarterly in arrears and payable in the month the invoice is received, as follows:

	Cashflow Month	Net £	VAT £	Total £
(Connection charge)	December	440.00	77.00	517.00
	March	360.00	63.00	423.00
	June	525.00	91.88	616.88
	Sept	675.00	118.13	793.13
	Y/E Creditor	825.00	144.37	969.37
		2,825.00	494.38	3,319.38

20. Motor Expenses

Motor expenses are assumed to be incurred and paid for in the same month and, for the cash flow forecast, are calculated as follows:

	Net £	VAT £	Total £	Memo-Tax/Ins. £
Dec	425.00	17.50	442.50	325.00
Jan	100.00	17.50	117.50	
Feb	100.00	17.50	117.50	
Mar	100.00	17.50	117.50	
Apr	100.00	17.50	117.50	
May	250.00	43.75	293.75	
June	100.00	17.50	117.50	
July	100.00	17.50	117.50	
Aug	100.00	17.50	117.50	
Sept	100.00	17.50	117.50	
Oct	100.00	17.50	117.50	
Nov	100.00	17.50	117.50	
	1,675.00	236.25	1,911.25	

No VAT is payable on car tax and car insurance.

21. Accountancy

A provision of £200 per month has been shown in the profit and loss account forecast to give a total fee of £2,400 in respect of preparation of the first year's accounts and reporting thereon. It is assumed that all this work is carried out early on in the second year of the business, invoiced once the work is completed and the fee then payable, together with VAT thereon, sometime soon after the invoice date. Therefore, nothing is reflected in the cash flow forecast for the first year of business.

22. Subscriptions

No subscriptions have been assumed in the profit and loss account forecast and, therefore, there is nothing to enter in the cashflow forecast.

23. Professional Indemnity Contribution

An amount of £504 is assumed to be payable in advance, during December, in respect of the first year.

24. Bad debts

Any adjustment in respect of expected bad debts would usually be shown by deducting the appropriate amounts from the forecast debtor collections. However, rather than complicate this forecast with bad debts, the amounts budgeted for in the profit and loss account forecast, have been deliberately left out.

25. Petty Cash (sundry expenses/periodicals)

Sundry expenses and periodicals are assumed to be paid for in cash, being incurred as shown in the profit and loss account forecast. VAT is assumed to be payable on the sundry expenses of £50 per month, but no VAT would be payable on periodicals. The figures are calculated as follows:

	Net	VAT	Total	Memo Non VAT
	£	£	£	£
Dec	70.00	8.75	78.75	20.00
Jan	70.00	8.75	78.75	20.00
Feb	70.00	8.75	78.75	20.00
Mar	70.00	8.75	78.75	20.00
Apr	70.00	8.75	78.75	20.00
May	70.00	8.75	78.75	20.00
June	70.00	8.75	78.75	20.00
July	70.00	8.75	78.75	20.00
Aug	70.00	8.75	78.75	20.00
Sept	70.00	8.75	78.75	20.00
Oct	70.00	8.75	78.75	20.00
Nov	70.00	8.75	78.75	20.00
	840.00	105.00	945.00	240.00

26. VAT

VAT is accountable to H.M. Customs & Excise, usually on a quarterly basis, often arranged in line with the business year end. The VAT payable or repayable, as the case may be, is due one month after the quarterly VAT accounting period.

The VAT figures, due on fee income and reclaimable on expenditure, have been assembled from the work already carried out in respect of the cash flow forecast. Details of how the quarterly figures have been arrived at are shown on the attached VAT schedule.

It will be seen that VAT of £753 is repayable by H.M. Customs & Excise in respect of the first VAT quarter to the end of February. This is not an unusual situation for the first quarter, as very often there will be some one-off large expenditure in respect of items such as fixed assets, telephone connection charges and printing and stationery set-up costs. At the same time, it is likely that fees invoiced for the first few months will be low.

Cash flow review

A. Total receipts:
   The total receipts are shown month by month together with the total receipts for the year.

B. Total payments:
   The total payments are shown month by month together with the total payments for the year.

C. Net cash flow (A - B):
   This shows the net cash inflow or outflow month by month together with the total net cash inflow or outflow for the year, being a net cash inflow of £6,455.

D. Opening bank balance:
   This gives the closing bank balance brought forward from the previous month. The total column shows a nil balance brought forward, which was the position at the start of the year prior to opening the bank account.

E. Closing bank balance (C +/- Line 27):
   This gives the closing bank balance at the end of each month. As will be seen from the forecast, there is a healthy bank balance at the end of each month which indicates, with capital introduced of £25,000 at the start of the business, the business will have no cash flow difficulties throughout the first year. However, this does assume that actual cash receipts come in as budgeted and that there is no unforeseen additional expenditure.

   The total column shows a closing bank balance, at the end of the first year, of £6,455 and this ties in with the bank balance at the end of November. These two figures should be identical and this acts as a cross check that no calculation errors have been made in the cash flow forecast.

Actual figures

When the business commences, the actual cash receipts and payments can be recorded month by month on the cash flow forecast and compared to the budgeted figures. This will enable the cash flow to be monitored each month and will be an indication of whether any problems are starting to come to light as regards the cash liquidity of the business.

Business premises

Details should be given of the proposed business premises. This should indicate whether they are freehold or leasehold, together with size in square feet.

If freehold, show value of property, giving basis and date of valuation. Show mortgage outstanding together with name of mortgagee, if applicable. Give details of rates payable.

If leasehold indicate lease terms together with annual rental and rent review dates.

Example

A firm of accountants, operating in the High Street, have office space surplus to their requirements. Therefore, a sub-lease is to be taken out with these accountants to obtain 500 sq.ft of office space on a leasehold basis.

The annual rent payable, inclusive of rates, will be £6,480. The premises are to be leased for a period of 10 years initially, with a rent review after the end of the fifth year.

The firm is to be charged for light and heat, property insurance and internal and external repairs on a proportionate basis, being a ratio of 500 sq.ft out of a total of 3,000 sq.ft.

Office furniture:

Office equipment:

Motor vehicles:

Details should be given of the office furniture, office equipment and motor vehicles to be acquired by the

Details of the office furniture, office equipment and motor vehicles required by the business are given on

243

business, giving a brief description of each item, the number required and the anticipated cost.

Assets available as security:

If any assets are available to be given as security against a mortgage or loan then details of those assets should be given together with a valuation, including the basis and date thereof. A note should also be made as to whether these are business or personal assets.

Financial requirements:

Details should be given of how the business is to be financed and whether this is to be provided from own resources, bank overdraft, bank loan or some other form of finance.

the fixed assets schedule which accompanies the monthly profit and loss account forecast.

The business is to be financed entirely out of the proprietor's capital savings and, therefore, this section is not applicable.

The proprietor is to finance the business with £25,000 cash from his own savings.

In addition, the proprietor is to introduce his existing personal car into the business. The market value of this car at the commencement of business is £10,000.

In total, the proprietor has introduced £35,000 into the business and this will ensure, as can be seen from the cash flow forecast, that the business is self-financing. This will save on bank charges and interest that would otherwise be incurred were the business to operate and make use of a bank overdraft facility.

M S J SMITH

PRACTISING AS MARTIN SMITH & CO

VALUE ADDED TAX

	Dec	Jan	Feb	Mar	Apr	May
	£	£	£	£	£	£
Output Vat						
Fee Income	175.00	350.00	481.25	350.00	962.50	1,181.25
Other						
TOTAL OUTPUT VAT	175.00	350.00	481.25	350.00	962.50	1,181.25
Input Vat						
Fixed Assets	1,136.80					
Light & Heat			23.62			19.25
Property Repairs					17.50	
Equipment Rental	78.75			78.75		
Equipment Maintenance	33.60					
Postage and Stationery		249.38	2.63	2.62	28.87	2.63
Advertising		43.75	35.00	8.75	8.75	8.75
Telephone	77.00			63.00		
Motor Expenses	17.50	17.50	17.50	17.50	17.50	43.75
Accountancy						
Petty Cash (Sundry Expenses)	8.75	8.75	8.75	8.75	8.75	8.75
TOTAL INPUT VAT	1,352.40	319.38	87.50	179.37	81.37	83.13
VAT PAYABLE/REPAYABLE	-1,177.40	30.62	393.75	170.63	881.13	1,098.12
QUARTERLY RETURN FIGURE			-753.03			2,149.88
PAYABLE/REPAYABLE			March			June

| Jun | Jul | Aug | Sep | Oct | Nov | Total |
£	£	£	£	£	£	£
700.00	1,137.50	586.25	525.00	612.50	288.75	7,350.00
700.00	1,137.50	586.25	525.00	612.50	288.75	7,350.00
						1,136.80
		15.75			18.38	77.00
		17.50				35.00
78.75			78.75			315.00
						33.60
2.62	2.63	28.88	2.62	2.63	2.62	328.13
35.00	8.75	8.75	8.75	8.75	35.00	210.00
91.88			118.13			350.01
17.50	17.50	17.50	17.50	17.50	17.50	236.25
8.75	8.75	8.75	8.75	8.75	8.75	105.00
234.50	37.63	97.13	234.50	37.63	82.25	2,826.79
465.50	1,099.87	489.12	290.50	574.87	206.50	4,523.21
		2,054.49			1,071.87	
		September			December	
					Year End	
					Creditor	

M S J SMITH

PRACTISING AS MARTIN SMITH & CO

MONTHLY PROFIT AND LOSS ACCOUNT FORECAST

Note Number	Month	December Budget	Actual	January Budget	Actual	February Budget	Actual	March Budget	Actual	April Budget	Actual	May Budget	Actual
		£	£	£	£	£	£	£	£	£	£	£	£
1	FEE INCOME	1,000		2,000		2,750		2,000		5,500		6,750	
	OTHER INCOME												
2	Interest Received	25											
	TOTAL INCOME	1,025		2,000		2,750		2,000		5,500		6,750	
	OVERHEADS												
3	Salaries and Employment Costs	432		432		432		1,762		1,762		1,762	
4	Rent and Rates	540		540		540		540		540		540	
5	Property Insurance	12		12		12		12		12		12	
6	Light and Heat	45		45		45		40		35		35	
7	Property Repairs							100					
8	Equipment Rental	150		150		150		150		150		150	
9	Equipment Maintenance	16		16		16		16		16		16	
10	Printing,Postage and Stationery	1,610		65		65		215		65		65	
11	Law Library and Books	500		30		30		30		30		30	
12	Periodicals	20		20		20		20		20		20	
13	Advertising	250		200		50		50		50		200	
14	Telephone	550		125		125		175		175		175	
15	Motor Expenses	425		100		100		100		100		250	
16	Accountancy	200		200		200		200		200		200	
17	Subscriptions												
18	Professional Insurances	42		42		42		42		42		42	
19	Bad Debts												
20	Sundry Expenses	50		50		50		50		50		50	
21	Depreciation:												
	Fixtures and Fittings	13		13		13		13		13		13	
	Plant and Equipment	82		82		82		82		82		82	
	Motor Vehicle	208		208		208		208		208		208	
	TOTAL OVERHEADS	5,145		2,330		2,180		3,805		3,550		3,850	
22	NET PROFIT/(LOSS)	-4,120		-330		570		-1,805		1,950		2,900	

June		July		August		September		October		November		Total	
Budget	Actual	Budget	Actual	Budget	Actual	Budget	Actual	Budget	Actual	Budget	Actual	Budget	Actual
£	£	£	£	£	£	£	£	£	£	£	£	£	£
4,000		6,500		3,350		3,000		3,500		1,650		42,000	
800												825	
4,800		6,500		3,350		3,000		3,500		1,650		42,825	
1,762		1,762		1,762		1,762		1,762		1,762		17,154	
540		540		540		540		540		540		6,480	
12		12		12		12		12		12		144	
30		30		30		30		35		40		440	
		100								100		300	
150		150		150		150		150		150		1,800	
16		16		16		16		16		16		192	
65		215		65		65		65		215		2,775	
30		30		30		30		30		30		830	
20		20		20		20		20		20		240	
50		50		50		50		200		50		1,250	
225		225		225		275		275		275		2,825	
100		100		100		100		100		100		1,675	
200		200		200		200		200		200		2,400	
42		42		42		42		42		42		504	
50		50		50		50		50		50		300	
50		50		50		50		50		50		600	
13		13		13		13		13		13		156	
82		82		82		82		82		82		984	
208		208		208		208		208		208		2,496	
3,645		3,895		3,645		3,695		3,850		3,955		43,545	
1,155		2,605		-295		-695		-350		-2,305		-720	

M S J SMITH

PRACTISING AS MARTIN SMITH & CO

MONTHLY CASHFLOW FORECAST

	Month	December		January		February		March		April		May	
		Budget £	Actual £	Budget £	Actual £	Budget £	Actual £	Budget £	Actual £	Budget £	Actual £	Budget £	Actual £
	RECEIPTS												
1	Fee Income (inc VAT) - Debtors			1,175		2,350		3,231		2,350		6,463	
	- Cash												
2	Capital Introduced	25,000											
3	Loans Received												
4	Disposal of Assets												
5	Interest Received	25											
A	TOTAL RECEIPTS	25,025		1,175		2,350		3,231		2,350		6,463	
	PAYMENTS												
6	Drawings	1,500		1,500		1,500		1,500		1,500		1,500	
7	Salaries (net)	369		369		369		1,265		1,265		1,265	
8	PAYE/NI			63		63		63		497		497	
9	Fixed Assets	7,633											
10	Rent and Rates	2,070						1,620					
11	Property Insurance	144											
12	Light and Heat					159						129	
13	Property Repairs									118			
14	Equipment Rental	529						529					
15	Equipment Maintenance	226											
16	Postage and Stationery	185		1,724		68		68		244		68	
17	Law Library and Books			500		30		30		30		30	
18	Advertising			294		235		59		59		59	
19	Telephone	517						423					
20	Motor Expenses	443		118		118		118		118		294	
21	Accountancy												
22	Subscriptions												
23	Professional Insurances	504											
24	Bad Debts												
25	Petty Cash (Sundry Expenses/Periodicals)	79		79		79		79		79		79	
26	VAT							-753					
B	TOTAL PAYMENTS	14,199		4,647		2,621		5,001		3,910		3,921	
C	NET CASHFLOW (A - B)	10,826		-3,472		-271		-1,770		-1,560		2,542	
27	Opening Bank Balance			10,826		7,354		7,083		5,313		3,753	
D	Closing Bank Balance (C +/- line 27)	10,826		7,354		7,083		5,313		3,753		6,295	

June		July		August		September		October		November		Total	
Budget	Actual	Budget	Actual	Budget	Actual	Budget	Actual	Budget	Actual	Budget	Actual	Budget	Actual
£	£	£	£	£	£	£	£	£	£	£	£	£	£
7,931		4,700		7,638		3,936		3,525		4,113		47,412	
												25,000	
800												825	
8,731		4,700		7,638		3,936		3,525		4,113		73,237	
1,500		1,500		1,500		1,500		1,500		1,500		18,000	
1,265		1,265		1,265		1,265		1,265		1,265		12,492	
497		497		497		497		497		497		4,165	
												7,633	
1,620						1,620						6,930	
												144	
				106						123		517	
				118								236	
529						529						2,116	
												226	
68		68		244		68		68		68		2,941	
30		30		30		30		30		30		800	
235		59		59		59		59		235		1,412	
617						793						2,350	
118		118		118		118		118		118		1,917	
												504	
79		79		79		79		79		79		948	
2,150						2,054						3,451	
8,708		3,616		4,016		8,612		3,616		3,915		66,782	
23		1,084		3,622		-4,676		-91		198		6,455	
6,295		6,318		7,402		11,024		6,348		6,257		0	
6,318		7,402		11,024		6,348		6,257		6,455		6,455	

Costings Plan for Setting Up a Small Practice

	£
Rent for 3 months	1625
Office space for:	
1 principal, 1/2 fee-earners and general office for 2 secretaries	
350 sq ft and business rates	
4-drawer filing cabinets	480
5 desks (second-hand)	300
2 secretaries'/typists' chairs	60
1 principal's chair	180
2 client chairs	100
2 fee-earners' chairs	170
2 storage cupboards for stationery	300
2 electric typewriters	700
1 word-processing system	
monitor with hard disk, keyboard	
bubble jet printer + Windows software)	1200
1 fax machine	1600
1 year service contract for fax	190
1 quarter's telephone line rental and connection charge	135

Incoming telephone line switchboard with 5 extensions
    1 quarter's rental + connection charge   380

1 principal's private telephone line + telephone   185
    (incl. connection charge + purchase of handset)

Cost of setting up and printing 1000 letterheads   150

Additional stationery:
Copy paper
File covers and correspondence files
Counsel's notebooks
Copy paper for word processor
Typewriter ribbons/envelopes/pens, etc.   160

3 months rental of photocopier   450

1 year membership of Document Exchange (one-off joining fee
    plus estimated usage charge)   500

3 months' worth postage stamps   185

4 dictating machines/transcribers + ancillary
    equipment (microphones/footpedals/headsets etc)   1406

Professional Indemnity Contribution (per principal)   500
(assumes SIF will treat the practice as brand new with no
clients being taken from a previous practice and no previous
adverse claims experience in relation to you or your former partners.
It is wise to get a written quotation)

Law Stationery Forms (wide range of commonly used
forms, sufficient for 3-6 months)   350

Manual accounts system   500

50 interview/attendance note pads   90
                                             11,896

NOTES

(a) All figures are approximate. The object of the exercise is to give you some idea of what your initial set-up costs are likely to be. Depending on your budget, you may wish to be more lavish or frugal, but at least you have a baseline figure to work from. There will undoubtedly be items you can omit and others you must add, depending on scale of operation and your priorities. Use the plan as a basic shopping list and add or subtract to suit your own circumstances. If you have all of the items in the plan when you open, you will at least be able to operate some kind of service.

(b) All prices are exclusive of VAT. VAT will be payable at point of sale and so the money must be found initially, but you will be able to reclaim it in your first VAT quarter.

(c) Substantial savings can be made by buying second-hand equipment or equipment of a low specification. The example tries to strike a balance between purchasing cheap, unreliable equipment of a low specification and high quality, new equipment whose specification may be greater than that required.

(d) You may wish to have a facility at home so that either you or your spouse or both (if your spouse is employed in the business) can work from home. This will be especially useful during school holidays if you have young children or if you need to get something done urgently out of hours. If you opt for this facility, allow for a proportion of the set-up costs, depending on how extensive the home facility is required.

(e) Fax machines can vary in price and sophistication. They start from as little as £200 and go up to £3,000. It is suggested that even at an early stage you will need a fairly robust machine for office use. As an alternative, buy a cheap machine for the office and then after six to nine months take it home and upgrade to a more expensive machine. The problem is you will be tempted to put off purchasing the bigger machine for yet another month because of something more pressing, and not get around to it. Some machines can double as computer printers and/or answerphones.

(f) Printers come in a variety of shapes and sizes (see Chapter 7 for more detailed information on printers):

Dot Matrix are fairly fast and very cheap but the finished product is often not quite as good as you might want. They are fine for drafts and may be up to letter standard. They are comparatively noisy.

Bubble Jet printers are quiet and produce a high quality product but not as good as a laser printer and are slower. They are much cheaper than laser printers.

Laser Printers are the quietest, highest quality, the most expensive and the fastest. You can easily pay £2,000 for one, as opposed to £200-£300 for a bubble jet. Whether the extra money is worth it is for you to judge. Certainly, there is no denying their performance and quality.

(g) Substantial savings can be made on telephone systems. I would advise against too small a system. Too many sole or small practices set up with one or two telephone lines. As with fax machines, the decision to upgrade is constantly deferred. Clients who cannot get through are unlikely to return calls. If you expand the practice, you will be busy - possibly too busy - to get around to inspecting other telephone systems and unwilling to undergo the disruption caused by implementing a new system. Build a certain amount of expansion into your system from the start, hence five extensions when two are probably sufficient for immediate needs. Line connection charges are about £115 per line (so a three-line switchboard's connection charge would be £345) and are a one-off charge. When calculating yearly expenses, deduct the connection and add estimated call charges.

(h) A photocopier is a substantial investment. A rental arrangement is likely to be the best answer. Alternatively, buy a small machine and take all your high volume copying to a professional copy shop. If you decide to buy instead of rent there are some good deals to be had with reconditioned machines from reputable suppliers.

(i) By buying (or leasing) transcribers rather than dictating machines (transcribers can only play back, dictating machines can record *and* play back) you can lower your costs. If, however, the dictating machine breaks down you cannot plunder your secretary's machine to bridge the gap. Always have at least one machine more than you need. Murphy's law will apply if you do not, and the machine will break down at the time you can least afford it to. Don't forget one or possibly two for home use. These can be your spare machines.

(j) Document Exchange joining fee £150*. Usage charge invoiced six months later, based on level of incoming and outgoing items at approximately 50 per cent of cost of first-class post.

* Since the business plan was prepared the fee has increased to £200.

Specimen Letters Chasing Unpaid Bills

LETTER 1

Dear Mr Ingrate

Re: **Outstanding Account**
        Date: 12 September 1995
        Amount: £448.00

My cashiers have reminded me that the above account remains outstanding. I would be most grateful if you would let me have a remittance in the next few days. A further copy of the account is enclosed for ease of reference.

Yours sincerely

LETTER 2

Dear Mr Ingrate

Re: **Outstanding Account**
        Date: 12 September 1995
        Amount: £448.00

I regret to note that my account is still outstanding despite an earlier reminder. In the circumstances, I would be grateful if you would let me have payment by return. May I remind you that interest is payable on overdue accounts. However, I will waive this requirement if payment is made as requested above. A further copy of the account is enclosed for your use.

Yours sincerely

LETTER 3

T.W. Ingrate, Esq.

Dear Sir

Re: **Outstanding Account**
        Date: 12 September 1995
        Amount: £448.00

We regret to note that the above account remains unpaid despite earlier reminders. We must inform you that unless this sum is paid to us within 7 days from the date of this letter, together with interest of £_____ making a total of £_____, proceedings for the recovery of the amount of the invoice, interest and costs are liable to be commenced against you without further notice.

Yours faithfully

APPENDIX 7

Specimen Default Summons

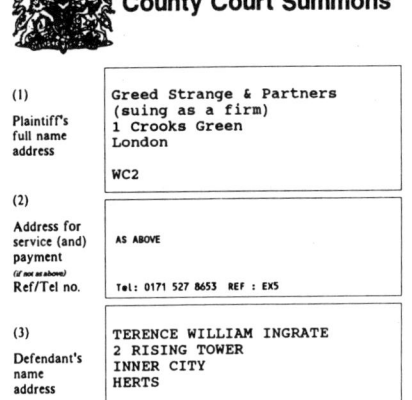

County Court Summons

Case Number	*Always quote this*

In the

EVEN HANDED

County Court

The court office is open from 10am to 4pm Monday to Friday

Telephone:

(1) Plaintiff's full name address

Greed Strange & Partners
(suing as a firm)
1 Crooks Green
London

WC2

(2) Address for service (and) payment
(if not as above)
Ref/Tel no.

AS ABOVE

Tel: 0171 527 8653   REF : EX5

Seal

This summons is only valid if sealed by the court. If it is not sealed it should be sent to the court.

(3) Defendant's name address

TERENCE WILLIAM INGRATE
2 RISING TOWER
INNER CITY
HERTS

What the plaintiff claims from you

Brief description of type of claim

Claim for Professional Fees

Particulars of the plaintiff's claim against you

See attached Particulars of Claim

Amount claimed	454.67
Court fee	50.00
Solicitor's costs	33.00
Total amount	537.67
Summons issued on	

What to do about this summons

You can

- dispute the claim
- make a claim against the plaintiff
- admit the claim in full and offer to pay
- pay the total amount shown above
- admit only part of the claim

For information on what to do or if you need further advice, please turn over.

Signed *Greed Strange and Partners.*
Plaintiff('s solicitor)
(or see enclosed particulars of claim)

N1 Default summons (fixed amount) (Order 3. rule 3(2)(b))

Keep this summons, you may need to refer to it

257

You have 21 days from the date of the postmark to reply to this summons

(A limited company served at its registered office has 16 days to reply)

If you do nothing	**Judgment may be entered against you without further notice.**
If you dispute the claim	Complete the white defence form (N9B) and return it to the court office. The notes on the form explain what you should do.
If you want to make a claim against the plaintiff (counterclaim)	Complete boxes 5 and 6 on the white defence form (N9B) and return the form to the court office. The notes at box 5 explain what you should do.
If you admit all of the claim and you are asking for time to pay	Fill in the blue admission form (N9A). The notes on the form explain what you should do and where you should send the completed form.
If you admit all of the claim and you wish to pay now	**Take or send the money to the person named at box (2) on the front of the summons.** If there is no address in box (2), send the money to the address in box (1). Read How to Pay below.
If you admit only part of the claim	Fill in the white defence form (N9B) saying how much you admit, then **either:** Pay the amount admitted as explained in the box above: **or** Fill in the blue admission form (N9A) if you need time to pay

Interest on Judgments

If judgment is entered against you and is for more than £5000, the plaintiff may be entitled to interest on the total amount.

Registration of Judgments

If the summons results in a judgment against you, your name and address may be entered in the Register of County Court Judgments. **This may make it difficult for you to get credit.** A leaflet giving further information can be obtained from the court.

Further Advice

You can get help to complete the reply forms and information about court procedures at any county court office or citizens' advice bureau. The address and telephone number of your local court is listed under "Courts" in the phone book. When corresponding with the court, please address forms or letters to the Chief Clerk. Always quote the whole of the case number which appears at the top right corner on the front of this form; the court is unable to trace your case without it.

How to Pay	**To be completed on the court copy only**
• PAYMENT(S) MUST BE MADE to the person named at the address for payment quoting their reference and the court case number.	**Served on**
• DO NOT bring or send payments to the court. THEY WILL NOT BE ACCEPTED.	**By posting on**
• You should allow at least 4 days for your payments to reach the plaintiff or his representative.	
• Make sure that you keep records and can account for all payments made. Proof may be required if there is any disagreement. It is not safe to send cash unless you use registered post.	**Officer**
• A leaflet giving further advice about payment can be obtained from the court.	**Marked "gone away" on**
• If you need more information you should contact the plaintiff or his representative.	

Laserform International 1991

258

APPENDIX 8

Specimen Particulars of Claim

<u>IN THE EVEN HANDED COUNTY COURT</u>   Case No.

B E T W E E N:

GREED STRANGE & PARTNERS
(suing as a firm)
<u>Plaintiffs</u>

- and -

TERENCE WILLIAM INGRATE

<u>Defendant</u>

PARTICULARS OF CLAIM

1.   At all material times the Plaintiffs were a firm of solicitors and the Defendant was the Plaintiffs' client. In July 1995 the Defendant instructed the Plaintiffs to act on his behalf in his defence of various prosecutions before The Severe Magistrates' Court. The Plaintiffs duly complied with the Defendant's instructions.

2.   On 12th September 1995 the Plaintiffs rendered to the Defendant an account numbered 523 in the sum of £448.00 (inclusive of VAT) in respect of the work carried out. The Defendant has failed to make payment of the sum due.

3.   The invoice was endorsed with a notice informing the Defendant of his right to have the bill taxed by the Court under the provisions of the Solicitors Act 1974.[1]

4.   The Plaintiffs claim interest on the sum owed at 8% per annum pursuant to Section 69 of the County Courts Act 1984.

AND THE PLAINTIFFS CLAIM:-

1. The said sum of £448.00[2]

2. Interest thereon of £6.67 pursuant to Section 69 of the County Courts Act 1984 at 8% from 12th September 1995 to the date hereof being 68 days at a daily rate of £0.98.

3. Costs.

Dated this 19th day of November 1995.

....

GREED STRANGE & PARTNERS
1 Crooks Green
London WC2
who will accept service of
proceedings herein
at the above address

To the District Judge of the Court
and to the Defendant

Notes:

1. This notice is not a requirement in relation to contentious business. If suing in a non-contentious bill add 'and the right to require the plaintiff to obtain a Certificate of Fair Remuneration'.

2. If the amount adjudged to be due is more than £5,000 you are entitled to interest on the judgment debt, in which case add as paragraph 3:-

    3. Interest on £_____ as aforesaid at 8% from the date hereof until judgment or sooner payment at a daily rate of £_____

    4. Costs.

N.B. The sum to be inserted is the amount of the invoice, not the aggregate of the invoice total and the interest to date, i.e. you cannot claim interest on interest.

APPENDIX 9

Accounts Packages for Small Practices

The following article by Charles Christian is taken from the Law Society's *Gazette* [1994] 25 May, 18 and contains updates from the *Gazette* [1994] 15 June and 6 July. You should contact the relevant suppliers for up-to-date information on prices and new products.

'Despite its relatively small size, the legal technology market is surprisingly dynamic in terms of the number of companies which enter and leave it each year. For this reason, the *Gazette* recently carried out a fresh survey of suppliers with low cost computerised accounts and time-recording systems suitable for sole practitioners and very small firms of solicitors. The definition of 'low cost' in this instance is a single user core accounts software package retailing for under £1,500.

The information contained in both the supplier/product profiles and comparison table should mostly be self-explanatory. 'DOS' means a stand-alone IBM PC compatible computer and 'Novell' is the most widely used make of local area network (LAN). However, there are two important caveats to make: all prices are quoted excluding VAT; and inclusion in this survey does not mean either suppliers or products are in any way endorsed by the *Gazette* .

Accounts/2

CPL Ltd's accounts system was originally developed in 1984 and is currently in use by 69 firms. The accounts system will support an unlimited number of matters, and time-recording, purchase ledger and legal aid franchising modules are available as optional extras. The single user system can be upgraded to run on a multi-user network. CPL has been involved in the legal market since 1980 and is a Law Society 'listed' supplier. The company also supplies systems for vets.

Lawbyte

Edgebyte Computers Ltd's accounts system, which includes an integrated time-recording module, was originally developed in 1990 and now has 93 users. It is one of a growing number of systems to have the Windows graphical user interface and can be upgraded to a multi-user version at a cost of £295 per user licence. It can support an unlimited number of clients and matters and can be linked to a conveyancing correspondence system. Edgebyte offers a complete hardware and software package from £1,695 and is a Law Society 'listed' supplier. There is also a user group.

Cashier

IT Accounting's Cashier system was originally developed in 1984 and is currently used by 187 firms. The company also develops accounts software for other markets. The accounts system will support 500 live matters but this can be doubled for an extra £150. It is also possible to rent the system from £26 per month. Time-recording is available as an extra and it will soon be possible to upgrade to a multi-user version. The business was established in 1982 and a user group is being formed.

C-Law

C-Law Solicitors Systems has been involved in the legal market for nearly 10 years, despite a low profile. The firm currently offers a stand-alone accounts system for £445 and an integrated accounts/time-recording package for £645.

This is a DOS-based system which will run on the most basic (and cheap) of 512K personal computers and will output data to a dot-matrix printer.

Cognito

Cognito Software has been making substantial inroads into the solicitors' market with its Cognito accounts package.

It is now distributed by a number of specialist suppliers, including Legal Systems in Swansea, JM Computing in Manchester, PCS in Birmingham and PCG in Bournemouth.

Although the standard Cognito product is intended for larger firms, the company has recently launched a DOS entry level integrated accounts and time-recording system for sole practitioners costing £1,500. The product comes complete with an integrated database.

Because it is a subset of a larger system, this is a product whose scope can be expanded as a practice grows.

Cognito has recently announced a link between the accounts package and the widely-used DPS range of case management software. This integration involves not just passing common data but provides a flexible means of utilising common information, handle time-records and access accounting figures.

Both C-Law and Cognito systems have no limits on the number of clients and matters the system can handle.

Legal Ledger

Jackson Computer Solutions (JCS) only entered the legal market in 1991 with an all-new Windows system that is now used by 20 firms. Time-recording is an integrated part of the system and it can support an unlimited number of clients and matters. A multi-user version is available and, during the next 12 months, JCS will be launching a practice database and documents register. JCS sells an entry level 'bundled' system (hardware, software, training and support) from £3,100 and can arrange credit terms. JCS is a Law Society 'listed' supplier and there is also an informal user group.

Solicitors Bookkeeping

Keith Simons, who lectures on legal accounts and is a driving force behind the Lawyers Amstrad PCW Club, originally developed the system in 1989 for a firm for which he was then working. It has been more widely available since 1992 and, despite its low price, is a full double-entry system with bank and client account reconciliations. Time-recording is not available but it can handle around 300 live matters at any given time and has been specifically designed for the Amstrad PCW. A full system (hardware, software and printer) could be bought for under £500.

LawPak '92

Lawmaster Software, which entered the legal market in the late 1980s with conveyancing, criminal law and probate support applications, has now taken over Harry Freeman's old Keendale Partnership, which has been selling solicitors' accounts software since 1982. The current product was rewritten in 1992 and has 180 users. The basic version can handle 3,000 live matters but this can be upgraded. Time-recording is integrated with the system but it has limited double-entry bookkeeping. Lawmaster is a Law Society 'listed' supplier.

AlphaLaw-PC

MSS Management Support Systems has been involved in the legal systems market since 1979 and there are now approximately 550 users of the AlphaLAW-PC accounts system.

Time-recording is an integrated part of the system and it can support an unlimited number of clients and matters. The system can be upgraded to a multi-user version running on a network, and can be fully integrated with the full range of MSS legal software applications including debt collection, conveyancing, database, case management and document image processing. MSS offer a 'buy-back' deal crediting AlphaLAW-PC users with the full cost of the software on upgrade. MSS is a Law Society 'listed' supplier and there is a user group.

Perfect Books 2

Perfect Software Ltd's Perfect Books, which grew out of the JC Legal Accounting bookkeeping service, now has 80 users. The system was launched in late 1992. Time-recording is an optional extra but it can support an unlimited number of clients and matters as well as handling client interest accounting and bank reconciliations. The software can also be linked to various databases and time-recording products.

The software is available direct from Perfect Books (software, hardware and printer from £14 per week) and Olivetti dealers. There is also a user group.

Legal Cashier

Professional Productivity Solutions plc was set up by solicitor Nicholas McFarlane-Watts in 1987 to develop and market legal software for the Apple Macintosh system (a Windows version is under development). Five firms currently use the accounts package, Legal Cashier, which is not a pure double-entry system. The system can, however, be fully integrated with a very wide range of legal and general business software and is now being distributed through a nationwide dealer network. The price is actually for a five-user licence as Macintosh hardware comes with built-in network support. PPS is a Law Society 'listed' supplier and there is a user group.

Quaestor

Professional Technology (UK) Ltd's Quaestor system was originally developed in 1986 and now has 225 users. Pricing is based on a sliding scale starting at £598 for 500 live matters rising to £2,177 for 2,000 live matters (ditto time-recording). The system will run on a wide range of hardware platforms, can be expanded to run on a Novell network, and even further expanded by upgrading to Professional Technology's Seriatim multi-user system.

All versions can be linked to standard database products as well as the widely used MCS Document Processing System. The company is planning to launch a voice-activated version of Quaestor later this year. Professional Technology is a Law Society 'listed' supplier and there is a user club.

Solpack and Pracctice Integrated

Solpack, from Solpack Systems is now used by around 300 practices and costs £1,750 for a software-only single user licence. Pracctice Integrated, from Pracctice Ltd costs £1,795 and is now used by 200 firms. Both run under DOS and feature time-recording software integrated with the core accounts system.

Strongbox II

James Strachan & Co.'s Strongbox was originally developed in 1987 and now has just over 200 users. Complete with integrated time-recording, the system can support an unlimited number of clients and matters. The system can also be linked to a Windows practice database and legal aid time-recording. The company is currently offering a number of price promotions, including software only for £595 and a complete package – hardware, software, printer and training – for £1,395. Bank reconciliation and database modules are currently under development and a full Windows version is planned this year.

SPAS

Wheatsheaf Professional System's Sole Practitioner Accounting System (SPAS) was launched in 1993. It is now used by 20 firms, the largest of which is a three-partner/five fee-earner practice. The system has been developed by David Salway and Graham Irwin, who both have extensive experience in IT consultancy for solicitors.

Reflecting this pedigree, SPAS has a number of sophisticated features including full nominal ledger, legal aid billing support and client account interest calculations. Complete with integrated time-recording, the system can support an unlimited number of clients and matters. A Windows version is under development and while the current version is only a single-user system, it can be run on a network.

Solledger

Textstore Ltd has released Version 4 of its Solledger integrated accounts and time-recording system, which now incorporates enhanced database facilities.

Over 120 firms now use this DOS-based package, which currently sells for £1,450 (including installation, training and six months' software support).

Textstore's Paul Ashley says recent changes to the time-recording software now make it particularly appropriate for legal aid work, while further enhancements and complementary software products are currently under development. There are no limits on the number of clients and matters the system can handle. A full multi-user version is available but Textstore say the more popular option is to have multi-enquiries running on a Novell network.

Tracpac Entry Level

Admiral Software has purchased the rights to Hay Logic's Tracpac legal accounting and Logit products.

Supplier	Telephone	Software	Price	Hardware	Time-recording
Admiral Software	01276 692269	Tracpac Entry Level	£1,500	DOS	Integrated
CPL	01758 613035	Accounts/2	£1,100	DOS/Novell	Extra £400
C-Law Solicitors Systems	01548 85775	C-Law	£645	DOS	Integrated
Cognito Software	01363 775582	Cognito	£1,500	DOS	Integrated
Edgebyte Computers	01253 899311	Lawbyte	£875	DOS/LAN/Windows	Integrated
IT Accounting	01803 856566	Cashier	£495	DOS/Windows/OS-2	Extra £200
Jackson Computer Solutions	0121-355 6789	Legal Ledger	£1,375	Windows	Integrated
Keith Simons	0161-485 2789	Solicitors Bookkeeping	£150	Amstrad PCW	Not available
Lawmaster Software	0181-658 5839	LawPak '92	£450	DOS	Integrated
MSS Management Support Systems	01276 451941	AlphaLaw-PC	£595	DOS/Windows	Integrated
Perfect Software	0181-546 7656	Perfect Books/2	£399	DOS/Windows	Extra £200
Practice Ltd	01432 351041	Practice Integrated	£1,795	DOS	Integrated
Professional Productivity Solutions	01865 784784	Legal Cashier	£995	Macintosh	Extra £995
Professional Technology	01634 815517	Quaestor	£598	DOS/Windows/OS-2/ LAN	Extra £399
Solpack Systems	01604 643033	Solpack	£1,750	DOS	Integrated
James Strachan & Co.	0181-336 2700	Strongbox II	£595	DOS/Windows	Integrated
Textstore Ltd	01403 257348	Solledger	£1,450	DOS	Integrated
Wheatsheaf Professional Systems	01600 860497	SPAS	£750	DOS	Integrated

Solicitors Act 1974, s.34 (Accountant's Report)

34. Accountants's reports

(1) Every solicitor shall once in each period of twelve months ending with 31st October, unless the Council are satisfied that it is unnecessary for him to do so, deliver to the Society, whether by post or otherwise, a report signed by an accountant (in this section referred to as an 'accountant's report') and containing such information as may be prescribed by rules made by the Council under this section.

(2) An accountant's report shall be delivered to the Society not more than six months (or such other period as may be prescribed by rules made under this section) after the end of the accounting period for the purposes of that report.

(3) Subject to any rules made under this section, the accounting period for the purposes of an accountant's report:

(a) shall begin at the expiry of the last preceding accounting period for which an accountant's report has been delivered

(b) shall cover not less than twelve months; and

(c) where possible, consistently with the preceding provisions of this section, shall correspond to a period or consecutive periods for which the accounts of the solicitor or his firm are ordinarily made up.

(4) The Council shall make rules to give effect to the provisions of this section, and those rules shall prescribe -

(a) the qualification to be held by an accountant by whom an accountant's report is given;

(b) the information to be contained in an accountant's report;

(c) the nature and extent of the examination to be made by an accountant of the books and accounts of a solicitor or his firm and of any other relevant documents with a view to the signing of an accountant's report;

(d) the form of an accountant's report; and

(e) the evidence, if any, which shall satisfy the Council that the delivery of an accountant's report is unnecessary and the cases in which such evidence is or is not required.

(5)   Rules under this section may include provision -

(a) permitting in such special circumstances as may be defined by the rules a different accounting period from that specified in subsection (3); and

(b) regulating any matters of procedure or matters incidental, ancillary or supplemental to the provisions of this section.

(5A) Without prejudice to the generality of subsection (5)(b), rules under this section may make provision requiring a solicitor in advance of delivering an accountant's report to notify the Society of the period which is to be the accounting period for the purposes of that report in accordance with the preceding provisions of this section.

(6)   If any solicitor fails to comply with the provisions of this section or of any rules made under it, a complaint in respect of that failure may be made to the Tribunal by or on behalf of the Society.

(7)   A certificate under the hand of the Secretary of the Society shall, until the contrary is proved, be evidence that a solicitor has or, as the case may be, has not delivered to the Society an accountant's report or supplied any evidence required under this section or any rules made under it.

(8)   Where a solicitor is exempt from rules under section 32:

(a) nothing in this section shall apply to him unless he takes out a practising certificate;

(b) an accountant's report shall in no case deal with books, accounts or documents kept by him in the course of employment by virtue of which he is exempt from those rules; and

(c) no examination shall be made of any such books, accounts and documents under any rules made under this section.

[NOTES

1. For a similar provision in relation to registered foreign lawyers see paragraph 8 of Schedule 14 to the Courts and Legal Services Act 1990.

2. By virtue of section 89(3) of the Courts and Legal Services Act 1990 the power to make rules under section 34 is also exercisable in relation to registered foreign lawyers.

3. For the application of section 34 to a recognised body see paragraph 5 of Schedule 2 to the Administration of Justice Act 1985.

4. By virtue of section 9(2)(f) of the Administration of Justice Act 1985 rules made under section 34 may be made to have effect in relation to a recognised body.]

APPENDIX 11

Town and Country Planning (Control of Advertisements) Regulations 1992, reg. 2B

Description

2B. An advertisement relating to any person, partnership or company separately carrying on a profession, business or trade at the premises where it is displayed.

Conditions and Limitations

2B.– (1) No advertisement may exceed 0.3. square metre in area.

(2) No character or symbol on the advertisement may be more than 0.75 metre in height, or 0.3 metre in an area of special control.

(3) No part of the advertisement may be more than 4.6 metres above ground level or 3.6 metres in an area of special control.

(4) Not more than one such advertisement is permitted for each person, partnership or company or, in the case of premises with entrances on different road frontages, one such advertisement at each of two such entrances.

(5) Illumination is not permitted unless the advertisement states that medical or similar services or supplies are available on the premises and the illumination is in a manner reasonably required to fulfil the purpose of the advertisement.

[Approximate imperial measurements
0.3 sq. metre   =   3¼ sq. ft
0.75 sq. metre   =   2ft 5½"
0.3 sq. metre   =   1ft ¾"
3.6 sq. metre   =   11ft 9¾"]

APPENDIX 12

Solicitors' Publicity Code 1990, Rule 3

3. Unsolicited visits and telephone calls

Solicitors may not publicise their practices or properties for sale or to let by means of unsolicited visits or telephone calls except:

(i) by means of a telephone call to a current or former client; or

(ii) by means of a visit or telephone call to another solicitor or to an existing or potential professional connection; or

(iii) by means of a visit or telephone call made to publicise a specific commercial property or properties the solicitor has for sale or to let.

Arrangements on death of sole principal

3.04 Arrangements on death of sole principal

Principle

A sole principal should make a will containing adequate provision for the running of the practice after his or her death.

Commentary

1. Clear instructions should be left by the sole principal to ensure that the executors are able to make arrangements immediately after his or her death to appoint a solicitor of sufficient seniority to run the practice, pending its disposal.

2. Although it is not essential to appoint a solicitor as executor, this would greatly facilitate the running of the practice. The will should include an authority for the solicitor-executor to purchase the practice if he or she desires.

3. An executor who is not a solicitor may not sign cheques on the client account of the deceased's practice.

4. In view of the provisions of Rule 9 of the Solicitors' Incorporated Practice Rules 1988 (Annex 3C) it is advisable for a solicitor shareholder in a recognised body to appoint a solicitor as executor in respect of his or her shares.

5. If no appointment of a suitable solicitor-manager is made, the Law Society may intervene in accordance with the provisions contained in Schedule 1 to the Solicitors Act 1974. The powers of intervention are available where

the Council of the Law Society have reason to suspect dishonesty on the part of the personal representatives, where there has been undue delay on the part of the personal representatives, or where the Schedule applied to the sole principal before his or her death. To avoid ensuing difficulties to clients following intervention, every effort should be made by the personal representative to find a solicitor-manager. In cases of difficulty, the honorary secretary of the local law society may be able to help.

6. If a sole principal dies intestate, those entitled to apply for a grant of letters of administration to the estate strictly have no right to take active steps in administering the estate until so authorised. However, in these circumstances the prospective administrators are encouraged to nominate a manager for the practice before the grant is obtained.

7. Where there is a failure, within a reasonable time of death, to apply for a grant of representation in respect of the estate of a deceased sole principal (whether under a will or an intestacy) the court has power to protect the interests of the clients. In exercise of the discretion conferred by section 116 of the Supreme Court Act 1981, the court can make an order for a grant in respect of the deceased solicitor's estate in favour of a nominee or nominees of the Law Society. The grant may be general or limited depending on the circumstances and the power is in addition to that conferred on the Law Society by paragraph 11 of Schedule 1 to the Solicitors Act 1974.